99 DRAMS OF WHISKEY

99 DRAMS OF WHISKEY

The **ACCIDENTAL HEDONIST'S**
Quest for the Perfect Shot
AND the History of the Drink

KATE HOPKINS

ST. MARTIN'S PRESS   NEW YORK

www.stmartins.com

Book design by Phil Mazzone
Photos courtesy of Glencairn Crystal

Library of Congress Cataloging-in-Publication Data

Hopkins, Kate.
    99 drams of whiskey : the accidental hedonist's quest for the perfect shot and the history of the drink / Kate Hopkins.—1st cd.
           p. cm.
    Includes bibliographical references.
    ISBN-13: 978-0-312-38108-0
    ISBN-10: 0-312-38108-5
    1. Whiskey—History.   I. Title.   II. Title: Ninety-nine drams of whiskey.
    TP605.H67 2009
    641.2'52—dc22

                               2009007174

First Edition: June 2009

10 9 8 7 6 5 4 3 2 1

To Mom and Dad

Contents

Preface

It's all about the stories.

Whiskey is many things to many people, but at the very root of its popularity lies the story. It could be a tale told at the bar in which the drink plays a supporting role. Perhaps it's an anecdote about the drink itself told by a fan of the drink in order to justify his or her fascination with it. Often it's the distilleries themselves who promote a story that highlights their tradition, their founders, or even the cat that had once roamed their halls. For example:

During Prohibition, a man by the name of Bill McCoy worked at the Hiram Walker Distillery in Windsor, Ontario. It was Bill who would ensure that his American cousins who came to visit him got only the best whiskey, rather than the "bathtub gin" that many folks who enjoyed their whiskey had to endure during this period.

Bill acquired a reputation for being honest, the one person in the whiskey industry who would not steer you wrong. His name became synonymous with authenticity, especially with regard to whiskey. To ask for the "real McCoy" meant that one was looking for real aged whiskey, not the stuff that was colored to look as if it had sat in the cask for several years.

The phrase soon took on a life of its own, and became a way to state that one was not willing to accept anything but the most authentic of products.

It's a cute story. Not overly funny, but clever in a modest way. Most importantly, it sounds as if it could be true.

It's not. The "real McCoy" has its roots in another whiskey, McKay, out of Scotland. "A drappie o' the real McKay" was the first written reference to the phrase, which comes out of the mid-nineteenth century.

But the fact that the story exists, as well as thousands like it, only adds to the mythology of whiskey. After reading and hearing only a few of these anecdotes, an image starts to appear that is far different from the reality of whiskey. People thrive on the stories, and indeed many companies spend and make millions of dollars propagating them. Take this bit of prose from Glenlivet's Web site:

> George Smith founded the Glenlivet distillery in 1824 to legitimise the whisky he was already making there. Other distillers built their premises near roads or railways, but George chose the most isolated glen. He understood the savage terrain and spiteful climate and what made them special.
>
> Local smugglers sampled George's whisky, and knew it would put them out of business. They threatened to burn down his distillery, even to kill him. The Laird of Aberlour gave George a pair of hair-trigger pistols for his protection. He kept them loaded day and night.
>
> Glenlivet was a dangerous place and George had to fire his weapons many times in self-defence. Eventually the smugglers gave up. George Smith's whisky, and pistols, had won the day.

Again, it's a cute story. But it's likely not 100 percent accurate. The truth isn't the point. It's the legend that demands our attention. To honor whiskey, I've decided to approach this book much in the same way that fans of whiskey treat these stories. This is a book for which a fair amount of research has been done. But whiskey works best when one doesn't take it too seriously. You, the reader, will be better served by treating this book as entertainment, rather than as a serious academic work.

In the end, it's the story that's important. With whiskey fans, it's almost always about the story, at least when they aren't drinking the stuff.

Note: There is a turf war of sorts when it comes to the spelling of whiskey. In some areas of the world, it's spelled "whiskey"; in others, "whisky." What determines the spelling is often arbitrary, based mostly on tradition rather than any claim to authenticity. I have chosen to use the "whiskey" spelling throughout most of the book, except in cases where I am speaking to a specific brand or organization that uses "whisky" in its name.

I chose the "whiskey" spelling mostly based on the fact that it's the preferred American style. Being American, this seemed the best option. Of course, having the world's best-selling grain spirit go by the "whiskey" spelling also goes a long way to defending my choice. If my preference is not your own, feel free to vent to me the next time we share a dram at your local hangout, your treat.

PART I

The Right Side of the Atlantic

1

To Ireland

I am in a surly mood.

One would think that a person who was off to distant lands to drink whiskey, and who was then off to write about the experience of drinking said whiskey, and who would then get paid for the aforementioned writing, would be as excited as a pug whose owner had just come home drenched in the odor of ground steak. And yes, a mere twelve hours ago, I was that thrilled.

But that was before the plane ride from Chicago to Dublin. About five hours into the flight, somewhere around 35,000 feet, and between the time when my "aisle buddy" started snoring and the child behind me began kicking the back of my seat and then sadistically counting along, I felt my anxiety slowly evolve into something more . . . menacing. This was never a good place for me to go, and quite frankly, it was only adding to the frustration that was my "Happy Travel Fun Day."

I have decided that everyone who claims to like to travel is lying. No one could like this torture, let alone love it. No, what they mean when they say that they "like to travel" is that they like being somewhere (Point B) that isn't where they spend the majority of their time

(Point A). But to get from Point A to Point B and back again requires a long series of frustrating and degrading activities. Whatever romance travel may have once held has now been stripped clean, dipped in an acid bath, and shoved out into the cold, where knowing businessmen point and stare at it, and say in hushed tones to their compatriots, "Hey, isn't that the romance of travel? I've often wondered what happened to it."

Like I said, I am in a surly mood.

As my annoyance swells, I am finding ways to blame anyone for my predicament. I could blame American Airlines, for having the cheapest flight to Ireland. I could blame the mother of the child behind me, who apparently has been born with a supermutant popliteal ligament and a predisposition for pulling wings off butterflies. Or I could blame myself, for not making enough money to afford first-class or chartered flights.

Instead, I do the reasonable thing and blame someone else—an anonymous man from round about Surrey, England.

On May 24, 2005, Pennyhill Park Hotel in Surrey, England, sold their only bottle of Dalmore 62 Single Highland Malt Scotch Whisky to a regular patron of their hotel. Their bar manager negotiated the price. This wasn't an auction or a convention. This was a bar at a hotel, where this anonymous ruiner of my travels saw this rare bottle of scotch (probably on more than one occasion) and thought to himself, "I want that. No matter what the cost."

This anonymous buyer (whom I'll henceforth refer to as "Mr. Disposable Income") ended up paying £32,000 (or a little more than $70,000) for the honor of owning the bottle of whiskey, one of only twelve bottles of Dalmore 62 Single Highland Malt Scotch Whisky then in existence.

Following the sale, Mr. Disposable Income opened the bottle and shared it with a few of his friends, including the bar manager. By the next morning, it was mostly gone. It is at this point that those who hear this story typically fall into one of three camps.

The first call Mr. Disposable Income insane for spending this amount of money on such a trivial item. Who in his right mind would spend that amount of money on a bottle of whiskey?

The second call Mr. Disposable Income insane for wasting such a fine investment. These are the collectors who most assuredly throw jokes around, wondering about the value of Mr. DI's urine soon after imbibing the rare liquor, and stating that the owners of the eleven other bottles of Dalmore 62 were most likely pleased because now their own bottles appreciated in value overnight.

Then there's the third camp. These are the folks who, upon hearing this story, think to themselves: "Damn, I bet that was the best £32,000 Mr. DI ever spent."

For reasons I cannot yet fathom, I find myself drawn to the people of the third camp. I'm not sure whether I am inquisitive about these types of folks in the way that Jane Goodall is fascinated by chimpanzees or whether I'm drawn to them because, somewhere deep within the darker recesses of my soul, I know that I am one of them.

What would drive a person to spend that amount of money on a drink? Breaking it down, there are only three answers I can come up with.

One: Mr. DI is indeed quite mad. If he is, then there's not much more to add to the story.

Two: Mr. DI wants to bask in the status afforded to him for having sipped one of the rarest of liquors. But since he purchased the whiskey outside the typical auction circuit, and he distinctly asked the management of the Pennyhill Park Hotel to keep his identity from the public, there's little status that can be afforded to him (outside that of those who partake of pricey drinks).

So that leaves me with the third reason: He felt that the drink, and the experience that it brought him, would be worth the money he had paid for it.

This conjecture on my part leaves me with several questions: Can a bottle of whiskey be worth this amount of money? What properties or characteristics does such a whiskey need in order to be considered "worth it"? Is the price paid for such a drink a reflection on the quality of the whiskey, or on its rarity? If it is the quality, does the price reflect that the whiskey is close to perfection? Is there such a thing as a perfect whiskey?

I am vexed by what a £32,000 bottle of whiskey means to my inner philosopher.

In the years after I heard this story, I created an agenda for myself. I needed to learn about whiskey as well as the associated passion for it that Mr. DI, and those like him, carry. I arranged various tours of whiskey distilleries and interviews with several folks who carry their own obsession for the spirit. I asked a friend to come along so that I wouldn't have to drink alone and so that she could, if needed, let me know when I was getting too obsessed about the drink. Finally, I made travel plans that would get me to the various destinations I had planned . . . which is how I ended up on an American Airlines 777 at around five o'clock in the morning Greenwich Mean Time getting kicked in the tuckus by Timmy the wonder kid with ligaments of industrialized rubber.

I decide to get out of my chair to flag down a flight attendant. I shoot Timmy a look that shows him a version of his future where he's forced to let me take a swing at his seat, and then I try to wake his mother.

"Your boy is kicking my chair. Could you get him to stop?"

She looks groggily over at her son and says, "Jons, bhve or tel dad," which I interpret as a passive-aggressive threat to Jonas that Dad is about to get involved, and apparently that means something dreadful. Jonas pouts to himself as I head to the flight attendant's station.

"Would it be possible to get a drink?" I ask. "For nerves," I add, as if I needed a reason.

The flight attendant nods in the affirmative, and I walk back to my seat with a tiny bottle of Glenlivet, an empty plastic glass, and a separate glass of water. I pour the Glenlivet into the glass and add a minimal amount of water. Life is a little better. There's no more kicking, there's no more snoring from my aisle mate, and I have a glass of whiskey.

I take a drink. It goes down nicely.

But there's no way in hell that a bottle of this stuff is worth £32,000.

Why am I heading to Ireland to start this journey, instead of Scotland? Isn't Scotland often seen as the preeminent area for all things whiskey? This needs a bit of explaining.

The Glenlivet 12-Year-Old

This is the bread and butter of the folks at Glenlivet, the one found in most liquor stores. It's popularity is such that one can find it on airplanes in tiny, 50-mL bottles that give many people the urge to pretend that they are giants holding a 750-mL bottle.

Nose: A sweet, fruity smell, almost like an apple orchard.

Taste: A lighter, sweeter Scotch whiskey, with the apples still making themselves apparent, along with a bit of vanilla.

Finish: Not so much a finish as an immediate vanishing act. Bright one minute, completely missing the next.

Character: The Glenlivet 12-year-old is the first college lit. class you took. At the beginning it seems quite vibrant and engaging, but it soon makes you realize that it lacks any depth, that those in charge are merely going through the motions. Its purpose is to set you up for bigger, better things down the road.

Whiskey is an item that engenders a fair amount of regional pride. Ask an Irishman where whiskey came from, and he'll state with pride, "Ireland!"

Ask a Scot a similar question, and he will also claim his land to be the true originator of the drink.

Ask an academic who has the best claim and he or she is likely to shrug and mumble, "Hell if I know. That part of the world wasn't too keen on keeping records of who was doing what." It's this lack of evidence that allows either region to claim whiskey as its creation without fear of contradiction.

So in the spirit of brotherhood, not only will I support both the Irish and Scottish claims that they are the originators of whiskey, I'll also support any future Welsh claim to the spirit, if only because there's no evidence saying they're not. They may as well add their name to the history books. What the hell, let's add the English, too.

The reality is that whiskey wasn't discovered at a specific moment. It evolved from a series of events that involve a wide array of characters, most of them alchemists, traders, and monks. Everyone from a Shia Muslim chemist to an Iberian alchemist to an Irish physician plays a part in the tale. But to connect these dots requires a bit of exposition.

The process of distillation is quite old. Early forms of distillation were known by the Chinese around 3000 BC, by Babylonian alchemists in Mesopotamia, where the process was developed sometime between 3000 and 2000 BC, and by Egyptian priests around 2000 BC. The Greeks were known to dabble in the process, and they were the first to attempt to develop large-scale distillation appliances. The first exact description of an apparatus for distillation is given by Zosimus of Alexandria in the fourth century AD. Distillation was further advanced by those renowned party animals, Muslim chemists, especially by the Arab chemist Abu Musa Jabir ibn Hayyan, in Iraq, around AD 800. The alcohol distilled would have been used in medicine and in the creation of perfumes.

Abu Musa Jabir ibn Hayyan lived sometime between 721 and 815. He was a prominent Shia Muslim polymath, chemist, alchemist, pharmacist, philosopher, astronomer, astrologer, engineer, physician, and physicist. He is seen by many to be the "father of chemistry" and had influenced and/or created a number of important processes used in modern chemistry, including the syntheses of hydrochloric and nitric acids, crystallization, and, for connoisseurs of aged spirits, distillation. His improvement to the alembic still is important to the history of whiskey, as the alembic was the precursor to the pot still. The pot still is a crucial tool in the development of whiskeys whose first use occurred somewhere in the British Isles, with the best guess being Ireland.

The question is, how did the alembic still, created by a man in Persia, end up as a pot still in the British Isles?

There are several thoughts, but the following seems the most likely to me.

In AD 711, the Moors conquered the Visigoths, mainly in Christian Hispania. Under their leader, an African Berber general named

Tariq ibn-Ziyad, they brought most of the Iberian Peninsula under Islamic rule during an eight-year campaign. The Moors ruled in the Iberian peninsula, the largely Basque regions in the Pyrenees, and North Africa for several decades. They likely brought their technologies into Europe at this time, with many of them eventually ending up in the hands of the Catholics. The still would have been one of those technologies.

The still ended up being of prime importance to monks, who often took responsibility for all things medicinal in Catholic hamlets and villages. Soon this new technology was introduced in the far corners of the Catholic empire—including places like Ireland and Scotland. That's how the still got to the British Isles. But who decided to make whiskey with it?

Arnaldus De Villa Nova, a Moorish alchemist, lived on the Iberian Peninsula during the thirteenth and early fourteenth centuries. He was fluent in both Latin and Arabic, and translated much knowledge from the Arab world into the Catholic one. Most assuredly in these translations were notes from Jabir ibn Hayyan concerning his process of distillation. But with regard to whiskey, it was his experiments undertaken around AD 1250 that are critical. For it was then that De Villa Nova first distilled wine, the end result of which was a precursor to brandy, meaning that De Villa Nova was indirectly responsible for the Busta Rhymes hit "Pass the Courvoiser Part Two."

Once the translated Arab texts became available to anyone who wrote and read Latin, it's likely that both alchemists and Catholic monks got their hands on most (if not all) of De Villa Nova's work. It was either the monks or the alchemists who posed the question: "If De Villa Nova could distill wine, what would happen if we distilled ale?"

The answer to that was the first production of whiskey. Somewhere in the British Isles, someone, either a monk or an alchemist, decided to distill beer.

It's probable that this is how the Beaton family in Ireland picked up on distilling. The Beatons, a family known for their various forays into alchemy, were renowned among tribal and clan leaders in both Ireland and Scotland. For generations they were the go-to folks for all things regarding converting one item into another. They were also likely well versed in both Latin and Gaelic, and could have translated various texts written in Latin by other alchemists, such as De Villa Nova.

It is due to this Irish family that I decided to wait for my friend Krysta at Dublin Airport instead of Edinburgh's. If pressed, I'll hedge my bet and state that whiskey was discovered/invented in Ireland, and not Scotland. Of course all of this is simply my own conjecture, based purely on well-known yet still circumstantial evidence. The fact is that the current lack of documentation makes tracking any evidence supporting either Scotland's or Ireland's claim impossible.

However, for those of you who are feeling their blood boil at my supposition, I do believe that the whiskey *industry* was formed in Scotland. The whiskey industry as we know it today can be traced back to the monopoly that James IV gave to the College of Barbers (later College of Surgeons) in Edinburgh. But I'm getting ahead of myself a bit.

Airports are a place of constant transition, an ever-changing dynamic fraught with emotional baggage as people either part with sadness or meet with joy. At least this is what I tell myself as I sit in the food court of Dublin Airport, waiting for Krysta's plane to land. Jet lag and anxiety often lead me to wax poetical.

As I take a bite of a chicken tandoori sandwich that I purchased at a snack shop, I begin to think about my own past with whiskey.

In the interest of saving my own reputation, it's best to assume that I have limited experience. On a scale of one to ten, with one being a drunken frat boy and ten being a master distiller at an award-winning distillery, I fall somewhere between a five and a six on this completely arbitrary scale. I know how whiskey is made and could name probably about three dozen different brands without looking in any literature. I've been able to pick up a decent read on its history, enough to annoy people at most whiskey tastings.

I think about what could be my weaknesses with whiskey, and tasting immediately comes to mind. My palate is . . . okay, but it could be much better. Mostly this weakness is due to a lack of comparison.

Whiskey has been in my life since I was a youngster. My father was a fan, with bottles of Jim Beam, Cutty Sark, and J&B appearing in the liquor cabinet at one time or another. As I grew older whiskey became a means of releasing a bit of stress and pressure common to college students across the world, and was likely the cause of my C grades and extra year and a half in school.

For a while after college, I did not drink at all, finding that losing control and then waking up with a hangover was not the way I wanted to go through life. Instead, I became interested in tastes and flavors of all things, not just spirits. It was the chasing of these flavors that led me to start my Web site, Accidental Hedonist, which allowed me to document my travels that concern all things food.

By the time I had reached middle age, alcohol was a treat to be respected, and whiskey was one that provided interesting flavors and contrasts. It became fun and compelling trying to determine its relevance in the world by examining its history. In short, I became a whiskey nerd. And it was in a nerd's quest for knowledge that I had arranged my trip to several whiskey-producing nations. Ireland, Scotland, the United States, and Canada have all added something to the history and culture of whiskey, and it was these four countries that I had decided to visit.

I had decided to omit from my journeys other countries that have minor whiskey production, either because they replicate processes already established elsewhere, as is the case with Japan, or because their processes deviate so far from established ones that I felt their products were no longer whiskeys in the traditional sense (such as in India, where sugar is used).

I asked Krysta to be my partner in crime on this journey, as she is a well-seasoned traveler. I felt she could help me with some of the basics of international travel, important things like companionship, shared experiences, and, of course, helping defray the cost of hotel rooms and car rentals.

She has told me of her own unique experiences with whiskey. She started, like many folks, drinking straight from a bottle or shot glass in her teenage years. By her thirties she was drinking it neat from a glass. She rates her knowledge of whiskey as a three. She can name about a dozen or so brands off the top of her head, and admits to being a "huge fan" of Bushmills white label. She has great memories surrounding Bushmills and sharing a bottle with another close friend one night in a graveyard near the University of New Mexico. Now, every time she goes group camping, she brings a bottle to share among her friends in hopes of replicating that evening in New Mexico, even if only a bit. From my perspective, she's the best person to bring along on this trip, as she's a fan of whiskey, has a great curiosity for it, but is aware of how much she doesn't know. To me, she best represents the consumer that every whiskey company should be aiming for. She'll drink the stuff for life, and will likely stay loyal to only one or two brands. She drinks for taste and not for the effects of alcohol, and will share her passions with all of her friends. To ignore her and those like her would be a huge mistake for any whiskey seller to make.

I hadn't seen Krysta in five years, since I fled Washington, D.C., for the damp confines of Seattle. It was she who encouraged my writing, it was she who led by example in regard to traveling. And it was she whom I first thought of whenever anyone mentioned the word whiskey. From my perspective, she absolutely had to come along.

And now, here I am waiting for her outside the gates of the customs lines at Dublin Airport, the doors emblazoned with ads for a better life in Dubai. For a second, I note the irony, as two women in Dubai would likely never be able to share in the experience on which we are about to embark. Seconds later, Krysta, with her shoulder-length and jealousy-inducing straight red hair, exits from customs, her eyes widen in excitement upon seeing me, and she drops her bags next to her ever-present Doc Martens. "We're in Ireland!" we both exclaim as we raise our arms in excitement.

We have arrived in the world of whiskey.

2

Dubliners

There are moments in one's life when sleep should not be a viable option, regardless of how tired one may be. The birth of a child certainly should qualify as such an event, as should the day that one graduates from college. But for me, nothing says "screw jet lag" like arriving in Dublin for the first time. With the vibrant pubs and the ghosts of Shaw, Joyce, and Wilde roaming around, my mind fought for consciousness. Sleep would have to wait, if only for a bit. After dropping off our luggage at the hotel, we went out to see what Dublin had to offer.

Those first moments in a new city are crucial to any tourist. They not only give the first impressions of the city (ones that will remain with the traveler for likely the rest of her life), but it will also set the tone for the rest of the trip. A bad first day can ruin one's fun for days afterward.

As we walked toward Trinity College, several concerns ran in the back of my mind. "Is this part of the city safe? Where did I store my money? Did I lock the hotel room? Oh look, a bookstore."

That was all that was needed to get my mind into the proper

mood. We entered and exited several shops that fit our desires. As dusk fell across the town, street lights and shop windows became ablaze. The city looked more vibrant, more energized than I thought possible. People of all ages and classes filled the sidewalks with purpose, as if they all, en masse, had somewhere else important to be, whether they were off to work, or heading to get a drink. Apparently, loitering was an unknown concept in Dublin.

We walked past the college and on toward the Temple Bar, an area in Dublin known as a tourist/drinking destination, and I noticed how gritty the city could be. But this wasn't a character flaw. It was as if the city had more important things to attend to, and didn't have time for public vanity.

After an hour of getting our first taste of the famous city, we decided to head back to the hotel. We walked down a side street filled with a variety of convenience stores and restaurants. It was difficult to walk more than a block without passing by a pub, church, or coffee shop. Dublin appears to be a city that loves to both celebrate and commiserate, and does both with a distinct sense of itself.

I found myself falling in love with the city for all the reasons mentioned above. This wasn't a city covered with new architecture. Nor was it excessively plastered with the international retail institutions that one might find in Times Square in New York City, or Piccadilly Circus in London. It seemed to be unpretentious and straightforward.

"Oi!" A yell broke into my daydreaming. Krysta and I kept walking to the hotel, not knowing whether the call was meant for us.

"OI!!!"

Apparently it was. We both turned to see who was trying to hail us. A girl who looked no more than fifteen-years-old looked at us, cigarette in one hand, and a flock of her compatriots behind her. "Can you get us some whiskey from the takeout?" She pointed at a liquor store papered with faded posters extolling the virtues of vodka. Krysta and I looked at each other. Several of her friends looked at us with a sense of expectation.

"Uh. No." We kept walking. The thought of contributing to the delinquency of a minor while in a foreign land was a little beyond the scope of what we wanted to accomplish in Ireland.

A slight murmur of disappoint came from her friends.

"Great. Thanks. THANKS!" was her sarcastic response as the distance between us increased.

As far as an introduction into Irish whiskey culture, this was admittedly less than what we had expected. "Did she have a stroller with her?" asked Krysta later when we were at dinner. "I think she had a stroller." It was possible that the legend of our whiskey gal was going to grow.

"C'mon. Let's order." I was famished. The long flight and then the arrival into Dublin was starting to catch up with me. It was time to eat. On the menu? Lamb stew and whiskey.

The waiter came to our table. "What kind of whiskey do you have?" I asked. Krysta chuckled a bit.

A brief moment of shock occurred when a French accent, not an Irish, responded with: "We have Jameson's, Johnnie Walker Red, and Chivas."

"Don't you have any Bushmills?" I said, surprised by the accent that seemed out of place.

"No. Only the three." This also surprised me a bit. I knew that there were only three whiskey companies in Ireland, but there were over thirty different brands of Irish whiskey out there. To have only one behind the bar was not only unfortunate but a bit of a slight to the heritage of the island.

"Jameson's, please," I said. There was no need to start accusing our waiter of how poorly I felt his bar was stocked. After a moment, two glasses of whiskey, straight with water back, were delivered to our table.

"So," said Krysta, "how do you drink this thing?"

"Carefully pour it in your mouth and then swallow," I said. She looked at me, annoyed yet bemused. I knew what she meant. She was asking how someone tastes whiskey.

There is a skill to tasting whiskey. Note the use of the word "tasting" as opposed to "enjoying," which is not the same thing.

Never was this fact as apparent to me as when, several years before, I was sitting in a bar in Sandusky, Ohio—an unfortunate participant in an impromptu lecture on the joys of whiskey given by someone I shall call Barry.

Barry clearly fancied himself a connoisseur, and I, for one, was not willing to challenge him on his self-proclaimed title. Part of it was because he was short-tempered and shouted down anyone who wanted a share of his spotlight. But another part was because he was slightly entertaining, in the same kind of way that someone performing Bach's *Cello Suite No. 1 in G major* on a banjo can be entertaining.

What made Barry's bartending skills and whiskey knowledge so compelling, in an oh-my-God-he's-really-going-to-do-it kind of way, was his insistence that the best way to enjoy whiskey was in one's choice of mixers for the liquor. Sour Mix was his preference, although the colas of the world could provide an equal amount of satisfaction. But Barry's joy was reserved for mixing whiskey with Sunny Delight, a citrus beverage best known for containing precious little natural citrus.

There's no shame in the way that Barry prefers his whiskey. After all, a person likes what he likes. But what mixers do is cover up the taste of the whiskey, a fact that was lost on the wannabe bartender, as he proved with his point that Canadian whiskey works best with colas while bourbons work best with the citrus mixers. The subtleties of scotches, bourbons, and ryes are oftentimes lost when they have to compete with the sour tastes of citrus or the savory taste of cola. When sugar is thrown into the mix, the sweetness will further dilute the flavors. If I wanted to learn how to taste whiskey, then mixers were out of the question.

I was saddened by this discovery, until I realized that mixers are sometimes used as a response to bad-tasting whiskeys. The cheaper whiskeys tend to be strong in alcohol, but either lacking in the nuances you find in many of the scotches or bourbons that have been aged several years in barrels, or having an excessive chemical taste about them. These mass-produced whiskeys have artificial flavorings and colors added to them, and often taste like what Dow Chemical would create if they ever got into the distillery business. Mixers, in these cases, were most often used to mask the flavor of whiskey, not highlight them.

The problem is that once a consumer gets used to the taste of, say, a whiskey sour, he'll stick with it, even when he can afford the higher-quality whiskeys. If you ever want to make a bartender cry, order a 21-year-old single malt and have him mix it with orange juice.

Not one to have a sobbing bartender on my conscience, I resolved not to add mixers to the whiskeys I drank while on our tour. But at the same time, I'm not sure that the bar is the best place to explore the spirit. These places are loud, busy, and, as I was finding out, rather overpriced when it comes to single drinks. Not only that, the list of whiskeys available is limited only to what will sell in any location. Finding the $500 shot of 50-year-old Macallan is the exception, not the rule. And quite frankly, I'm not all that fond of bar food when tasting the grain. If I wanted to learn how to taste whiskey, I would have to leave the place where most whiskey is consumed—the bar. But where was I to turn to learn how to taste?

Being the geek that I am, I turned to the Internet. A quick search on Google brought up several options, of varying degrees of usefulness. The one that caught my attention was a site that demonstrated how to determine quality whiskeys by breaking each whiskey you taste down into several categories, such as Bouquet/Aroma, Appearance, Flavor, Body, Drinkability, and Overall Impression. Each of these categories then had several subcategories, in which one would apply a point rating system.

Once a rating had been applied in each subcategory, one would then presumably add these numbers together and compare the total with scores awarded to other whiskeys. From this process, one should be able to determine the better whiskeys out there.

While there may be some professional applications for this process, I have to admit to finding several flaws with it for my own personal use. Namely:

1. Judging flavor is a subjective experience. One person's preference for smokiness is another person's preference for a nice piquant clove undercurrent.
2. How does one define "drinkability"?

3. After one or two drinks, math and I become the most vicious of archenemies.

No, this process would not do at all. I wanted to learn how to taste whiskey. And although I wanted to find the best shot of whiskey, a micro-rating system such as the one mentioned above removes the romance from the search. Not only is a shot enjoyed for its taste, it's also enjoyable in the environment in which it's tasted. In other words, whiskey is as much about the moment during which it is consumed as it is about the flavor. And any moment that involves writing down numbers and notes is a moment that almost always can be improved upon by not writing down numbers and notes.

So I was back to square one. I still needed to learn how to taste the whiskey before setting off to find the best place to consume it. While thinking on this problem, I poured myself a shot of Bulleit Bourbon, hoping that just by looking at the glass of the tawny liquor I could suss out what I needed to learn.

Judging the quality of a product is simply a matter of an individual taking two similar experiences and comparing the relevant perceptions that were involved in those experiences. From these perceptions a person can determine whether something is "better than," "worse than," or "equal to" something else. This is a philosophical overgeneralization, to be sure, but it does provide a nice starting point when looking at something as deceptively simple as whiskey.

The key to the matter is determining what perceptions are relevant in the consumption of whiskey. Taste is the most important, but people also use their senses of sight, smell, and touch when consuming almost every edible product. In shorthand, that would read: Sight + smell + touch + taste = whiskey experience.

Sight: Although there is some information a person can glean from looking at a shot of whiskey, very little in the way of quality can be determined. The variations among ryes, scotches, and bourbons, not to mention the variations allowed within each of these types of whiskey, makes claiming any one color or one opacity as "the best" laughable.

But there is information one can get from looking at whiskey.

The multitude of colors can indicate everything from how long an unblended whiskey has been casked to how much flavor a drink should or should not have. Much like honeys, the darker colors in whiskey generally indicate stronger, more robust flavors, while the lighter colors indicate more subtlety.

However, it should be noted that many distilleries add artificial coloring to their whiskeys in order to ensure that each batch looks the same as the next. Some people claim to be able to taste this addition, but the producers who partake in this behavior say that it's not possible. The exception to the coloring technique are the bourbon producers, who, by law, cannot add anything to their whiskey beyond what is codified into American law.

Then there's a whiskey's opacity. Most whiskeys are chill filtered prior to bottling. On the bottling line the spirit's temperature is reduced to close to freezing. In this state a number of impurities can be filtered out. These impurities cause the whiskey to go very slightly cloudy when water and/or ice are added. Unfortunately, the impurities are, in some cases, flavor elements that may have been better left in.

Smell: At the back of almost every human's nose is a fleshy bulb called the olfactory epithelium, a specialized tissue inside our nasal cavity that is involved in smell. Where humans can sense variations of five different tastes, it is said that we can distinguish as many as thirty-two base aromas.

The difficulty in this is that there are some smells that are physically harmful, at least for a short period of time. This includes aromas that contain a fair amount of alcohol. If the whiskey has been bottled directly from the cask it may be as much as 63 percent alcohol by volume, and too powerful a sniff can anesthetize the sense of smell for several minutes or even as long as an hour. As smell and taste are connected, this will affect one's appreciation of the whiskey.

Professional tasters will often water down the drink to as little as 20 percent alcohol by volume in order to dilute it enough to get an accurate read on the other aromas. Conversely, too much water, especially in older whiskeys, can affect and even "break down" aromas.

Once a person is able to sniff beyond the alcohol, some of the aromas that may be found include vanilla, smoke, flowers, even tobacco. The trick is to be able to have the vocabulary to match the scent.

Touch: It's a sensation that many of us forget, but our mouth is capable not only of tasting but feeling. "Mouthfeel" is the term often used to describe the way our tongues, palate, and throat interpret the way they "touch" whatever is in the mouth.

For whiskey, the mouthfeel may be smooth, viscous, spirity, vaporous, astringent, or dry. It may also burn, which is less a flavor and more of an irritation to the mouth's sense of touch. It is not uncommon for people to describe whiskey as being "hot." One could say that this means, in essence, "Good God! There's a lot of alcohol in this shot!"

Taste: The primary tastes are registered by tiny sensory receptors on our tongues and palates. These set off electrical impulses in our brains that allow us to categorize the sensory experience into one of a combination of the five tastes that we can register—sweet, salty, bitter, sour and savory/umami. The amount of time it takes to stimulate the receptors of the tongue varies according to taste, with the bitter receptor taking the longest. Often this means that if one wishes to fully explore the taste of a whiskey, the drink should sit within the mouth for several seconds.

It takes more than simply putting whiskey into the mouth and swallowing to taste it. Much as with wine, there are three distinct moments that a person can taste whatever is in his mouth, and each moment can provide different experiences.

The first moment is when the whiskey first hits the tongue and shocks the taste buds into action. The second moment is after the whiskey has had several seconds to coat the tongue and mixes with the saliva. The final moment is after the drink has been swallowed (or spat out, if tasting professionally) and the aftertaste slowly dissipates. Each of these moments allows for new flavors to reveal themselves while others fade away.

What tastes are likely to fall upon the tongue? Dr. David Wishart, author of *Whisky Classified: Choosing Single Malts by Flavour*, has sampled whiskeys at over 100 distilleries, and says that most flavors will fall under the following categories: smoky, honey, sweetness, medicinal, tobacco, spicy, winey, nutty, malty, fruity, and floral. Although his list is applied to scotches, it is a great starting point for other whiskeys as well.

But the real question is: How much does all of this matter to someone who is carefully stepping her toes into the whiskey world?

"Whoa, whoa. Wait," Krysta said. "Are you seriously telling me that to taste whiskey I'll have to pay attention to how it feels in my mouth?"

I nodded my head. "It's a common tasting procedure for all food critics. Not just whiskey."

Krysta looked at me like a dog being shown a card trick. She took a quick drink and swallowed and returned her glass on the table. "It feels like liquid," she explained to me, as if I were a kindergartner.

"Well, yeah . . . but."

"And I have to note the way it smells, and the way it tastes?" she continued.

"Uh-huh."

"Then, and let me get this right, I have to note not just how it tastes, but how it tastes at three different times when it's in my mouth?" she asked.

"If you want to be a professional whiskey taster, then yes."

"I'll never remember all of that."

I smiled. "Luckily for you, you are not a professional whiskey taster. You, as a nonwhiskey professional, can drink it any way you like. There's no wrong way to drink whiskey. Just wrong ways to taste it." I poured a bit of water into the Jameson's.

"You are such a nerd," she said to me, shaking her head. Considering that I had contemplated using a rating system that involved math, it was difficult to argue her statement.

After a night's sleep that, due to jet lag, was less efficient than I had wished, we awoke to our only day in Ireland on which we had no officially planned whiskey events. It was our day to explore the area, with the plan to fit in as much Irish culture as we could.

Jameson Irish Whiskey

A blended Irish whiskey that is the big moneymaker for the folks at Pernod Ricard, the French company that owns the brand. This is the best-known Irish whiskey in the United States.

Nose: Citrusy, with more lemon than orange.

Taste: Very grainy, with the barley being somewhat apparent. Starts off a little peppery, but that quickly fades.

Finish: Short and incomplete, almost as if it was a missing third act.

Character: Jameson should be the table wine for the whiskey set. It's dependable, not bad, but not great either. It's the type of whiskey you give to friends of friends, while saving the really good stuff for yourself and those you deem worthy.

As we sat over a plate of black pudding and fried eggs, we discussed our plans.

"Okay, we have several options," Krysta said. "I suggest doing one thing I like, one thing you like, and one thing we both agree upon."

I nodded. Part of the deal I had with Krysta in getting her to come on this trip with me was that, since the research for this book dictated a fair bit of our schedule, she would be in charge of any free time that we could scrounge up.

"The only thing I really want to do is head to a pub later in the day. Other than that, we can do whatever you want," I said.

"Okay, then I have a few ideas," she said, pulling out a guidebook that she had stored away deep within the recesses of her purse. As she read it, she removed a sheet of paper with several lists on it.

"As I was doing research on things to do, I divided things we could do into several categories, including cultural, culinary, and shopping," she said.

I looked at her book, and saw that she had color-coded tabs on several dozen of the pages. "What does the blue tab mean?" I asked.

"That's stuff I could do anywhere, like see a musical, or watch a play. The ones we want to focus on are the green and yellow ones. Since you're the one with the food blog, I figured you would have the places we will eat at covered."

I swallowed. Since my idea essentially boiled down to "let's go eat at a pub," I felt a bit insufficient in my own planning. I didn't even know what pub I wanted to eat at, let alone having a color-coded list that had categories and subcategories. I tried to play it off.

"Oh, yeah. Not a problem." A small, nervous laugh escaped from my mouth.

Not having noticed, Krysta continued, "For culture, we could do recent history or ancient history. What I would like to do is head to Newgrange, just a little north of here. When we head back, we could get a bit of shopping in, and then take a nap. Then we could top off the night at your pub."

This is how we found ourselves leaving Dublin city limits at eight a.m. on a Sunday morning. We were heading to the prehistoric sites of Ireland.

Being an average American, with a below-average knowledge of the Emerald Isle, the only thing I could say with any certainty about the country before landing was this: They dig the color green.

This isn't the most profound of observations, nor is it even rooted in knowing anything directly about the country. This knowledge comes from the many over-the-top celebrations of St. Patrick's Day in the United States, where we Americans decide to celebrate the cultural heritage that is Ireland by putting on green clothing, heading to a parade route lined with bunting colored with several different shades of green, and proceeding to get soused on weak American-brewed beer that has had green food coloring liberally added to it. It is on this day that phrases such as "the wearin' o' th' green" are tossed around so often that nearly everyone in America knows, even on a subconscious level, "Ireland? Ireland equals green."

I write the above so that you, as the reader, can appreciate the following exchange that took place as we found ourselves traveling along the back roads of County Meath, looking for the temples and tombs of folks who had died five thousand years back.

"Kate?" asked Krysta, her eyes on the road ahead as our rental

car crested the latest of several rolling hills that our GPS had said we
needed to take.

"Yes," I responded, letting her know that I was seeing the same
thing she was.

"Holy shit, this is green," she noted with a sense of awe.

"Oh my," I said by way of agreement.

Here we were, in the middle of February, where, back home in
the United States, our respective hometowns would be swathed in
various shades of gray and brown, waiting for spring to come forth
before the various indigenous vegetation would turn into any sort of
aesthetically pleasing color. But in Ireland, in the middle of winter,
on an early Sunday morning with frost slowly melting away into dew,
the fields that were dotted with various flocks of sheep were a magnificent shade . . . of green. From forest to emerald, jade to British
Racing, green was everywhere.

As we arrived at Newgrange and put on our amateur archaeologist
hats, I thought back to an article that I had recently read. Billy Quinn
and Declan Moore, two Irish archaeologists based out of Galway, believe that an extensive brewing tradition existed in Ireland as far back
as 2500 BC, roughly the same time that most people in the know agree
that it was being developed in the Tigris-Euphrates area. Using tools
that were known to have existed at the time, Bill and Declan demonstrated that it was quite possible that a rudimentary ale could have
been easily made back during the start of the Bronze Age. If true, then
Ireland would have had the primary ingredient for whiskey long before the still was introduced to the area. While the timeline would
make it unlikely that the long-dead folks at Newgrange knew about
brewing, it's quite possible that their descendants did.

As we spent the rest of the morning crawling through ancient
tombs, and walking through fields topped with frost and dew, various
questions went through my mind. Could Ireland have discovered beer
at roughly the same time that it was being consumed twenty-eight
hundred miles away? What role did beer play with respect to religious
ceremonies? And most importantly, what would it have tasted like?

When we returned to Dublin, it seemed a little less impressive than it had the night before. I chalked this up to the recent country excursion as well as to the "Every city looks better at night" maxim. I had little in the way of concern with how the city looked, as we had two weeks of city to explore, and only an afternoon in which to fit it. Next on the agenda? Shopping.

"There is one place where I would like to stop," I said to Krysta as we walked toward Grafton Street, after having entered and exited several bookstores and shoe shops along the way. "There's a whiskey store around here somewhere."

She checked her watch. "Oh yeah! Absolutely!" she said, as we nudged ourselves past a few of the buskers who had taken up residence on the crowded sidewalk.

I can say with a fair amount of confidence that most American whiskey fans have not had the joy of entering a shop dedicated solely to the sale of a specific type of liquor. In the United States, liquor is often distributed and sold under strict government supervision, with many individual states still operating under laws put forth following the failure that was Prohibition. If my experiences with liquor stores bear any resemblance to most people's in the United States, a liquor store comes across as only slightly more reputable than the local strip club.

The last time I had entered a state-run store in Seattle, the place was dark and muted, even as several fluorescent lights strained to provide an adequate amount of lighting for the customers to read the labels on the bottles they were purchasing. Lottery tickets adorned the counters, and the shelves were lined with mostly cheap bottles of vodka, most flavored, some not. For every bottle of decent whiskey, there were three bottles of whiskey that were renowned for how inexpensive they were, and five bottles of vodka flavored with some sort of chemical additive. The deep green carpet was matted with age and had not been cleaned in several years. Marks on the linoleum floor had likely been there since the Reagan administration. Liquor stores in America are, for the most part, fairly sketchy places to congregate.

That's not to say that Irish liquor stores are much better. The corner shop in which we were "invited" to purchase whiskey for the

fifteen-year-old mother the night before bears a resemblance to its
Seattle counterpart, with the added touch of having a Plexiglas window from which transactions could occur.

But my notion of what a liquor store could look like changed the
moment I opened the door of the Celtic Whiskey Shop. As we walked
in, it was as if angels started singing. From floor to ceiling, there
were bottles of whiskey, some no larger than the size of the bottles
sold on airlines. Others were sold in wooden boxes, giving the
whiskey an added status. For every label that I recognized, there were
several that were unknown to me. I felt my knees wobble a bit.

"Steady. Steady," said Krysta, as she grabbed my arm.

I looked at the Irish whiskeys, each with its own section on the
shelves, walled off as if to prevent them from being influenced by
each other. There were the familiar brands—Jameson, Bushmills,
Tyrconnel. Those that were new to me included Inishowen, Shana-
hans, and a brand called Feckin.

To explain "feckin'," one has to know a bit about Irish slang. Replace the *e* with a *u*, and one understands the bit of controversy that
the brand has brought upon itself. Some see it as a brilliant move to
get younger people to start drinking whiskey, others see it as a bit
slanderous by not treating whiskey with the respect it's due. And others?

"You don't want to buy that." I looked up from the bottle and
glanced over at the older gentleman who was walking our way. Twenty
four-hours in the country, and I still was getting used to the Irish accents.

"There are better-tasting bottles over there, for roughly the same
price," he said. This was new—a liquor store employee who was pointing me away from a brand because . . . well . . . it wasn't any good.

"Good to know," I said, placing the bottle back upon the shelf. I
looked around. There was something new and interesting everywhere
my eyes roamed. "Is there something you can recommend to someone who doesn't know much about whiskey?"

His head cocked. "Not from around here, are you?" he asked. I
blinked. Oh, right. Krysta and I were the ones with the accents.

"We're here to do research on whiskey," said Krysta, who was showing fewer effects from jet lag than I. "She's writing a book," she said, pointing to me.

The man smiled. "Are you now? Well, you came to the right place, that's for sure. Let's see what I can find for you." He shuffled toward the back of the shop.

I smiled back, and took a quick look around the store. There were two rooms, one with wine, brandies, and other upscale liquors. The room I was in had nothing but whiskey: Irish, Scotch whiskey, bourbon, Japanese single malts, a few from India and New Zealand. I was awestruck and speechless.

"Are you an Irish whiskey fan, or do you prefer the scotches?" the older gentleman asked when he returned.

To this question, I already knew the answer. When traveling, always show preference for the whiskey created in the country in which you are located.

"I'm a big Irish fan," I said.

The shopkeeper smiled. "Good answer." He pulled a thick, dark-green bottle off the shelf.

"This here is my current favorite, a Connemara single malt," he said, looking at the bottle with a bit of reverence. "These folks have changed the way people are looking at Irish whiskey."

"Are these the folks at Cooley?" I asked.

His eyebrows rose. "So you have been doing a bit of research, haven't you?"

I gave him my "aw shucks" look, and blushed a bit. "We're planning on heading out to their Kilbeggan location later this week," I said.

"Ah. It's a great place out there. You're sure to like it."

We shuffled around the crowded shop looking for some of the more rare and expensive bottles that were on display. There was a 30-year-old bottle of Midleton whiskey that was going for two thousand euros, a black label bottle of Maker's Mark bourbon that was going for around one hundred euros.

"What's the most expensive whiskey that this place has sold?" I asked.

"Oh, that's hard to say. Typically the higher-end, more collectible whiskey sales are handled by the owner of the shop."

I nodded. From what was out on display, there was little here that would compete with Mr. Disposable Income's level of purchase, but the sheer number of brands of whiskey still held me in place enough that we spent nearly thirty minutes just looking at what they did have.

I purchased the bottle of Connemara and thanked the shopkeeper for his time.

Exhaustion had set in far sooner than either Krysta or I had expected, and we headed back to the popular Temple Bar. We wanted to drink and we wanted to have a decent meal constituting what one would consider a basic Irish dinner, while downing yet another whiskey.

We walked through the cobbled streets of the area, looking very much like the tourists that we were, and we came across a place called the Oliver St. John Gogarty, a larger-than-life pub/restaurant/hostel that seemed to attract a fair number of tourists and locals. Much like the bars back in the United States, sports blared out of the half dozen or so flat-screen televisions, while a group of twenty-something women sang along with pop hits from the 1980s that were being piped in over the PA system.

Connemara Single Malt Irish Whiskey
Depending upon your point of view, this is either a return to tradition or a novelty for Irish whiskeys. Either way, it is a bit of a risky venture for the folks at Cooley, and they are likely the only Irish whiskey producer who has the nerve to take said risk.

Nose: The briny peat wafts over a bit of vanilla.

Taste: There's a bit of an oily texture, with dark honey balanced by a nice bit of smoke.

Finish: The smoke decrescendos smoothly into a bit of vanilla and oak.

Character: Connemara single malt is like the eccentric literature professor who has a preference for science fiction over the classics of Joyce or Dostoevsky. It would be easy to dismiss him if he weren't so smart. As it is, he's the most interesting teacher in the department.

This was my first Dublin pub experience, one that I tried to savor as much as possible. As Krysta and I found a seat and looked over a menu, I tried to put my finger on the cultural differences between a bar in America and a Dublin pub.

In hindsight, it was perhaps a bit unfair to do this in a well-known tourist neighborhood, so the signifiers of what defines a "pub" would be colored by this. But even so, I noticed that families and couples, both young and old, had taken up residence both at the bar and at the tables. An older couple shared a smaller table with us, telling Krysta (who once again had no problem in starting up a conversation with complete strangers) that they recommended Trinity College Chicken, as they had had it on several occasions and found it "quite good, especially for a pub."

The other thing I noticed was that nearly every alcoholic beverage being sold was a beer, and nearly every beer sold was Dublin's favorite stout, Guinness. Mixed drinks were nowhere to be seen, and no one that I could see was drinking whiskey. Perhaps it was too early.

"Hey, Kate. Look." Krysta pointed to the wall. Sitting upon the inset shelves were several different bottles of Bushmills. A mental note sounded in the back of each of our minds, stating that this was the first restaurant or bar in Ireland that we had been to that sold the stuff. That this was only the second restaurant or bar that we had been to did nothing to downplay the significance of this.

Back in the States, both Krysta and I were told that one should be careful when ordering whiskey in certain bars, as a simple choice of dram would paint your particular political persuasion. Order a Jameson in front of the wrong person, and you would be forever deemed a Republican. If Bushmills is more your fancy, then you would be labeled a loyalist to the crown. For a country that has recently gotten over "the Troubles," this sounded like sage advice.

It was also likely bullshit, a simple misunderstanding of history and business played up to heighten a tourist's fear of being caught in the wrong place at the wrong time. That a pub named after a prominent Republican politician and advocate would sell a whiskey that purportedly defines a loyalist perspective should have been enough evidence. But I looked around for signs of Jameson anyway.

Krysta brought out her day planner as the dinner plates were re-moved from our table. "What time should we be leaving tomor-row?" she asked.

"I think it's a three- to four-hour drive to Bushmills from here, so to be there at ten, we should be leaving around . . . I don't know . . . six?" I said this more as a guess than anything.

She wrote down the time. "Any time for sightseeing afterward?"

I picked up the glass of Bushmills that I had ordered with my Dublin Coddle, and Krysta lifted her glass of Guinness. "After whiskey, there's always time for sightseeing," I said. We clinked our glasses as a means of acknowledging our agreement.

3

The Promised Land

While it is easy to get lost in the history surrounding the still, there is one additional component that is equally important to the history of whiskey that is often forgotten or, at the very least, glossed over: barley.

I understand why. Technology is sexy. Grains? Meh, not so much.

The reality is that whiskey (or aqua vitae, as it was known back then by Latin scribes, or usquebaugh, which is how Gaelic speakers referred to it in the early 1500s) started as the drink of the farmers. The agricultural environments of Ireland and Scotland were nearly completely pastoral. The land lent itself to the raising of sheep and cattle, and much of the farming in these regions revolved around these animals.

From the late medieval period through to the eighteenth century, the principal cereals grown in these countries were oats and a primitive barley called bere. Oats were the staple food for all classes, and were referred to as a food crop. Bere was considered inferior food, likely due to having a low yield. Brought over to the British Isles by the Vikings around AD 800, it was often left as a livestock crop. When other grains were not an option, it was used in some foods, such as broth, and in some places made into bannocks, a sconelike flat bread.

That is, until someone discovered that bere could be used to make a decent drink. It was somewhere within the British Isles that it was discovered to have the inherent talent of being a better fermentable product for making ale. Then, when someone added this ale to the still he found out that the end result was palatable enough to drink. Once consumed, this usquebaugh provided some intoxicating effects that could best be charitably called "pleasant."

More importantly, the farmers discovered that their friends and neighbors were willing to pay them for this new drink, oftentimes more than they would have gotten for the grain itself. It also likely meant that their friends and neighbors would end up knocking at their doors at all hours of the day stating things such as, "I love you man. No really. I love you *hiccup*."

But the introduction of distillation to the farmers was more than a luxury. It was more than a means to provide alcohol to the masses. For people who had little in the way of money or assets, producing whiskey became an economic necessity.

For the farmers who grew the bere, drying and storing grains had always been a problem in the damp climates. Harvests often arrived late, and when grain was stored, extra attention had to be paid to prevent the grains from growing moldy and rotting. Moldy and rotted grain meant lost revenue. The easiest way to maintain the value of a harvested crop over an extended period of time was to convert the grains into alcohol. Whiskey was the better solution than ale, as ale itself could still go bad (the idea of using hops as a preservative had not yet made it to these regions).

Additionally, the residue from distilling—the barley husks— were (and are) highly nutritious animal food. This proved to be a boon for the livestock farmers. As hay could be difficult to find, the "draff" (as barley husks were known) helped feed livestock during the winter months, when food for animals was nearly impossible to find. So, in essence, not only were the farms extending the value of their crop by converting it to whiskey, the livestock farmers were also able to maintain their highly valued animals instead of slaughtering them and selling them prior to the winter months. In other words, the introduction of distilling to the farm culture increased the long-term value of the farms where barley was grown and live-stock was raised.

That the usquebaugh also happened to be a source of entertainment and provided a bit of social lubrication at get-togethers, that was simply an added benefit.

To the ruling class, it looked the opposite. The Highlanders in Scotland and the Gaels in Ireland were seen as savages by the lords and nobles in England, and it was whiskey that greased the wheels of opposition to the English invasions of these lands.

Almost immediately upon the introduction of whiskey into the lower classes, the ruling class tried to control the level of both its distillation and its consumption. In 1556, legislation was introduced by the English-influenced parliament in Ireland that stated, "aqua vitae as drink nothing profitable to be daily drunken and used is now universally throughout the realm of Ireland." To put this into modern terms, Parliament was saying that whiskey provided no public good, yet for some reason, it was very popular. Clearly Parliament had yet to be invited to the really good parties.

The 1556 act tried to implement licensing by requiring appropriate documentation from a lord deputy before distillation was allowed. According to this act, peers, borough freeman, and property owners of lands worth greater than ten pounds were the only folks allowed to make aqua vitae without a license. Everyone else needed to cough up the dough.

Luckily for everyone else, the English lacked the personnel to enforce the act. Distilling went on, pretty much as before, only this time with the added bonus of breaking a law set up by a semi-occupying country. As E. B. McGuire writes in *Irish Whiskey: A History of Distilling, the Spirit Trade and Excise Controls in Ireland*:

> The Machinery for enforcing the spirit licenses or any other laws was utterly inadequate. Wardens of the peace were named for every county following the statute of Kilkenney in 1367 and in the sixteenth century were still nominally operating, but

by then Ireland was in a state of anarchy. Laws, at least those by
the Dublin Government, were not even nominally observed.

By the late sixteenth century, the conflict between the English
occupiers and the residents of Ireland became more intense. The
English, in their wisdom, blamed whiskey, in part, for the "rebellion." In 1580, the English government in Ireland issued a directive
that in Munster, martial law was to be applied to "idle persons . . .
aiders of rebels . . . makers of aqua vitae." This edict did accomplish
a decrease in the amount of aqua vitae produced in the region.
However, it also resulted in the increase of smuggled aqua vitae
from other parts of the country. And thus started one of the longer
conflicts in the history of the world: that between a government and
a person who wants a drink of whiskey.

It wasn't just in Ireland that the government wanted to restrict
production of aqua vitae. Scotland, too, had issues with the government controlling production of the drink. An act of the Scottish parliament in 1555 allowed the inhabitants of the western burghs to
trade bread, ale, and aqua vitae with residents of the isles. In 1556,
Edinburgh Town Council fined one Besse Campbell for making aqua
vitae, thus violating the monopoly that had been granted to the sur-
geon barbers by James IV in 1506. Over the following years, such
convictions became increasingly common.

An act of 1579 indicates that distillation was becoming even
more popular. The act stated that in expectation of a poor harvest,
the making, brewing, or distilling of aqua vitae would be restricted
to earls, lords, barons, and gentlemen for their own use. Or, to put it
another way, so much aqua vitae was being made that it was causing
grain shortages in years of poor crop returns and the government
wished to ensure the ability to feed the citizens. It also demonstrated
that the upper class had the legal wherewithal to ensure that they
could still get their drink on in the lean years.

And it wasn't just the Irish that the English considered ill fit for
whiskey consumption, it was also many of the Scots, who were often
disparaged as acting too "Irish." In 1609, King James I of England
ruled Scotland via a privy council that had been staffed with his own

nominees. One of these representatives, a Bishop Knox, held court in Iona, located on the western isles of Scotland. He wrote nine statutes "of the utmost importance for the improvement of the Isles" that were to be enacted. The legislation embodied in the Statutes of Iona stigmatized what it called "Irish" manners, dress, and customs. The fifth statute relates to whiskey.

> One of the chief causes of the great poverty of the Isles and the cruelty and inhuman barbarity practiced in their feuds, was their inordinate love of the strong wines and aquavite, which they purchased partly from dealers amongst themselves, partly from merchants belonging to the mainland.

From these statutes came the restrictions that individuals were permitted to brew as much aqua vitae as their family needed, but the importation of wines and spirits was banned, as was the selling of any home brew. Of course an exclusion was made for barons, landowners, and other wealthy gentlemen.

This statute was even more of a failure than the bans on whiskey production in Munster.

By the start of the seventeenth century, whiskey had become an established commodity. People made it, people drank it, and the English government was trying to make money off it. But the English were in a precarious position. The distillation of whiskey came with issues. Allow too much whiskey to be made and it would lead to an increase of drunkenness. Decrease the production of whiskey by too much, and the money collected from the tax on the spirit would affect the government budget. Oh, and that would run the risk of making the citizens a tad unruly.

At first the English implemented the process of selling monopolies, a practice they had used back in England. These monopolies were sold to anyone who was held in favor by the right people. It worked like this: A man, typically a royal, was granted the rights to a certain industry by the crown, typically after paying a set amount of money or promising a percentage of the profits. The new owner of this monopoly could in turn sell licenses to this patent to anyone who paid enough money. Typically these licenses were sold, in a given area, to one individual, who could sublicense.

In 1608, the first whiskey patent in Ireland was granted by the lord deputy, Sir Arthur Chichester, to a Charles Waterhouse in Munster. Later that same year, Sir Thomas Phillipps, in likely need of some revenue to keep his occupying forces located in Ulster paid and fed, bought his own license, a patent to distill in County Antrim. It's this license that Bushmills claims as their own heritage, and it is why they plaster their bottles with the year 1608. Of course they do this without reminding the public that there wasn't a brand of whiskey called Bushmills until the early nineteenth century, and that the company that currently owns Bushmills didn't exist until late 1997. But hey, that's modern marketing.

At 4:15 a.m. the alarm goes off.

At 4:30 a.m., the front desk rings up. Holy Christ, it's early. Driving from Dublin to Bushmills, with the intent of being at the distillery by ten o'clock in the morning, initially seemed like a good idea. But any activity that requires you to be awake and in the shower before five a.m. needs to have all aspects seriously considered. For example, will waking up this early in a city that doesn't have a decent coffee shop open before sunlight encourage smaller acts of violence? Does getting caught in rush-hour traffic really make for the start of a good day? What are the odds of having the car trapped in the parking garage for forty-five minutes while dealing with a card reader that has decided that it doesn't want to work anymore? The answers were yes, no, and, well, pretty good, actually.

After having dislodged the car from the parking garage, we finally find our way to the various motorways and regional routes needed to arrive at our destination, the voice of our good-natured GPS happy to tell us which way to turn and how soon we should expect to turn right at the "fohk in the road." It was this morning that we christened the GPS "Molly."

Molly was part of the rental package that we had entitled the "Junior Whiskey Mobile Command Force 2000," a package that was comprised of the rental car and a GPS. Since the car had no voice, we had little need for it to be anthropomorphous. We had initially named the car Seamus Finnegan, hoping that the spirit of Seamus, however he manifested himself, would protect us from harm. Inside was Molly, the mouthy, know-it-all wife of Seamus.

We were quickly to discover that Molly was a temperamental bitch. Sometimes she would just sit there, saying we were still in Dublin when in fact we were a couple of dozen kilometers outside the city limit. She also gave us alerts that said something along the lines of "In five hundred meters, you will stay on the road you are already on." Other times she had no clue where to go, especially when newly developed roads appeared. As Molly was our primary means of navigation, we needed for her to work nonstop. She, on the other hand, worked when she felt like it.

Her work ethic soon became the reason we blamed her for anything bad happening, such as arriving in Ireland during the "spread fertilizer on every acre of farmland festival." By the time we reached Bushmills after four hours of driving (thanks to a hiccup or two by Molly) it became rather apparent to us Yanks that sheep were used for more than wool and meat.

"Can we stop to take pictures of the sheep?" asked Krysta as we both noted the local aroma.

I shook my head. We had a scheduled appointment, and I did not wish to miss it.

The Bushmills distillery is located in the far north of Northern Ireland, in County Antrim. In the village of Bushmills (so named because of the mill on the River Bush), various tourist signs pointed us to the correct location of the distillery. It was a crisp morning, close to forty-one degrees Fahrenheit, when we walked through the front door.

We met Sam, an older, retired gentleman who worked at Bushmills as a tour guide only a few days a week as a means to bring in a little extra money. But mostly, he said, it allowed him to get away from his wife a few times a week, and have access to his favorite drink.

"Now, ladies," he said to us, "we're going to be going through areas where work is going on, so I have to ask you to stay in the areas where directed."

He paused, winked, and then grinned at us.

"But don't you worry," he continued. "We'll get you safely to the tasting at the end."

Any tour of a distillery should include an explanation of the process of distillation. Without it, it's difficult to explain where the flavor of the drink comes from.

Whiskey has evolved over its lifespan. Back in the day, people would drink it almost directly from the still. They would make it with herbs and fruits in the mash. Today it is made from a grain of some sort, with corn, barley, rye, wheat, and even oats being the primary ones used. But the basic process of distillation is roughly the same as it was back when it was first discovered. It's the efficiency and the scale of the process that has seen tremendous change.

Whiskey is made from water, a grain, and yeast. Have those three items, and you are at the start of the whiskey journey.

But if the grain you use is barley, the next question you must answer is "are you going to malt your barley?"—which sounds like a euphemism of some sort. In fact, malting is a means of germinating grains, a necessary step in getting the grain to provide sugars for when the yeast is added.

Malting is the act of steeping the grain in water and then draining said water. The end result is that the barley seeds are tricked into germinating—the process where the plant starts to grow shoots. In order to grow the shoots, enzymes are produced in the seed, which convert some of the stored starch into sugar—sugar that is critical for fermentation. The trick here is to stop the germination at the point where there is still sugar left in the seeds. Intentionally drying the barley accomplishes this. Sometimes hot air is used, other times smoke from peat fires is added. Smoke will leave a distinctive taste, but the hot air by itself will add nothing to the overall flavor. Bushmills does not use peat fires. In fact, the majority of Irish whiskeys no longer use peat to dry their malted barley. However, back in 1608 and for hundreds of years afterward, it's likely that a great amount of Irish whiskeys, both legitimate and illegal, used peat.

Sam made a small face when I brought up peat smoke, as we were walking into their cask house. "It covers the taste of the whiskey," he said.

"Does this mean you think that the peated Scotch whiskeys are covering up their flavor?" I asked.

"Oh, you won't get me to answer that," he laughed. "I've too many friends who like their scotch."

The malted grain is ground into a rough flour called a grist. This is poured into a tub, where hot water is added. This mixture, called a mash, is then agitated regularly in order to encourage further conversion of starch into sugar. The water is drained and saved.

Most of the water is transferred into fermenters. The remaining water is held until the next batch of grain is put into the tub, where it will be used in the mashing of the grist, much in the way a piece of sourdough is set aside and saved as a starter for the next batch of bread to be made. While there are several variations to the process, this is the basic principle of creating what is known as the wort.

Back at the fermenters, yeast is added to the wort. Yeast, being live bacteria, begins to look for something to chow down on. Lo and behold, the sugars that were created from both the malting and the agitation are sitting there, waiting to become a buffet for some very hungry yeast.

This will be recognizable to some as a basic beer or ale recipe. When one thinks of whiskey, one should think "distilled beer," the same way that one should think "distilled wine" when one thinks of brandy. It's not a coincidence that whiskey most often comes from countries with a strong beer/ale culture.

However, the proper term for this fermented liquid is not beer. It's referred to as wash.

Once the wash is made, it has an alcohol content of roughly 9 percent, give or take. In order to make it a stronger drink, a large percentage of the water content must be removed. This is where distillation comes into the picture.

The wash is transferred to the still. The still is then heated, and takes advantage of the fact that alcohol boils at a lower temperature than water, 173.3°F to water's 212°F. First distillation is done in the wash still and will transform the wash into what is termed a "low wine," which has an alcohol content of roughly 21 percent.

The low wine is transferred to a second still (or returned to the first, if only one still is available), where it undergoes the same process. In Ireland, as well as at least one distillery in Scotland, it is distilled for a third and final time. The Irish say that this helps take the edge off the alcohol. Everyone else says that it's simply the Irish showing off.

This is the process that is explained on most tours, and Bushmills was no exception. Sam walked us through each stage, showing an appropriate part of their operation for the topic at hand. In one building we saw the mash tuns. In another, the tall copper stills. In yet another, we saw the bottling operation. Krysta took pictures while I hung on Sam's every word.

As we walked upon a catwalk above the bottling operation, I looked down. My mouth was agape.

"They're Jameson's!" I pointed at the bottles of whiskey that the folks below us were labeling. I looked again, to make sure I was seeing things properly. Yes, Bushmills was busy bottling Jameson whiskey.

"Ah, yes. Well." Sam hemmed and hawed for a moment. "Well, y'see. Before Diageo bought us, we were owned by the same company who owns Jameson's. And we contracted to do some work for them, sort of our version of outsourcing. No pictures, please."

Krysta gave a small pout, and lowered her camera as Sam hurried us out of the room.

The next stop was the tasting room, where we were introduced to George, a taster who had been tasked to give us a tasting tour of Bushmills. In front of us sat eight drams of whiskey. Our goal? Find our favorite, under the tutelage of George.

Krysta looked at me and then back at the drinks. Her glance contained a mix of fear and bliss. She mouthed the word "Eight?" I nodded and pretended to look as if this were normal. Inside I was anxious. Eight glasses of whiskey? Were they trying to kill us?

For drink one, we followed George's lead and added a bit of water to Bushmills primary brand, sometimes called their white label.

"Sniff," he suggested, passing the glass beneath his nose with the grace of a ballet dancer. We tried to emulate him.

"What aromas did you get?"

"It's sweet." said Krysta.

"There's hints of vanilla," I added, not wanting to seem ignorant.

George nodded and looked pleased. "Give it a small taste." We did.

"This is quite smooth," said Krysta, looking over at me.

"A nice finish. It's not long, but it's satisfying," I said. George looked pleased.

At first I thought that Krysta and I cheated somewhat, as we were already well versed in Bushmills white. But over the next few drinks, we seemed to hit our stride in the tasting. Black Bush, their 10-year-old single malt (which I found to be a bit spicy, but good), their 12-year-old single malt (a little sweeter than I expected, but good), and their 21-year-old single malt all passed through our lips, and we both gave intelligent, well thought out responses. I was surprised at how much I enjoyed the 21-year-old, how well I explained what I had tasted, and how much George agreed with

Bushmills White Label

I have a bias towards Bushmills for reasons I cannot explain. Bushmills white label is Diageo's foremost blended Irish whiskey brand. And between you and me, neither Bushmills nor Diageo has anything to do with the 1608 date that they stamp on their bottle.

Nose: A little floral, a little medicinal, a little nutty.

Taste: The mouthfeel is a wee bit viscous, and brings a very sweet vanilla to the back of the mouth. It is also a very light drink, almost dainty.

Finish: A quick finish that is sweet but also comes across as a bit musty.

Character: To me, Bushmills white label is the Julia Roberts of the whiskey world. Beautiful to look at, fun to be around, pleasant to talk to, but really not as talented as one might be led to believe. She can certainly hold her own onscreen, and can demand top billing (and get it), but there are other actors who have far more range and are far more talented.

what I said. I believe one of the phrases that came out my mouth was something along the lines of "a ribbon of near caramel-like flavor that falls upon the tongue like silk, fills the mouth nicely, and lasts as long as a movie." Yes, I can be expressive when I need to, but it helped that the 21-year-old Bushmills is an excellent drink. Out of all the samples on the mat in front of me, this was the only one I finished.

George looked at the last glass and said: "We have a new bottle out to celebrate our four hundredth anniversary, called the 1608, and that is made from a crystal barley. Tell me what you think."

I poured a little water into my drink, thinking to myself: "What the hell is crystal barley?" Distracted, I did not add enough water, so when I took a drink, it went down hot and spicy. I told George as much.

He reminded me gently that it's okay to add more water to a drink if needed, in order to remove the edge. He then asked me to find the one previously consumed dram that was similar to the 1608. He turned his attention to Krysta, as I tried to compare the various Bushmills.

Was it like the Black Bush? Or like the 12-year-old? I started to panic. I thought I was doing so well! None of the other glasses had tasted so overtly spicy. What was I doing wrong? George turned his attention back to me. "Well, what did you get?" he asked.

"Ummm . . ."

He looked at me suspiciously.

"I think it's the Black Bush," I said. "But none of them were as spicy as the 1608."

George gave a small look that showed his disappointment. "As I said before," he repeated, "it's okay to add water to take the edge off."

For a brief moment, I felt like I had let George down. It's an odd feeling, trying to impress a professional taster. Being around him made me feel as if I should have known everything there is to know about tasting, and that not knowing these things made me a bit of a whiskey fraud. But then I kicked myself. Drinking whiskey is not about impressing others. It's about enjoying yourself. And while an educated palate may help increase one's exploration of whiskey, it is *not* a requirement. If one wants the ability to taste the majority of tastes and flavors available in the whiskey world, then yes, an educated palate helps. But if one doesn't aspire to be a master taster, then not getting the flavors of a handful of whiskeys is okay. In fact, it's part of the education process.

"Are you enjoying yourself?" said an unfamiliar voice. George looked up to see who was asking the question, resulting in an acknowledging smile.

"Kate, Krysta," said George, extending his hand to the forty-something male who stood beside our table, "This is Colum Egan, the master distiller here at Bushmills."

Krysta, for whom Bushmills is akin to ambrosia that comes directly from the gods, let out a little gasp.

"How goes the tasting?" Colum asked of all of us as he took a seat. Both Krysta and I offered "Good, really good," with our faces contorted into a mixture of awe and giddiness.

"Oh, you're Americans! I'm heading off to your fine country in the next few weeks to do some promotion."

"Promotion?" I asked.

"St. Patrick's Day events mostly," he said.

"Are our celebrations kinda weird to people who actually live in Ireland?" I wondered aloud.

"It is, really," he said. "Imagine you traveling to here and everyone celebrating America." Images appeared in my head of parades of twenty-something Irish filling the streets of Belfast and Dublin, getting drunk on beer dyed either red or blue, and I began to understand the small cultural dissonance Mr. Egan might be feeling when visiting the U.S.A. on March 17.

"Do you do a lot of promotion?" asked Krysta, giving her red hair a twirl with her fingers.

"A bit."

"Do you get some of the rock-star treatment when you do these events?" I asked.

"Well, I do sign a lot of bottles, more than I thought I would. It does get a little weird, if that's what you mean. I had one man bring me into his bedroom to sign a bottle. That was odd," he said, looking a little distant as he remembered the experience.

Just as quickly, he brought himself back into the present. "So what brings you to Bushmillls in the off season?" he asked.

"She's writing a book on whiskey," Krysta offered, still somewhat starstruck. I blushed a bit as I had when she had mentioned the book the previous day.

"Really? What's it called?" he asked, as George excused himself from the table to head to other responsibilities.

"Well," I said. "I'm thinking of calling it *The Search for the Perfect Shot.*"

Colum looked a bit uneasy, as if I said something that breached some unwritten etiquette.

"What? Don't you like it?" I asked.

"No, no. It's fine. It's just that . . . ," he paused, clearly not wanting to offend me. "Having a shot isn't the best way to have whiskey. In fact, most people will have a *glass* of whiskey, and drink it slowly."

I smiled and offered a lame explanation. "Well, it's sort of a play on words. I'm not tied to it or anything," I said. Meanwhile, in my

 Bushmills 21-Year-Old Single Malt
Whenever people insult or demean Irish whiskey, this is the bottle I point them to. It has been finished in a Madeira cask that must have been blessed by the whiskey gods.

Nose: A choir of grapes, molasses, oak, and a bit of pepper, with other aromas playfully jumping in and out.

Taste: Smooth as silk, and yet manages to get juicier throughout. Flavors such as caramel, chocolate, and raisins all play with each other nicely and the balance here is sublime. The consistency of the drink is near liqueur-like.

Finish: A long, pleasant finish that starts out like a spice cake topped with raisins and ends up with the oak showing up as it fades from the palate.

Character: This whiskey is Christmas and your birthday on the same day, and everyone giving you two gifts in order to celebrate. It is the anticipation and the fond memories of celebrations both in the future and in the past. It is fun, fun, fun.

mind I thought "Great, the first big distillery I go to and the master distiller tells me the title of my book is factually incorrect."

"Could I get a picture of you?" asked Krysta, who had already taken out her camera and began fiddling with her camera's settings.

"Of course, of course," said Colum, ever the diplomat. He picked up one of the several glasses of whiskey that George had left behind, and looked at me. "Shall we toast?"

All thoughts about new book titles went out of my mind, and I smiled. "Oh yes." I said, picking up the glass filled with rest of the 21-year-old.

"To your book!" he said, as he clinked my glass.

"To your whiskey," I offered back.

4

The British Influence

There is an underlying truth about the history of whiskey that is sure to make both the Irish and Scots bristle. For all of the influence that both of these regions have had upon the development of this grain spirit, the English had as much, if not more affect upon the evolution of the drink to modern-day standards.

There are reasons why this fact is not made readily available to consumers. For one, the English influences don't really lend themselves to the underlying mythology of whiskey being the drink of Irish or Scottish rebels. For two, the English accomplished their influence mostly through rules, regulations, and tax laws, laws that the the Irish and Scottish had little to no say in implementing. The English influence on Irish Whiskey is particularly interesting as it speaks to those aspects of Irish national identity that feature rowdiness and rebelliousness. Often when legends are written, the rowdy and rebellious get better press.

Ireland in the 1600s and 1700s was a mishmash of law and chaos; there were Irish chiefs looking to hold on to what was theirs, and British lords and other interlopers looking to increase their own

land and power. Dermot MacMurrough, an ousted Irish king looking to regain leadership, invited English mercenaries to Ireland to
help him with his local problems during the twelfth century, and
the English, ever the gracious guests, decided to seize large tracts of
land from the Irish chiefs they defeated in battle. This started the
ongoing battle wherein every time the Irish revolted against the
newly established English and their laws, which they did with a fair
amount of regularity, more English soldiers were sent over to put
down the rebellion. After the Irish were successfully subdued, the
conquering soldiers were rewarded with even more land taken from
the rebel Irish they had just defeated. By 1640, it is said that 35 percent of all the tillable land in Ireland was owned by invaders or
English soldiers and settlers. The more land the English took, the
more they wanted to impose their own laws. They formed their
own "Irish" parliament, which was merely an extension of Britain's.
They went about passing laws and acts, including those relating to
taxation.

As whiskey demand and production increased, mostly by those
who lived beyond the pale of British-controlled Dublin, the British
government saw an opportunity to bring more money into their cof-
fers. The Irish Parliament introduced an act in 1634 regulating inns
and taverns that were selling whiskey in addition to the more popular ales. The impetus for this act was to ensure the public good by
limiting the number of these places and guaranteeing that the operators of these establishments were good, upstanding citizens. What
makes this act important for the history of whiskey is that it would
eventually set the pattern for controlling all retailing operations that
sold liquor.

After the act was implemented, it soon became apparent that
British-controlled Dublin lacked the resources to collect any of the
taxes due. The act was enforced on a limited basis, essentially when
a) The tax assayers outnumbered the crowd at the inn, and b) when
the inn owners didn't aggressively show their club, knife, and/or
gun collections to the tax men.

Meanwhile, the practice of giving out patents and collecting
monies from the licenses started to fail miserably. Any enforcement

of these regulations worked so poorly that, by 1641, when the Dublin government needed to fund the English troops to put down a revolt of Irish chiefs, all they could collect was fifty pounds. Though the rebellion was eventually quelled several years later, it was clear from an English perspective that more efficient excise controls needed to be put into place.

It was Charles I who introduced "excise" into the legal vernacular. Or, more specifically, it was Charles I's treasurer, the earl of Bedford, who was aware of a practice of obtaining revenue used by the Dutch. It was the Dutch who imposed the first excise duty—the word coming from the Dutch word "excijs" or "exziis." It is a duty charged on any domestically produced good, especially alcohol.

When Parliament got hold of the earl's plan, it complained that these practices amounted to little more than "unjust and pernicious attempts to extort great payments from the subjects by way of excise." These strong words rang hollow two years later, when Parliament enacted the excise.

The regulation of the collection of customs was entrusted to a parliamentary committee whose members were appointed commissioners and collectors of customs, forming in effect a Board of Excise. Everyone who now complains about taxes on alcohol and tobacco can blame the Dutch and the English, for they were the first to implement institutional policies seeking to enrich the government and to control public consumption by making products financially unappealing to purchase on a regular basis.

But before they could implement these changes in Ireland, all hell broke loose back in London. Oliver Cromwell helped initiate the execution of King Charles I. To help pay for his new government, Cromwell left the Board of Excise intact, to organize the collection of duties in London as well as Wales, Scotland, and Ireland. At first a wide range of commodities was covered, but when the duties were extended beyond the districts Parliament controlled to cover the whole country, they were confined to alcoholic liquor. Originally intended for one year only, these duties have remained in effect to this day.

After a decade, the Royalists took back England from the puritanical Roundheads. When Charles II took the throne, he not only maintained the Board of Excise, he furthered its control. On Christmas Day in 1661 the English government tried to exert their control over the Irish whiskey trade, with a tax of four pence on every gallon of whiskey distilled. The monopolies that had been abused by Chichester were abolished. The Excise Department became ensconced within the English government, and gaugers—revenue officers who inspect goods subject to the excise—were introduced to Ireland.

Unfortunately (or fortunately, depending upon one's point of view), the act of 1661 made several errors. First, it made the distinction between higher-quality whiskeys and those of a lower quality, giving limited direction on how to determine one from the other. The purpose was to tax the higher-quality whiskey at a higher rate than the lower-quality, with the intent of giving distillers an economic "leg up" over imported liquors. What happened, though, was that, through haggling, bribery, and possibly threats, many higher-quality whiskeys were taxed at a lower rate.

Second, there were no provisions in the act for distillers or importers to register with the excise office. Registering was strictly a voluntary activity.

Third, the act did not require a distiller to show any sign that stated his trade. So if a gauger wished to check in on a registered distillery, or locate a newcomer to the industry, it would be up to the gauger to locate the premises on which the still was stored.

Fourth, even if they could locate the distillery, the excise officer had no authority to enter the premises without the distiller being present. This later added to the popular problem of the distiller being regularly "absent" from the site whenever the gauger appeared.

Finally, if the gauger wanted to pursue action against illegal activities, he would have to bring his case before magistrates who were likely prejudiced more toward the locals than a person representing the occupying Crown.

So what they had was a situation where the collection of revenue depended upon the trustworthiness of the distillers, and the lack of bias in the enforcers of the law. In other words, the system put in place was perfect for people to abuse the system . . . which is exactly what happened.

A distiller had two options when he decided to make whiskey. He could either be legitimate and pay the tax, or decide to go against the law. The choice made by the distiller would likely determine how much money he could make as well as how long he could operate his distillery.

Those who paid the tax made whiskey that was called "parliament whiskey." The quality of parliament whiskey should not be inferred simply because its makers decided to stay above the law. However, as the act of 1661 detailed that higher quality would be taxed at a higher rate, it can be assumed that there were distillers who practiced techniques that resulted in a better-tasting whiskey. Included in these techniques would likely be the act of storing and aging the whiskey in casks for a period of time.

The aging of whiskey in casks was a known process by this time, even before the popularity of whiskey exploded within the British Isles, as it was an understood technique with brandy. The discovery of the benefits of aging in casks occurred when spirits exported from the wine regions of France ended up hundreds of miles away, several months or even years after the spirit had been put in the cask. Those who sampled the aged drink found it smoother than liquor straight from the still, and found that the wood of the cask provided additional flavor. Aged liquor, whether brandy or whiskey, soon became a valuable commodity.

That's not to say that aged whiskey made up the majority of the market. There was plenty of demand for unaged whiskey, and many producers of the drink simply could not afford to keep their product for any extended period of time. Unaged whiskey was the norm, with aged whiskey likely being rare, and only affordable by the wealthy who had a taste for it. As whiskey was seen during this era as a drink of the lower class, very few wealthy individuals partook of the spirit.

The distillers who chose to not pay the tax went underground to areas of the country were the gaugers feared to tread. It is these folks who introduced poteen, an illegally made whiskey similar in spirit to

American moonshine. And, as with parliament whiskey, one should not infer any lack of quality in the drink simply because it was made illegally. In fact, later in the book we'll discover that there would be a period of time when the best Irish whiskey to be had was poteen.

It is important to note that these acts introduced by the government were not the work of incompetent men. This was a new system that was being implemented in a country by an unwanted occupying government. The excise department began without the benefit of experience, without trained staff, and without the knowledge of the resources required to make this system of taxation work. The experiences of the men who established these precedents would have an effect on distillers throughout the world of whiskey, and these effects are still felt as part of the day-to-day life of the alcohol industry today.

But by the late seventeenth century, England regarded Ireland as more of a place to do battle than as a source of taxes from whiskey revenue. As King James and Prince William sought to engage one another on battle in the fields of Ireland, it became clear that England's priorities lay elsewhere. Enforcing excise fell by the wayside, and by 1700 Ireland could be considered a country without a centralized government.

That didn't stop the Irish Parliament from trying to take up the whiskey issue, on several occasions. The intent of their attempts was to fix the various failures of the 1661 act. In 1717, an act was introduced that changed the role of the gauger from that of an observer of the distillation process to that of hands-on participant. Gaugers no longer visited farms and distilleries infrequently. Now they showed up on a regular basis. The responsibility of reporting the amount of wash created was taken out of the hands of the distiller and put into the hands of the taxmen. The gaugers had to know the distilling process inside and out, and act accordingly. Paperwork increased, as did the tax, as well as the belief that tax men were somewhere between "garden slug" and "rabid mongrel" on the scale of "animals that common folk would kick if given half a chance."

The distillers soon learned their ways around the loopholes of the implemented acts. The early eighteenth century saw a game of cat and mouse between the legal distillers, looking to exploit the laws and make as much money as possible, and the government, who were looking for their share of the money made. Every year that the distillery laws were addressed, the government had to deal with the ways that many were flouting them, and yet acknowledge the place that the still had in everyday farm life.

In 1719, a regulation was enacted that stated that no distiller could work or deliver his spirits at night unless a gauger had been notified.

In 1731 another act was implemented that said that it was illegal to distill in areas where gaugers could not exert their authority.

A clarification to the 1731 act stated that stills could only exist within a two-mile radius of established market towns, unless a still made so little spirit that it could only provide drink for the farm in which it was located.

The governments of both Ireland and England were in reactionary mode, never quite getting ahead of the distillers, who were looking for ways to circumvent paying the excise. Every time those in Parliament sought to address the failures and loopholes of past acts, they added new interpretations of the law and, with it, new ways for the whiskey distillers to flout authority.

Take the act of 1717: The gauger had to keep track of the wash within the still, and tax the differences between visits. For example, if he observed three gallons of wash on one visit, and then two gallons of wash during the next visit, he assessed a tax based on the one gallon that was no longer present. Distillers caught on to this loophole fairly quickly. Between visits, distillers would replace the sold wash with previously undisclosed wash that was not in a still. They would add just enough to the still so that it would show a token decrease. The gauger, instead of noting a gallon decrease on his next visit, would note only a half-gallon decrease, even though the distiller had sold a gallon.

This loophole was addressed by an act of 1742, which required not only a duty charge on the decrease of the wash but a tax on the spirit that had remained in the still. The result of this was that now excise officers had to measure still capacity, an act that was to have ramifications in the industry later on in the century.

But by this time, whiskey was not the primary liquor on the mind of the British. That honor instead went to gin.

Much like their counterparts in Scotland and Ireland, farmers in England found that the production of spirits was an effective way of using surplus grains as well as increasing the value of their crops. However, they didn't produce straight whiskey. Instead they focused on whiskey's juniper-flavored cousin, Genever, later known as gin.

When King William III came to the English throne in 1689, he wrote a series of statutes actively encouraging the distillation of English spirits. Anyone could now distill by simply posting a notice in public and waiting ten days. William also restricted the importation of brandy into England, in the hopes that this would reduce some of the income that the French were making off English subjects. Additionally, it would serve to tweak the nose of the French, a sport which the English have always seemed to relish. The side effect of this restriction was that brandy, still available in England due to smuggling, was only affordable to those who had the money to pay smuggler's prices. The poor turned to gin. From there, gin's popularity took off.

At the height of the craze London was full of backstreet dram shops and peddlers selling small amounts. Illicit stills competed with the big distillers—in 1726 there were 1,500 stills in London and 6,287 places where gin was sold, much of it adulterated with turpentine, alum, and sulfuric acid. Abuse was rampant among the poor, and deaths due to overconsumption and excessive violence were common.

The problem was tackled by introducing the Gin Act, which made gin prohibitively expensive. At midnight on September 29, 1736, the act went into effect, and soon it became clear that the fans of gin did not take kindly to this government interference. Riots broke out and the law was widely and openly broken. About this time, eleven million gallons of gin were distilled yearly in London, which was over twenty times the 1690 figure and has been estimated to be the equivalent of fourteen gallons annually for each adult male. Within six years of the Gin Act's being introduced, only two distillers took out licences, yet over the same period of time production rose by almost fifty percent.

However, the Gin Act of 1736 did not mention the usquebaugh. As gin at the time was essentially straight whiskey macerated with juniper berries (and other herbs), whiskey producers in Ireland and Scotland sought to cash in on the craze going on in London. With an eye on exporting their drink to Britain's capital, they increased whiskey production from about 100,000 gallons in 1708 to 250,000 gallons in 1736.

Most of the new whiskey never left the regions where it was made. According to contemporary documents the great majority of the production was absorbed by the local market. While their intent was to sell to London in order to take advantage of the loophole created by the Gin Act, distillers soon found that they had little problem in selling at home. If they didn't know they could make money at making whiskey beforehand, they certainly did now.

The Gin Act of 1736 was an unmitigated failure. It led to social unrest and riots, and it never achieved its primary goal—to reduce drunkenness. Illegal gin was still made, was still available, and was still drunk. Eleven million gallons of gin were annually distilled in London, nearly all of which went untaxed. It was the same story for the increased production of whiskey in Ireland and Scotland. As more whiskey found its way into the market, more people began consuming it, increasing the drunkenness of the citizenry. And due to a lack of resources, most of the increased whiskey production also went untaxed. It was at this point that the English government decided that they loved money more than the appearance of having a stiff upper lip.

The prime minister, Sir Robert Walpole, opposed the Gin Act as unenforceable and against the will of the people. With the evidence of the failure of the Gin Act so readily apparent, he was able to get it repealed in 1742. With the help of distillers, a new policy was introduced that set up reasonable prices, reasonable excise duties, and licensed retailers under the supervision of magistrates.

For a brief time, the British parliament learned its lesson, and did not seek to reduce the consumption of alcohol. The Irish House of Commons in 1771 made an attack upon drunkenness, and passed a bill to suspend all whiskey distilling, claiming it was having a demoralizing effect upon the country. Lord Townshend, then viceroy, informed the English ministry back in London that the House had the bill exceedingly at heart, that it was generally popular, and would give contentment and satisfaction throughout the kingdom. All they needed for it to pass was the go-ahead from London.

When the British looked at the bill, they had to dismiss it. Besides the interference with the natural liberty of the Irish, it was found that it would involve a loss of excise tax. In a choice between sober citizens and regular income from excise, what the British government really wanted was more money from the taxation of whiskey.

This was the environment that John Jameson entered into when he landed in Dublin to start his own distillery.

5

This . . . Is John Jameson

When one is reliant on an unreliable GPS, certain allowances must be made. For one, a map should be purchased, essentially making the GPS redundant. As we headed to the Cork area of Ireland, some 160 miles south of Dublin, this is exactly what we did. We didn't turn off Molly, as both Krysta and I thought this cruel, but we did use her more as a backup. Every time she got something wrong, we'd pat her on her system and tell her in the most patronizing tone: "That's okay, Molly, we know you tried your hardest."

To be honest, we were a little hard on her, because with the influx of money into Ireland as a result of the Celtic Tiger—the rapid period of economic growth—the government has had money to invest in the infrastructure. Everywhere we went on the west coast of Ireland showed signs of new motorways. These roads now go a long way to shortening drives from north and south of Dublin. Sadly, as Molly's maps had not been updated in some time, we found that quite often she had no idea where we were going. Many times, she was simply not needed. Thanks to the new motorways, we made it south in very good time, and we pulled into the parking lot of the Midleton distillery at 10:30 a.m.

Jameson has two different locations for whiskey folks in Ireland, one in Dublin and one in Midleton. We had decided to go to Midleton, as the Dublin location had a decidedly tourist-trap aroma about it. The distillery in Dublin had long been closed, and no production officially went on. Rather, it had been refurbished with models and mannequins demonstrating what a distillery could look like. Krysta and I agreed that it would be best to see an actual distillery, even if it was one that was no longer producing whiskey. The Midleton location also had the added benefit of being next to the production plant where Jameson's *was* made.

In 1966, John Power & Son, John Jameson & Son, and the Cork Distillers company (which owned the Midleton Distillery) merged to form the Irish Distillers Group. The board of the newly formed company decided to close their existing distilleries and consolidate all production at a new facility. This was built at Midleton, directly behind an older distillery, as it was the only existing site with room for expansion. In July 1975, production ended at the old distillery and began in the new. The old distillery sat unused for a period of time until 1992, when it was converted into a visitors' center.

We walked in, impressed by what they had done to the place. It looked like how I imagined a distillery should look, albeit refurbished for tourism. On the outside, slate gray and crimson dominated the building fronts. Inside, a green similar to that of the Jameson's bottle was everywhere. Krysta looked at the clock on the wall.

"We're early," she said.

Indeed we were. The first tour didn't start until eleven o'clock.

"Well . . ." I said. "Do you want to look around at the trinkets, or shall we get a drink?"

"Both," Krysta said, and I agreed. We headed back to the bar and restaurant area of the visitors' center, giving a quick glance to all of the displays of paraphernalia that an old distillery can collect.

"Look! An old bottle top," Krysta pointed out in mock delight.

"Oooo. An ad from the nineteen-seventies!" I responded.

"Ahh, a bottle of whiskey from the nineteen-hundreds!" Krysta said.

"Hey, a glass from . . . wait, what?"

She pointed at a crusty bottle of Midleton with the label aged to a nearly decrepit state, where there was any label at all. My mock sincerity turned to honest interest.

"Good lord," I said. "I wonder what it tastes like."

Having given the items the proper respect, we headed back to the bar to share a glass of Redbreast, their Irish pot still whiskey. Thoughts of one hundred-year-old whiskey jumped through my head.

As we sat at the table, Krysta looked at me with an impish grin. "We're drinking at 10:30 in the morning."

"And no one is looking at us as if we're insane," I added. "Isn't it great!" We acted like teenagers who had been given their first beer at a family reunion—respectful, yet thrilled at breaking our American taboo.

 Redbreast 12-Year-Old Pot Still Whiskey
Redbreast is Pernod Ricard's nod to Irish whiskey heritage. There's no use of the continuous still, so it's produced like a single malt. However, they use a single mash made up of both malted and unmalted barley. This is why they cannot call it single malt.

Nose: Strong honey aroma, with a little bit of spiciness underneath it.

Taste: Butterscotch mixed with a slight dose of pepper at the end.

Finish: Great finish, lasts almost a minute or so after swallowing, with the sweetness combining with a small hint of licorice at the end.

Character: Redbreast is the secret restaurant tucked away in the back of a strip mall that only a handful of people know about. The atmosphere is great and the food divine, but no one is sure that they should tell other people about it because either it'll become too crowded (and thus it will be impossible to get a table) or the increased production by the staff in the back will affect the overall quality of the place.

Krysta pulled out her tour book to look for new sightseeing opportunities. She turned to a page with a blue tab at the top.

"Y'know," she said in such a way that it sounded both offhanded
and intentional. "We could make it to the Drombeg stone circle before dusk if we're lucky."

When we weren't researching whiskey, Ireland was quickly becoming our stop for all things prehistoric. Two days prior we had
been at the tombs of Newgrange. The day before, after visiting
Bushmills,we had climbed the rocks at the Giant's Causeway, a series of forty thousand interlocking basalt columns that formed the
basis for the legend of Finn McCool. Today it would be looking at
monoliths in the southern region of Ireland. Each stop, Krysta had
filled me in on some legend or story associated with the area we
were visiting. Where she was learning loads about whiskey, I was
learning loads about faeries, giants, and the Irish gods of Tuatha Dé
Danann.

I looked at the clock on the wall. "Can we get lunch in Cork before heading out?" I asked.

"Oh sure!" Krysta said. "Of course."

"Then let's do it."

Krysta clapped, saying "Yay!!!" as we gathered our stuff before
heading to the area where the tour was to start.

The visitors' center promoted several different brands owned by
the Irish Distillers and, by extension, Pernod Ricard. Tullamore Dew,
Paddy's, and Power's all had a bit of a presence. But it was Jameson
that was the headliner at Midleton. As Jameson's sells nearly two million cases of whiskey a year, they knew who paid the bills around here.

We returned to the front of the distillery, where guides ushered us
into the theater. A younger woman with black hair and the look of a
person who wished she were somewhere else greeted us and asked
us to take a seat.

"Before we go on the tour, we have a brief movie to show you,
about ten minutes long. As I've already seen this movie a few dozen
times, I'm going to step out and return when it has completed." She
turned down the lights and, as promised, left the room.

The movie was bad. Not poorly constructed bad, as it was apparent that a fair amount had been invested in production costs. But over-the-top exaltation of the founder as the next messiah kind of bad. The film had a self-consciously artistic quality and featured an out-of-focus, rarely in frame John Jameson who never spoke, and a voiceover that was seemingly sucking up to the corporate board of Pernod Ricard. It repeated Jameson's name over and over at the start of each sentence. "John Jameson came to Ireland with nothing but skill and a dream," it said in a booming voice. "A chemist once offered John Jameson an additive that could make one-week-old whiskey taste like five-year-old whiskey, but John Jameson refused," and "John Jameson knew quality when he tasted it." Halfway through the video, I almost expected the booming voice to say, "John Jameson once saved two orphans from a burning bog, while discovering the cure for bubonic plague! You are not fit to stare at the shoes of John Jameson! Look away! Look away!"

I groaned aloud. Krysta elbowed me in the ribs, and we both started laughing, annoying the Canadian family behind us. Well, not so much annoyed as . . . politely distressed.

After ten more minutes of this propoganda, I was highly annoyed, and needed a drink. When the tour guide returned and asked for volunteers for the tasting that was to occur at the end of the tour, I quickly raised my hand. Krysta, who was suffering from the same case of *over-propagandus annoyus*, also raised her hand. We were both chosen.

As we started the actual tour, we found ourselves even more paranoid about the quality of the exhibition. But an odd thing happened . . . the tour became interesting. It wasn't due to the tour guide, who seemed to be literally running us through the old distillery, and showed no interest in going into great detail in any answer to any question posed.

"Do they make single malts here?" asked a small man with a British accent.

"No," was the terse response from the guide.

Nor was it due to the the topics covered by the tour guide, who gave the standard "this is how you make whiskey" script.

"You need three and only three ingredients to make whiskey here at Jameson," she said.

"Barley, yeast, and water," Krysta and I mouthed at each other, thinking back to the previous day's tour at Bushmills.

"Barley, yeast, and time," said the tour guide, intentionally ignoring us while still walking forward at such a pace that some of the tour group had to jog to keep up.

What made the tour interesting was the distillery itself, stuck in time from when it closed. It was an untended museum with a tended-to tour thrust upon it. Every sign and display seemed out of place in the remains. From the water wheel to the home of the master distiller, each place within the distillery seemed a bit, well, sacred. And the group who had taken it upon themselves to tend to these buildings, I thought, could be doing better.

Throughout the tour, I found myself turning to Krysta, correcting various errors. When they talked about the fall of Irish whiskey in the early twentieth century, they made it seem like everyone's fault but the owners of the Irish distilleries. When they talked about the concept of "triple distilled," they failed to mention that this was a bigger issue when whiskey was distilled in pot stills, and that continuous stills have made this much less of an important point.

There were many parts of the distillery where the tour did not go, areas that, because we didn't get to see them, immediately made me wish I had several hours to explore the place on my own.

The most interesting part of the tour was not even located within the old distillery. Outside in the courtyard, which had an old smokestack, we were told to look about five hundred yards or so beyond the distillery. There, in the distance, was roughly 5 percent of the new, more modern-looking, industrial-sized distillery, which has been in operation since 1975, when the group transferred operations from the old distillery. Midleton is one of the most modern distilleries in the world and, with a production capacity of five million gallons per year, is the largest in Ireland. The distillery boasts thirteen 75,000-liter stills, both pot and column, which are used in combination to produce several different types of whiskey, as well as a gin and a vodka. Jameson is obviously made here, as well as Power's,

Paddy, Tullamore Dew, Redbreast, Midleton Rare, and even the grain whiskey used in Jameson's chief Irish whiskey rival, Bushmills. It looked huge—or at least as huge as one can surmise by only viewing 5 percent of a building.

Outside of the small corner that we could make out by the smokestack, the rest of the new distillery was left unseen. It was as if the industrialized image ran contrary to the image of tradition and heritage that Pernod Ricard would prefer to sell. Pernod Ricard, the owner of all of the brands mentioned in the above paragraphs, as well as several other brands of spirit, was not mentioned at all. Learning that the owners of Jameson also owned The Glenlivet, a single malt Scotch whiskey from the Speyside region of Scotland, as well as Chivas Regal, yet another Scotch whiskey, would also play a bit of havoc with the image that the Jameson whiskey wishes to sell. Out of courtesy, I declined bringing up to the tour guide the fact that the world's most popular Irish whiskey is actually owned by the French.

After showing us a display of false casks filled with a lighting display used to demonstrate just how much whiskey is lost due to evaporation, the guide asked those of us who volunteered for the tasting to separate ourselves from the rest of the tour group. "So who wants to do a tasting?" she said with a little more enthusiasm than she had for the tour. She guided us into their bar, strategically located directly next to the gift shop.

For the tasting, they pitted three of their own Irish whiskeys against Johnny Walker and Jack Daniel's, designed to illustrate just how much better Irish whiskey is than both Scotch whiskey and American whiskey. Had they wanted to impress me, they should have pitted the Irish spirits against The Glenlivet Scotch and Wild Turkey Bourbon, as both of these are also Pernod Ricard products.

The whiskey tasting did me in. Not only did I taste-test the five different whiskeys, the volunteer taste testers also received the standard free drink at the end of the tour. The next thing I found myself wandering aimlessly in the Jameson gift shop trying to figure out if I could afford both the Reserve and a twenty-five-euro T-shirt with "Jameson" sewn across the chest. In the light of sobriety, it seems laughable that I would give them money so I could advertise for their product. But I

Powers Gold Label

Ask several Americans what brand they think of when they hear the phrase "Irish whiskey," and Jameson's and perhaps Bushmills may come to mind. In Ireland, Powers Gold Label is likely to come to the forefront. Owned by Pernod Ricard, and produced at the Midleton Distillery, the spirit is a blend of pot still whiskey and grain whiskey.

Nose: Full and spicy, with the grain being very apparent.

Taste: If you like barley, this is the drink for you. This whiskey fills the mouth, and is quite vibrant.

Finish: A bit of caramel in the back, but this is really all about the barley.

Character: Rough and fun, playful without being overly clever, smart without being smug, this whiskey is Ireland.

---

had just paid eleven and a half euros for the honor of viewing a company's models of the distillation process and a "free drink." I had bypassed the right to be holier than thou the moment I sat in the cushioned theater to watch a ten-minute commercial.

They extolled the virtue of their drink over that of Johnnie Walker Red and Jack Daniel's, and the tour guide prompted some of the volunteers to suggest that, even out of the brands of Irish whiskey owned by Pernod Ricard, Jameson was superior. Krysta and I shared our free drink, taking in the spiel. I thought that Jameson as a drink was okay, but I much preferred the Redbreast. Hell, I'd even promote the Power's label over Jameson. But the tour guide would have none of it. Jameson was king.

And they had the movie to prove it.

6

Locke's and Loaded

In 1779, the inefficient and toothless tax upon any whiskey that was voluntarily announced as being distilled was still in effect. Taking advantage of the various loopholes, the amount of retailers selling whiskey had increased dramatically. With more liquor shops available and, as a result, more liquor available for consumption, a rise in drinking of whiskey occurred. Not so coincidentally, a rise in drunkenness also occurred.

By this time, taverns had not just become a place to take a drink or two. They became the de facto meeting place for the professional classes throughout the United Kingdom and Ireland. Part of this was certainly due to the use of the drink in professional matters. Whiskey was used to loosen inhibitions in order to help foster complicated and risky deals. It was also used to celebrate when the deals were signed.

Whiskey also became present in other day-to-day matters. It was taken when one felt ill, and when one wished to celebrate. A dram or two was had before one went to work, and for breaks and lunches. Workplace drinking was ever-present, and on-the-job inebriation was common. This drunkenness led to inefficiency in the workplace, which in turn harmed the economy.

It also led to more crime. With the demand for whiskey increasing, those who were motivated by greed tried to take advantage of the lax laws surrounding whiskey production. These were the types of folks who would try to put anything into the wort, using cheaper ingredients and cheaper alternatives to grain to create the alcohol, all in the hope of squeezing every last penny from the profit margin. Peter Mulryan, author of *The Whiskeys of Ireland*, wrote of this time that ". . . the standard of whiskey being produced in Ireland was so dismal and dangerous that [Irish] parliament was forced to pass an Act prohibiting distillers from using any ingredient except malt, grain, potatoes and sugar."

The money raised by taxes on liquor was also needed, especially as the British had to fund a war that was taking place an ocean's distance away, and to protect themselves from their neighbors in France, who were always looking to make their life difficult. The British government and, by extension, the Irish Parliament, soon found themselves in a predicament. The revenue was badly needed, but so was a sober, productive, law-abiding citizenry. Some distillers only announced a small percentage of their whiskey, others did not declare anything. Money from the excise was not pouring in, even though a quick walk into a local pub or inn would convince even the most skeptical that the whiskey producers were somewhat less than ethical.

Britain's answer? They decided to mess with the tax laws in order to reduce consumption, but not so drastically that it would lead to an effective black market similar to the ones that thrived during the time of the gin riots. The British government decided to overhaul the excise tax regarding whiskey production. Their goal was to start bringing in enough money from whiskey production to pay not only for the enforcement of the excise but for the prosecution of those producing whiskey outside the law. Once prosecuted, they could confiscate the stills and remove the product from the marketplace. Less alcohol on the market would mean fewer people drinking, which would mean more people sober and contributing to society.

This was the idea behind the act. But as with many other of the previous tax plans, it fell apart in implementation.

The act of 1779 was novel in the fact that it called for a stop to the taxation of the whiskey itself, and instead taxed the size of the still and the amount that might be produced from that still. The larger the still, the larger the tax. It was an attempt to limit the number of distillers who were avoiding taxation through means of giving inaccurate or inadequate measures of their wash. Prior to this act, distillers would go out of their way to avoid showing the gaugers just how much wash they had on hand. The extent of this avoidance went so far as to introduce a new profession into the communities—the sugar bakers.

Essentially the sugar bakers were people, either brewers or bakers, who made wort for their own businesses, and made distiller's wash on the side. The benefit for the distiller is easy to see: The distillers could not be taxed for wash that was not on the premises. And the sugar bakers were not covered by the act of 1661. So they became a third-party, untaxed storage house for a distiller's wash. This was exactly the sort of behavior that the new act sought to address.

The act of 1779 changed the focus from the amount of alcohol that was made from a still to the amount of alcohol that could be made, making it one of few laws on the book that required that the government had a proficient skill in predicting the future.

The initial interpretation of the act worked like this: A still of a certain size was determined to have the capacity to make x number of batches (called "charges") over a twenty-eight-day-period. This was the basis of the license duty. During this period, the distiller continued to pay duty on decreases of his wash for the first three weeks of the month, much as he had over the previous century. But it was the fourth week, when he paid duty on the difference between what was produced and what it was determined that he could produce, that became the thorn in the side of the government. Eventually the assessment of the decrease of the wash became less important, and soon these assessments became secondary to excise control, as the license duty became the primary means of revenue generation.

Those distillers who registered with the government did everything they could to increase their profits. A typical way of eluding the taxman went as follows: If the government said a still could produce x gallons of whiskey per year, then the distillers tried to produce x plus an additional y amount of whiskey. This resulted in paying taxes on x, and y providing revenue that was not taxed. The more y a distiller produced, the more money they would make. The distiller had every financial motivation to work his still as much as possible to produce as much whiskey as time would allow. This resulted in a fair amount of liquor escaping duty. Since liquor escaping duty was one of the primary reasons for the act of 1779, Parliament soon raised the number of charges to be taxed.

Over the next several years, the distillers and Parliament engaged in a constant struggle. Each year, Parliament increased the number of charges that the distiller could be taxed, and each year the distillers would find new ways to hack their stills in order to increase their yields, and then thumb their noses at the taxmen.

The initial rate of taxation was reasonable, given the profit margins of the distillers, so the effects upon the industry were negligent. But when the number of charges saw a drastic rise in 1780, the effect was immediate. Distillers who did not have the capital or the skill to increase production went out of business or went underground. Twenty-five percent of the industry either closed shop or went underground. In 1780 there were 1,228 registered distilleries. By 1790, there were 246. But these statistics do not tell the full story. One thousand stills had not disappeared. Instead, most simply no longer reported to the government. The whiskey produced at these unregistered locations went to the last place where the government wished them to go: the black market.

Meanwhile, the distillers who had remained registered worked faster and harder to increase the numbers of their charges. Known as makers of parliament whiskey, they introduced technological improvements to the still, all with the goal of producing more alcohol in a shorter amount of time. And if the still couldn't work fast enough, then production techniques and ingredients were changed, cut, or ignored. Poor production techniques soon became common practice. Higher heat was applied to the still so that the alcohol would evaporate more quickly. But quicker evaporation led to frothing, which in turn slowed down distillation. So to cut the foaming, soap was added to the mix. This reduced the froth, but now the whiskey tasted like dish soap. Quantity became the order of the day, and the quality of the whiskey produced suffered.

It didn't take long for people to realize that Parliament whiskey tasted vaguely of soap, kerosene, and a touch of muskrat innards. If people wanted a better-tasting whiskey, they turned to the black market for poteen. Those who were producing poteen could produce whiskey on their own timetable and sell a higher-quality product. The market for parliament whiskey fell, while the sellers of illegal whiskey were making a good amount of the money that the British government wanted. The 1779 act had backfired, and the English parliament needed to fix it.

Their first thought? Go after those distillers who were underground. In 1783, the government introduced a penalty of £20 on any town where an illegal still was discovered. This resulted in nefarious folks placing illegal distilling apparatuses into the possession of innocent individuals and communities. So much for that idea.

In 1791 the license period was reduced from twenty-eight days to twenty-five, and the number of charges allowed was once again increased. But a new twist was added to the regulations—a distiller had to work his still for a minimum of 112 days out of the year, or pay the still license for the periods of time the still lay dormant up to the 112th day. This was a horrible law for the small hamlets and counties with smaller marketplaces. If distilleries were forced to make an excess of whiskey and yet had no one to sell it to, the spirit would go unsold. Faced with the decision to either produce whiskey that no one would buy or pay taxes on a still that was not in use, people simply opted out of the government rules. Again, distilleries either went onto the black market or closed. This aspect of the act of 1791 essentially shut down the smaller market distilleries.

After finding out that they were closing more distilleries than was economically beneficial, the government tried to fix this in 1797 by lowering the minimum active days to 100. But by then it was too late. Illicit distilleries had filled in the demand that the parliament distilleries had lost. The British had to deal with illicit distilleries in both Scotland and Ireland, and they found themselves having to increase the presences of the law to deal with smuggling. Once again, Britain's attempt to tax whiskey had been a complete and utter failure.

The next day saw us leave the confines of Cork, where we had stayed after the visits to Midleton and the Dromberg stone circle. We got into our car and drove north to Kilbeggan, in County Westmeath, about fifty miles east of Dublin. Molly, being fairly well rested, gave us little in the way of problems, and we found ourselves there in no time at all, even with the steady pitter-patter of rain that seemed to follow us.

We were off to see Locke's Distillery, owned by Cooley, the only Irish-run whiskey company on the entire island. Looking to expand their product line and purchase their own bit of heritage, the young company of Cooley had bought Locke's several years prior and was in the midst of restoring the distillery to its old glory. If the site contained as many historical knickknacks as Jameson's had the day before, I was promised a good time.

We passed through the town of Tullamore, where we stopped to have a bit of breakfast before heading out to nearby Kilbeggan. Locke's distillery was situated on the River Brusna, which seemed more creek- than river-sized. I looked over my notes about the distillery as Krysta looked for a place to park.

"A small pot still distillery, it is the oldest licensed distillery in the world. The license to distill dates to 1759, a copy of which can be seen in the distillery," I read to Krysta from the notes I had copied from Wikipedia.

"If there's anyone even here to show us around," she said in response as she set the parking brake.

I looked up. She was right. The place looked quite deserted. Steven Hynes, the marketing director of Cooley (which also owns the Kilbeggan Distillery), had said that I was to meet with Brian Quinn at the office, but it didn't look as if anyone was around.

We got out and walked to the front gate. The office was situated just off the distillery, across a service access road. There, almost camouflaged, was the front door to the office. I knocked on the door, and when there was no answer, I opened the door into the foyer. There was a doorbell located by a small window and I rang.

From the distance we heard footsteps clamoring down the steps, and soon we were greeted by an older gentlemen with a sunny disposition and a slightly red nose.

"Hello! Hello!" he said to us, his Irish brogue strong and distinct. "You must be Kate! I'm Brian. Brian Quinn."

Krysta and I introduced ourselves, and we followed up with the ritual of the business card exchange.

"We've got a lot to do today, including a tour of the distillery, a bit of tasting, and then a lunch with me and my wife. Are you up for that?"

We both nodded.

"Good. Keep your coats on, and let's get started."

We soon found ourselves being shown an older distillery, close in age to Midleton. As we walked the grounds, Brian talked about the history of the location. This was interspersed with quick explanations of the distilling process.

"Before there was a Locke's here, the distillery actually dates back to Matthias McManus, who started distilling here back in 1757," Brian said, as we walked through the courtyard to the milling area. "We don't know how successful they were at it, but we know they didn't get out of the business because they weren't making any money at it. Matthias's son, John McManus, got himself into a bit of trouble with the English, and found himself executed just down the street there." He pointed out an open window to a place I couldn't see.

"The McManus family's heart wasn't into distilling any more, and in 1794, the Codd family, long associated with the local malting trade, took a stake in the place."

As he continued, Krysta and I found ourselves entranced. Not five minutes into the tour, and we were listening to a story about an Irish rebel who had died for the cause, and the subsequent family strife. The history offered by Mr. Quinn and his storytelling skills kept us both silent and respectful, a rare combination for us.

Over the course of the next hour or so, Brian told us about heroes and villains, good times and bad, weddings and funerals, every few moments taking a second to clear his throat, or point out a unique aspect of the old distillery.

And oh, what a distillery! It was cold, full of cobwebs, with small pockets of activity taking place, as limited production was ongoing. It was more of an archaeological site than a place of business.

In other words, it was fantastic. Everywhere we were discouraged to go on the Midleton tour, we were encouraged to explore at Kilbeggan. Each place we found, Brian had a story to go along with it.

"Did you know they tried to find ghosts here?" he said suddenly, as we were looking over an old malting vat.

Krysta's eyes lit up, hopeful of a story about faeries.

"Oh I'm not sure if I believe the stuff that they were saying, but they said that they were able to talk with John Locke himself," he said, as we walked steadily down some old stairs.

We continued on.

"You want to taste some whiskey straight from the still?" he asked us.

Krysta and I nodded like children who had been asked if they wanted to go to McDonald's.

He guided us to the spirit safe, open and unlocked as they were testing a run and not operating it for production. The aroma that came out of the still enrobed us. It was then and there that I decided that the aroma of freshly distilled spirits is one of the better ones on the planet. The strong scent of the grain used permeated the air, giving out a breadlike scent, yet beneath sits a more nefarious aroma, threatening to kick the ass of those who don't treat it with respect. The scent around the spirit still is inviting and taboo at the same time.

The gentleman doing the testing was introduced to me, but I was too caught up in the moment to catch his name. He had poured a bit of the fresh spirit into the glass. Brian graciously took the drink and passed it to me. I sniffed and took in its smell, and I shook a bit with pleasure.

"Go on. Take a drink," said Brian, smiling. I wasn't sure if it was a command or a dare. Either way, I let a little bit of the drink pass my lips.

Electricity seemed to shoot through my mouth, followed by a hint of the warm, sweet, grainy flavor that the air around me foretold.

"Oh, that's good," I said, passing the glass to Krysta. She took a drink and smiled . . . and took another drink. Both of the men laughed. Brian thanked the tester and we continued on our tour.

We walked to a colder part of the distillery, where various hands-on displays had been set up. Brian spoke up. "We've even had spies here."

After hearing about Irish rebels and ghosts, I was hoping that this would be true.

"Really?"

He smiled, and looked at the ground. "Ah. No. Not really. But Locke's was accused of dealing with them."

He continued. After Ireland and England went their separate ways, Lockes' went into a decline. Two of the Locke's sons who had run the distillery passed away, and the company seemed to be directionless. Day-to-day operations fell to a company secretary, while some shareholders sold their part of Locke's. Further blows came due to Prohibition in America, and years of strife following Ireland's quest for independence. Between 1924 and 1931, no whiskey was distilled, and

High Wine Whiskey (Straight from the Still)
Everyone should take the chance to try whiskey straight from the still.
Nose: Warmth and grain, with the spiciness of the alcohol hanging out for fun. In my opinion, this is the best aroma in the world, especially if it is smelled around the spirit safe of a distillery.
Taste: Unaged whiskey is like liquid electricity with a hint of a barley scone beneath it all. Hot and spicy, and a little bit dangerous (in a good way).
Finish: Finish? What finish?
Character: High wine is the rebel no one wants you to date, yet something still compels you to see what all the fuss is about. You realize he's a bit dangerous and quite illicit, but he is so much fun to hang around.

the company relied upon the stock of whiskey aging in their warehouse.

The 1930s saw a little improvement in the company's fortunes, mostly due to the master distiller's illicit nocturnal whiskey operation that he ran on site. Helped by a corruptible exciseman, he made illegal whiskey throughout the late thirties and throughout World War II. He made a killing, but Locke's saw just enough consumers to keep them afloat.

But it wasn't the bootlegging that brought down Locke's. The place had fallen into disrepair, and no one had invested in the distillery since the 1890s. The owners looked for new buyers. A Swiss investor who used an English front man by the name of Horace Smith claimed that he wanted to buy the company and the distillery for just over £300,000. His unstated intent was to immediately sell the whiskey aging in the warehouse, and clear a profit of 100 percent.

However, neither the Swiss investor nor Smith could come up with the deposit, and soon both found themselves running from the law for fraud. The Swiss man was caught and released. Mr. Smith turned out to have a decent criminal record at Scotland Yard. As he was being extradited back to England, he jumped overboard and escaped with the help of accomplices.

In Dublin, Oliver Flanagan found out that the Swiss gentleman had offered several members of the government gold watches. Using the minor news story to fling some mud at his political foes, Flanagan proceeded to paint members of the government as dupes. Rumors spread, with one stating that the Swiss gentleman wasn't Swiss at all but a spy from behind the iron curtain, looking to infiltrate Ireland.

The Locke's scandal stayed in the press for months, ruining many reputations, including that of Locke's Distillery. Interested buyers disappeared, and the company went deeper into debt. The Irish Distillers Group, the monopoly that was purchasing companies and brands at an alarming rate, steered clear of the troubled company. By 1953 Locke's had stopped distilling whiskey, and in 1958, they closed their doors. The stills remained silent until Cooley, having acquired Locke's assets, ran them again in 2007.

I was in love with the distillery, and a little reticent to head back to the office when the tour was complete, even if we were going to do a tasting. Locke's was a time machine. I felt all aspects of whiskey's history throughout the site, from the boom years of the late 1800s to the failures of the mid-twentieth century. I wanted to explore more of the place. I didn't want to return to anyplace that would bring me back to the twenty-first century. As Brian led us back to where we met him only an hour before, I started to think up ways to excuse myself. As he brought us into the warmth of the office building, and up the back steps, I thought of reasons I could give to explain my disappearance. As he opened the door to a small room filled with nearly twenty bottles of different whiskeys and stated that we were about to do some tasting, all thoughts of escape left my mind. Twenty whiskeys? How the hell were we going to taste twenty whiskeys?

Brian's plan was to have us taste a little bit from each bottle, and spit out the drink into a shared bucket. Decorum never entered our decision making, and Krysta and I both sat down at the table. Various bottles of Kilbeggan, Locke's, Tyrconnel, and Michael Collins were all in front of us. Several peated malts from the Cooley collection also loomed large off to the right. Off in the back was an unlabeled clear bottle that had only about one eighth of its golden content left.

Brian oversaw the drinking, with him pouring and explaining, and us tasting and determining which we liked best. The 15-year-old Kilbeggan was tasty and the sherry-finished Tyrconnel was also quite nice. The peated whiskeys were okay, with the Locke's aged 8-year-old single malt giving a nice introduction to peated whiskeys for the newcomer. And instead of rushing us, Brian took his time, explaining each whiskey and how it fit among the others. Krysta and I took drinks, noted the flavors, and spat out what we didn't want to swallow, both of us aware we still had to drive back to Dublin after we were done here.

I was enthralled. For the first time on the tour, I felt like a whiskey professional. I knew Brian was giving me a sales job, but he was damn good at it. As I was reflecting upon my blissful state of mind, Brian lifted up the unlabeled bottle, displayed it to us, and started to speak, only to stop before any sound came out of his mouth.

He paused.

Krysta and I looked at each other, confused by the fact that this man who had been so talkative suddenly found himself speechless.

"A few years ago," he finally said, staring at the table in front of us, empty glasses all around, "we were told of several casks of whiskey being stored at a local police warehouse that had been left there for decades. We went down and picked up the casks. These were whiskeys from several different companies, including that of Locke's."

I did a quick calculation in my head. Locke's had stopped distilling in 1954, making the whiskey in his hand at least fifty years old.

"It's sixty-three years old," he said, guessing my next question. He lifted the bottle. "After hiring someone from Louisville to make it drinkable, we found ourselves with only a handful of bottles." I presumed he meant Louisville, Kentucky, as I had never heard of a Louisville, Ireland.

He paused again, looking at me, over at Krysta, and then back at me.

"Here . . . ," he said, pausing long enough for effect, "is the last of this whiskey on our premises."

He lowered the lip of the bottle to a glass, as if to pour, and then pulled up again, as if he had reconsidered his decision. He then lowered the lip again, and poured two glasses. He passed one to each of us.

Normally I pride myself on being quite aware of when I'm being oversold. In the back of my head, I heard a voice telling me, "He's overselling it. Can't you see that?!?" I told my inner voice to pack it in for the day. I lifted my glass to him and said, "Sláinte." He nodded, smiled, and left the room, allowing Krysta and me to share the moment alone.

We both drank. What entered our mouth was a thick, buttery whiskey that coated my tongue. It was both sweet and full of character. I could not taste any of the alcohol, but I knew it was there. My eyes rolled back into my head. I smiled and swallowed.

We had our lunch with Mr. Quinn and his wife, and we talked about restaurants and the state of food. They were both quite cordial and wanted to hear of our plans for other tours. Soon, we found

Locke's 63-Year-Old (Not Publicly Available)
If anyone ever asks you to sample a whiskey over the age of forty, the answer should always be "yes"! Keep in mind that this whiskey had to be fixed in order for it to have the flavors mentioned below.

Nose: Deep and complex. Both butter and vanilla were jumping to the forefront, with a multitude of other aromas playing in the background.
Taste: Buttery with a bit of heat. Thick on the tongue, yet full of character. A little grainy, but very present in the mouth.
Finish: The finish was sweet and warm, but ended quicker than I both expected and hoped.
Character: This whiskey was the brightest star in a sky that was full of them. It was like an old man who could dance exquisitely, as long as he had a little help from someone else.

ourselves shaking hands good-bye and giving our thanks. It had gone by so fast. All throughout, I was on a high that Brian had created. Authentic or manufactured, it mattered not, for it was a near-perfect moment. Life presents these times so rarely that I didn't have any desire to question it. We got into the car and drove back to Dublin in silence, both of us reveling in the day.

7

Two Irish Men

In the beginning of the nineteenth century, there were two Irish gentlemen who would go on to change the whiskey world and help it evolve into the one we know today. One of the men helped increase production of the liquor. The other man helped decrease its consumption.

The problem in trying to determine how much the consumption of whiskey was an issue is that one has to separate evidence into two categories. The first category would be based in reality, and provides evidence that shows overconsumption by a country's citizenry. The second category would be any anecdote with a hidden agenda that can be told/written/communicated. There are a multitude of examples of the latter group throughout history, the best example being that of the English. A typical statement said anywhere between the seventeenth through the twentieth centuries would have been along the lines of "When it comes to the Irish, the drinking of whiskey is continual and extraordinary and impoverishes the country, and moreover is indulged in excessively by the most rebellious parts of the population." Statements similar to this were used both to justify implementing stricter regulatory oversight over the Irish whiskey industry and to paint those who were seeking Irish independence as inebriates. Nothing says "Our conquest of Ireland is just" better than "The people we're fighting and trying to civilize are drunks." This attitude, whether it was England's occupation of Ireland or the Anti-Saloon League's quest to instill their morality upon others in North America has been, is, and always will be part of the arguments of temperance and prohibition. That these are also the same tactics used by powerful institutions to bully the weak and the voiceless is only a slight coincidence.

Such arguments are also problematic, as they paint everyone who drinks as a sinner, never acknowledging that there are many individuals who are responsible when it comes to drink. Responsible people temper their drinking. They know their limitations and rarely, if ever, exceed them.

The 1700s had seen a substantial increase in alcohol consumption, mostly in spirits, a trend that was both recognized and condemned at the time. Though he is relatively unknown today, it was Dr. William Henry who set forth the first arguments for national temperance in Ireland. Born in England, Dr. Henry spent a fair amount of his life in Ireland. He was educated at Trinity College in Dublin and later spent more than thirty years as a rector of parishes in Counties Fermanagh and Tyrone. He was appointed Dean of Killaloe in 1761, and wrote at least four pamphlets in the 1750s attacking excessive spirit consumption.

He mentions correspondence between himself and a Dr. Stephen Hales, indicating more than a passing knowledge of the campaign against gin drinking in England going on at that time. In fact, Elizabeth Malcolm writes, in *Ireland Sober, Ireland Free*, "This familiarity with the English Campaign probably accounts for the sophistication of Henry's arguments."

He noted the increase of drinking, which he argued had only occurred in recent times. According to him, spirits had "under the various names and kinds of brandy, rum, gin, usque baugh, and above all, of whiskey, had spread over all parts of Ireland; nor is there any place from Cape Clear in the County of Cork, to Fair Head, the north-ernmost promontory in Antrim, wherein it had not shed its poison."

Henry stated that a government had three principal aims: to increase the number of its inhabitants; to keep them well employed, so as to make them rich; and to preserve them in good humor in a temper amenable to the laws. The consumption of spirits, he argued, undermined all three. To him, liquor in any form was bad. Ale, on the other hand, was perfectly okay. Spirit consumption, he said, used up a vast amount of grain that should have gone into the making of bread and beer. He complained that so much grain went into spirits that "scarce a drop of good ale is to be got even in our market towns but what is imported from England."

And while he conceded that a man can get drunk on ale he argued it was a form of drunkenness different from that produced by spirits. "He that gets drunk from ale is a stupid inoffensive sot; but the man who has his brain inflamed with hot spirits, is above the laws, is a madman," he wrote, demonstrating that rationalization and hypocrisy could even afflict the sober.

Dr. Henry set forth the arguments that would affect Ireland several generations later. The temperance movement in Ireland is traditionally considered to have picked up steam in the 1820s, with the establishment of the first anti-spirits societies in New Ross, Belfast, and Dublin. Influenced by the successes of the anti-spirits movement in the United States, these may have been the first significant Irish temperance societies. What made these movements notable was their less than subtle response to the recent Catholic emancipation.

To many in the movement, temperance offered the Protestants a means of proving their superiority and of thereby bolstering their status during an era when Catholics were getting their legal rights in Ireland, achieving equality with the already established Protestants. The movement ultimately failed to take hold in the Protestant upper classes, for a variety of reasons, chief among them the failure of several leaders to renounce wine and ale, in addition to the lower-class drink of whiskey. But what makes the Protestant temperance movement notable is its effect upon a Capuchin monk from Cork by the name of Theobald Mathew.

Theobald Mathew, later known simply as Father Mathew, was born at Thomastown, near Golden, County Tipperary, on October 10, 1790. He received his schooling in Kilkenny, and from 1808 to 1814 he studied in Dublin, where in the latter years he was ordained to the priesthood. Having entered the Capuchin order, an offshoot of the Franciscan, both of whom reported to the papacy, Mathew spent a brief period of time in service at Kilkenny, then joined a mission in Cork.

Mathew's involvement in the temperance movement began in April of 1838, after he heard of anti-Catholic sentiments being expressed by a Protestant minister at a temperance meeting. After taking advisement from several ranking members of the movement, he committed himself to the Cork Teetotal Abstinence Society. By the fall, he had changed the approach of the movement by highlighting the benefits of sobriety rather than the sins of drunkenness. Twenty-five thousand people had already taken his pledge that stated:

I promise to abstain from all intoxicating drinks
except when used medicinally and by order of a medical man,
and to discountenance the cause and practice of intemperance.

The promise was akin to a marriage vow, and Father Mathew advocated it as such, giving blessing to all who made it. The vow was to be a permanent commitment, and, with discipline, could be followed easily over the course of a lifetime.

His approach worked, and over the course of the next few years, thousands upon thousands of the Irish took the pledge. As John F. Quinn notes in his book *Father Mathew's Crusade: Temperance in Nineteenth-century Ireland and Irish America*, in two and a half years, Mathew had committed 2.5 million countrymen to his cause, nearly 30 percent of the Irish population.

The news of Father Mathew's success spread around the world, and he became a celebrity among the teetotaler set. In 1844 he visited Liverpool, Manchester, and London with almost equal success. Soon he was traveling throughout much of England, as well as the United States, where he influenced the temperance societies that would have input into the Prohibition debate to come fifty years later.

Mathew's influence was so great that two communities felt compelled to honor him with a statue of his likeness, one in Cork, the other in Salem, Massachusetts. And while his effectiveness in the nineteenth century is undeniable, his effectiveness today can be best demonstrated by the several pubs and clubs within eyeshot of his statue in Cork.

The first half of the nineteenth century in Ireland was a period of chaos and uncertainty. Catholics and Presbyterians—who together made up a large majority of the Irish population—were completely excluded from public life at this time under the Penal Laws, in force in Ireland from 1691 until the early 1800s. The Anglican minority made all political decisions in Ireland. These elites, whose families had emigrated to Ireland in the seventeenth and eighteenth centuries, no longer saw England as their homeland. Folks in Parliament, including one Henry Grattan, sought greater independence from England.

However, when Grattan sought rights for the Catholics, the more corruptible members of the Irish Parliament were influenced by London to limit any such independence from being instituted. Grattan's proposals were often shot down, and, as frequently happens when compromises cannot be reached, more extreme positions by all parties began to emerge. Influenced by America's and France's recent revolutions, the Irish rebelled in 1798. However, they did not have the same success as their spiritual cousins, and the English quelled the revolution after several battles and losses of between 15,000 and 30,000 Irish lives.

The end result of this failed rebellion was the Act of Union, which merged the Kingdom of Ireland and the Kingdom of Great Britain, itself a union of England and Scotland, formed almost 100 years earlier. This created the United Kingdom of Great Britain and Ireland. Having been passed in August 1800, the act came into effect on January 1, 1801.

For the first time in history, Ireland, Scotland, and England were all ruled by one centralized government. Granted, many in Ireland were suspicious, and others were outright hostile to British rule, but it did consolidate the laws under one government. This included the areas of excise and spirit regulation.

England and Ireland may have been separated by a mere fifty miles by sea, but they could not have been more different from a cultural point of view. While England was in the midst of its industrial revolution, Ireland saw little of the technological advancements that were now available. Belfast benefited some, but the rest of Ireland remained a rural backwater when compared with the wealth of London. Poverty was rampant and living conditions were abhorrent. The economy of Ireland was so bad that Dublin, once the second largest city of the British empire, lost citizens to areas in England that were able to provide the work that Ireland could not.

It was this lack of an industrial evolution that allowed whiskey to thrive in Ireland. Distilling was still very much an act of the farmer, requiring only grains, yeast, and water. The majority of the initial distilleries were small operations, serving smaller farms and communities and small businesses. The lack of roads made it difficult to travel to cities and towns not located on the eastern seaboard of Ireland. Government oversight of these communities was either limited or nonexistent. Collection of taxes on stills, especially when undertaken by non-Irish individuals, was a difficult, if impossible, task.

Poteen, the Irish moonshine, flowed freely. By its nature, it was made in secret. Illicit stills, whether formerly licensed and operating in the wee hours of the morning or hidden deep within caves and behind camouflage, could be kept far from prying eyes. Sometimes secret rooms were built into houses where the distiller could work entirely unseen, as long as someone could account for the smoke and ever-present smell, a problem today's pot smokers can likely appreciate.

One legend has it that a distiller inhabited a structure that was attached to the local revenue house, with which it shared a chimney. The distillery lasted several years without being detected, even though the still was under the revenuer's nose, quite literally if one considered the smoke from the fire of the still. When the distiller was finally caught, it is said that he was let go without trial, as to have public record would have been an embarrassment to the revenuer's office.

There was no organized police department to enforce the laws, so the excise men could not pursue the poteen makers without military assistance. The military was not happy with this duty, as the poteen makers were well organized, well acquainted with the land, and quite often well armed.

In County Armagh in 1797 several militia on revenue duty were killed in a clash with a mob when an excise man tried to collect some taxes. In 1819, a force of 140 infantry and 40 cavalry were repulsed and forced to flee by the people of Buncrana and Culdaff. A government report of 1824 states that gangs of 60 to 80 men "so ferocious they needed an army to defeat them" often engaged the revenuers and excise men sent to collect the taxes..

One of the most important people in the history of distilling came from the ranks of these revenuers and excise men, and he would change the landscape of whiskey forever.

Little is known of the life of Aeneas Coffey, outside of some small pieces of information gathered from public records. It is known that he was born in Dublin in 1780 and, by the time of the act of Union, was a gauger at the excise office. He married in 1808, and had one son, likely his only child. By 1813, he was appointed the subcommissioner of Inland Excises and Taxes for the district of Drogheda. In 1824, he resigned from the service at his own request.

It is likely he spent the next few years working on a way to create a device that allowed for continuous distilling. Before 1830, the most widely used distilling vessel was the copper pot still. The pot still's greatest virtue was that it produced a full-flavored spirit, but it also had several weaknesses. As a discontinuous process the still had to be filled, distilled, emptied, and recharged, which delayed the rest of the production process, limiting economies of scale from larger maltings, mash tuns, and fermenting backs. The first distillation produces a weak concentration of alcohol and a second or even third distillation is needed to raise the alcoholic strength. Recharging and inadequate concentration raised the cost of fuel and labor in making alcohol on a large scale. Ensuring that the final product did not contain too large a proportion of secondary constituents was difficult in a pot still. When lower-quality raw materials were used, it was easy for the still to leave a spirit tainted by the flavor of the second-rate ingredients.

Additionally, the pot still was heated by fire, and raising the contents to boiling point was a slow process. Wear and tear on the still from repeated heating and cooling was high, as was the danger of spoiling the spirit by charring the solid matter in the wash. It was these limitations that the process known as continuous distillation sought to overcome. The principle of distillation (that the boiling point of alcohol is lower than that of water) was widely understood. The problem was how to turn principle into an efficient practice.

An efficient means of distillation was an attractive goal for several reasons. There was an economic benefit to reducing the work and resources needed to distill. In areas of the United Kingdom and the world where neutral grain spirits were desired, a person who invented a process that created such a high alcohol content would have been richly rewarded. In England, where spirit drinkers remained wedded to gin, distillers used large-capacity pot stills and a high-gravity wash to make a harsh, undrinkable spirit that was sent to rectifiers to be re-distilled in the presence of flavoring agents such as juniper berries and coriander seeds. A continuous still would remove the need to have the gin spirit redistilled.

This was the golden egg that many inventors were seeking to create, and many different models were made and patents submitted. It was Coffey's continuous still that took hold in the marketplace.

His efforts were not without difficulties. Coffey was no chemist. According to Ronald Weir's *The History of the Distillers Company, 1877–1939*, Coffey made his first still from iron instead of the more efficient copper. As soon as "it came into contact with the wash . . . the acid of the wash, acting on the iron, produced hydrogen gas, which made the whiskey taste like rotten eggs." This failed attempt would be akin to the Wright Brothers making their first plane out of lead.

What Coffey eventually came up with was a two-column still. The first column has steam rising and the wash descending through several levels. The second column is used to carry the alcohol from the wash, and circulates it until it can condense at the required strength. It essentially behaves like a series of pot stills, except in a vertical tube that can be several stories tall. As long as the still is fed wash, it will create a constant stream of alcohol.

It has been said by some that Coffey's still was a unique invention. But this is untrue. Coffey's still was not the first continuous still; several other patents of the era show that others were thinking along the same lines. What really distinguished Coffey's still as an important technological achievement was its extraordinary efficiency. It produced a concentrated spirit containing between 86 and 96 percent alcohol in a continuous and quick manner. Its heat exchange from the steam helped cut fuel costs.

While Coffey is now as highly regarded in Ireland as Eli Whitney is in the United States, when he introduced his new still, he was rejected by the distillers of Ireland, both large and small. They eschewed progress in the name of flavor and tradition. At the time, it was seen as the right thing to do. The Scotch whiskey industry had yet to develop to the level of the Irish. The larger distilleries were starting to make their wealth. So why risk losing a good thing?

To make his fortune, Aeneas Coffey headed to England. It was a decision that would come back to haunt the Irish generations later.

By no coincidence, Krysta and I were going to the United Kingdom as well, not to chase fortune, as Coffey had. Rather, we were heading to the Highlands of Scotland to see just how Coffey changed the playing field, and allowed Scotland to become the whiskey producing capital of the world.

8

Kings and Snobs

When it comes to talking about Scotch whiskey, the topic of kings and queens comes up quite often. James IV is frequently mentioned, as he happened to be king when the first documented evidence of whiskey having been produced. "To Friar John Cor, by order of the King to make aqua vitae, VIII bolts of malt" was written in the Exchequer Roll in 1494, and ever since then, every book about the history of Scotch whiskey mentions this passage and ties the name of King James to whiskey.

Queen Victoria's name also pops up from time to time in the whiskey history books, for her preference for the drink is often cited as the key for elevating whiskey from the drink of the commoner to that of the upper class.

But in my mind, the most relevant royal event occurred in 1822, when King George IV made a visit to Scotland, the first monarch to visit there since 1607. During this visit, writer Sir Walter Scott encouraged the king to embrace everything related to Highland culture. The king wore Highland dress and was received in a tartan-bedecked Edinburgh.

The weird thing? Not sixty-two years earlier, the Highland culture and the Catholic ideology that it embraced was roundly rejected by the Lowland, Protestant and Presbyterian culture.

In 1740 the Highlanders were seen often seen as rebels and, worse, Papists. They were the last remaining Catholic enclave in Great Britain. And they were still bitter about the 1688 overthrow of King James II of England (a Catholic) by a union of Parliamentarians and William III of Orange-Nassau (a Protestant). Later, the English royalty did not look kindly upon the Highlanders supporting bonnie Prince Charlie's bid to retake the throne, and as a result, they outlawed many aspects of Highland culture, including the iconic regalia that King George donned in 1822.

The reasons for the royal visit were purely political. After a decade of ruling as prince regent, George IV was widely unpopular when he ascended to the throne. The royalty was seen as a corrupt oligarchy by many Scots, whose increasing unrest following the revolutions that shook America, France, and Ireland culminated in the Scottish Insurrection of 1820, wherein some of the radicals initiated a nationwide strike, and some even tried to take to arms. This insurrection was quickly quelled, but it terrified the gentry, who were still dealing with the aftereffects of the French and American revolutions. The king's inner circle wished to keep control of affairs and pressed the king to head to Scotland to help calm the unrest.

The stroke of genius was when someone told Sir Walter Scott what was going to happen. A baronet who just happened to be a well-regarded and prolific Scottish historical novelist and poet popular throughout Europe, Scott saw this visit as an opportunity to reinvent the Scottish image. When his advice was sought, he helped create a splendid pageant wherein ancient Scotland would be reborn, and the presence of the king would give credibility to the Highlanders and their culture by being surrounded by its imagery.

From most accounts, the event was a success. Various Highland chieftains sought to prove their allegiance to the king, and while he was mocked by some, no one remarked that he wore the garb of a group of people who would have been seen as his enemies a mere sixty years prior. The effect of the event was an increase in goodwill and a newfound Scottish national identity uniting Highlander and Lowlander in sharing the iconic symbolism of kilts and tartans. The pride the clan chieftains had in their heritage was reinvigorated. Soon, everyone wanted to be Scottish. And the whiskey makers, sensing an opportunity, began using the iconic images of their homeland to sell their spirits. This visit by the king would lay the foundation for Scotland becoming ground zero for all things whiskey.

Krysta and I received far less fanfare as we entered Edinburgh.

The previous day had been a sort of a day off for us, and, finished with our time in Ireland, we dropped off Molly and the car, and hopped a plane over to Edinburgh.

When I say "hopped," I mean it almost literally. With wind gusts approaching sixty miles per hour, smaller planes, such as the one we were on, were being tossed around the sky like batons being thrown by a juggler.

Add to this scene a group of twenty women of varying ages who were indulging in some of the pleasures that Ireland has to offer, mostly tacky Irish souvenirs and excessive amounts of Guinness. They were quite vocal, quite exuberant, and quite drunk.

"Bachelorette party?" I asked Krysta as we stood in line at the airline gate.

She shrugged. "Likely. I just hope we don't get seated near them."

Krysta's fear of being in close proximity to drunk bachelorettes on an airplane was well founded. While being tossed up and down and left and right by the aircraft, shouts of "Wheeeee!!!" and "Whooo!!" with a few faux screams of terror thrown in came from their section. The rest of the passengers were less than thrilled with having these revelers onboard, and by the time the plane landed, nerves had been clearly frayed, mine included.

We picked up the next rental car, dubbed the GPS "Emma" and the car "Mackenzie Cook," and headed into the grand city of Edinburgh. First stop? The hotel. Second stop? The Scotch Whisky Heritage Centre. I questioned if I had my priorities straight.

Located on the Royal Mile, next door to Edinburgh Castle, the

Scotch Whisky Heritage Centre is aimed squarely at the millions of tourists who walk by its door every year. But I wasn't here to play the tourist. I was here to get some advice from Susan Morrison, the director. Driving into the largest region of whiskey producers in the world was a little daunting, and I wanted to make sure that I was going in with the right attitude and state of mind.

We sat down in the coffee shop in the basement, and I explained to Susan my plan to find the best whiskey in the world, and how I had chosen to visit several of the distilleries of Scotland in order to accomplish this task.

"What should I be aware of while out and about in Scotland?" I asked.

Without hesitating, she responded, "Beware of the snobs."

Ah, yes. The snobs. I thought to myself. I had been waiting for this. These were the folks who unknowingly made it difficult for new folks to enter the world of whiskey. They judged what you drank and how you drank it. Some would comment if you drank anything less than a single malt, and others would mock you if you only drank single malts. Some would shake their heads if you drank whiskey straight, and others would scream blasphemy if anything was added to your drink. The snobs, in my opinion, are the largest reason regular folks seem to be intimidated by whiskey.

This discussion on snobs was similar to an e-mail exchange I had with Kevin Erskine, author of *Instant Expert's Guide to Single Malt Scotch* and owner of and primary contributor to The Scotch Blog.

When I asked him what advice he would give a newcomer to whiskey, his answer was direct. "Don't listen to any snobs. Drink what you like. Mix it if you like. Try new things." When I asked him to explain his position on snobbery, he wrote back, "I'm sure very few people would classify themselves as whisky snobs . . . and there are a variety of ways the affliction manifests itself: The People who will ONLY drink Johnnie Walker Blue; the people who WON'T drink Johnnie Walker Blue because of the people who will drink it; the people who won't drink anything under a certain price range; the people who dismiss all blends as inferior; the people who turn their nose up at mixing whisky."

"Of course, this is not particular to Scotch," he continued. "There is similar snobbery in EVERY aspect of life. Shoe snobs, car snobs, neighborhood snobs. These are the judgmental; the prejudiced; the ignorant. Not all collectors are snobs, but the very vocal online community-involved snobs can certainly sway the snob-in-training. Some of the more vocal snobs can, through the bully pulpit of the Internet, have an effect on the smaller producer—as the snobs are the most likely audience of the small producer."

Snobbery plays an odd part in the whiskey industry. It seems that whiskey connoisseurs are prevalent wherever one goes. Levels of connoisseurship range anywhere from someone telling you to not add water to your whiskey to others telling whiskey producers not to add coloring and not to chill filter the spirit. They exist solely to remind people that their way of enjoying whiskey is the best way for others to enjoy whiskey. Sometimes, as a distiller once told me, they are quite annoying. On rare occasions, much to the industry's chagrin, they can be right.

But mostly they're annoying.

Take, for example, the idea that whiskey should only be drunk straight. To some, adding anything to the whiskey, even if only water, is blasphemous. The problem here is that many whiskeys are simply too strong in alcohol content for anyone to be able to taste the flavor. If you were to take a whiff of a whiskey at say, 60 percent alcohol by volume (ABV), or 120 proof, your nose would be numbed by the excessive alcoholic vapors. The same will happen to your taste buds when a whiskey with a high ABV is drunk. The flavor is missed because the taste buds are still recovering from the anesthetic properties of the alcohol.

Probably the most frequent mistake that many connoisseurs make is one of philosophy. To them, "tasting" whiskey is the primary goal of drinking whiskey, being able to discern the various characteristics and nuances another comparing them to other whiskeys.

But many people enjoy whiskey without ever comparing their drink of choice to any other. Their enjoyment is derived from other means entirely, whether it's feeling local pride when drinking a spirit from a local distiller, or spending a simple evening out with friends.

"Tasting" whiskey requires a fair amount of thought, and, quite frankly, many people don't wish to put forth that level of effort when they have a drink. It's much more enjoyable to savor the moment when one is drinking whiskey than it is to deconstruct the nuances of the whiskey being consumed.

Susan provided a great example of this. When I asked her what kind of whiskey she enjoys and how she enjoyed it, she said: "It depends on my state of mind. If I want to relax by myself on a cold day, I might have a smokier malt from out of the islands with a bit of water. If it's a summer day, and I'm with my friends, I might have a lemonade mixed with the whiskey. I don't think there is any one 'best' way to have a drink."

I thanked her for her time, and Krysta and I got up to head to the tour the Heritage Centre provides.

"One warning about the tour," Susan said before we left. "It's a rather old one, being twenty years old. We're in the process of changing it, and by this time next year, it will be much different. The tour you're about to go on is a little outdated." Her words seemed more of an apology than a warning, and Krysta and I shared a glance of concern.

Her words were true. The tour was far more Disneyland than Speyside in its approach. It started with a shot of Dewar's, which was a little outside the norm, as most places give you a drink at the end of the tour. But soon it became apparent why they wanted us to have a drink beforehand. The video was less cheesy than Jameson's, but the production values were a little lower. By the time we reached the talking ghost who was once a master blender we began to realize the tour was getting a bit silly, and by the time they put us in a tracked car that ran us by about a dozen or so scenes of whiskey history I was able to come up with Kate's Law of whiskey tours: The enjoyment of any tour is inversely proportional to the number of mannequins used within said tour.

After the tour, Krysta and I headed to the gift shop. As I walked through the door, my mind played Handel's *Messiah*, specifically the "Hallelujah" chorus. With soft track lighting, the entire shop took on an otherworldly glow. Spread out in front of me and the dozen or so other tourists were hundreds of brands of Scotch whiskey. There were brands from the Lowlands, the Highlands, and the islands. There were single malts and blends. There were the standard 750-ml bottles as well as the tiny 50-ml bottles similar to the bottle of Glenlivet I had had on the flight to Ireland. I stood there, awed by the selection in front of me.

"Steady now, Kate," Krysta said, alerting me to my state of mind much as she had done at the whiskey shop in Dublin.

"It's, it's . . . so beautiful!" I said, walking slowly forward.

For someone used to having only a dozen or so options at the local liquor store, this shop represented the holy land, the adult version of a candy shop. Part of me wanted to squeal with delight, another wanted to weep with what I had been missing back in the States. We Americans may do many things well, but running liquor stores is not one of them.

We easily spent an hour in the shop, carefully selecting the bottles that we would be taking with us for the rest of the journey, some to consume during our stay in Scotland, some to put into our suitcases for our trip back home.

By the time we were done, the sun had nearly set upon the city of Edinburgh, and we decided to have dinner at a pub off of Royal Mile. With dusk casting dark orange shadows upon the shops that stood in deference to the looming castle located at the end of the Mile, we scoured the many tourist businesses. After finding several more whiskey shops, and twice as many places that sold either kilts or tweed jackets (sometimes both), we found a small place that had just put out a sandwich board promoting their menu.

Krysta and I were shown a table in the back of the pub, where we both ordered the haggis, and I asked for a glass of 10-year-old Bruichladdich.

Krysta pulled out a new tour book, with various places highlighted and the ever-present tabs sticking out from the pages. We had less than forty hours in Edinburgh, and she wanted to make the most of it. As we would be doing a fair bit of book research over the course of the next week, we both decided that Edinburgh would be less about whiskey, and more about being a tourist. We had also decided

Bruichladdich 10-Year-Old

Some consider Bruichladdich to be the the quintessential Islay whiskey. It is also the only distillery operation that I am aware of that was monitored by American intelligence services during George W. Bush's first administration, under the mistaken impression that Bruichladdich either could be or was making weapons of mass destruction.

Nose: Quite floral, with a hint of lemon at the end. Very light and not as strong as I expected for an island whiskey.

Taste: Both sharp and light, with a hint of malt in the back, cream soda and citrus in the front.

Finish: Very clean and direct, with the initial tastes combining nicely. Not long but not short.

Character: Bruichladdich is a morning person, the type of person who is thrilled to be starting the day when the alarm goes off at five a.m. Perky and happy, this whiskey is bound to frustrate those of us who are not happy with morning people.

that since we had spent most of the past week in the car, and would spend most of the coming week in the same state, we would stay in Edinburgh and walk everywhere.

"So," Krysta said as the food was delivered to our table. "Edinburgh Castle tomorrow?"

I nodded, taking a bite of my dinner. But I didn't care where we went. Here I was, at a pub on the Royal Mile, drinking whiskey and eating haggis. The outside had a brisk chill to the air, and inside was warm and comforting. Edinburgh had already delivered on its promise.

9

The Dance of The Grouse

It became clear by 1823 that the British way of dealing with collecting excise from whiskey was deficient on many, many levels. A generation of Scotsmen and Irishmen had lived contrary to the laws of their land, and were making a decent living doing so. Violence surrounding the smuggling trade increased, as did the severity of the violence. Meanwhile, the excisemen were understaffed and underfunded. The lawlessness surrounding smuggling and illegal distilling not only became embarrassing to the government, it illustrated how impotent they were to enforce the laws on the books. As Charles Maclean writes in *Scotch Whisky: A Liquid History:* "If smugglers could bring the excise laws into disrepute, all laws would be brought into disrepute."

In Ireland there were only twenty distilleries recognized by the government, and yet Aeneas Coffey reported eight hundred illegal stills on the Inishowen Peninsula alone. Landowners were getting tired of the lawlessness on their property. They began petitioning Parliament to change the laws.

In 1822, the same year as King George's visit, the Illicit Distillation Act was implemented in Scotland, raising the penalties associated with smuggling and illicit distilling. Equally important, the landowners who sanctioned or turned a blind eye to the illicit behavior were also made culpable, and fines would be levied against them as well. The results of this act were reported back to the chancellor of the exchequer, who, satisfied with the results, rolled them into an 1823 Excise Act that encompassed all of Great Britain.

The importance of this act cannot be underestimated. The system reverted to taxing the amount of whiskey produced, although the law still required the distillers to pay a basic license fee. No longer did the size of the still matter, nor the amount of possible production. Duty was halved. Exports were allowed throughout the land and duty-free storing of spirits was also allowed. A distillery, whether Scottish, Irish, or even English, could make as much or as little whiskey as they wished, and the marketplace would determine who would survive. A distillery could decide how long they wished to age their whiskeys, if at all. Each distillery would be responsible for the quality of their drink. It was as if the government of Great Britain realized that whiskey was here to stay. That it took them over four hundred years to come to that realization is a discussion for a far different book.

High-quality whiskey was no longer the exclusive province of the illegal distiller, and the legal distilleries could now undercut the pricing of the smugglers who had been bringing the poteen into Scotland from Ireland or from the Highlands the year before. Soon the illegal distilleries began to vanish and the legitimate ones thrived. In Scotland, over 125 distilleries started up between 1823 and 1825. By 1835, Ireland had 93 distilleries operating above board. Irish distilleries saw the popularity of their whiskeys grow worldwide, even as the rest of the country fell into destitution. Irish whiskey was so popular that it even outsold Scotch whiskey in Scotland.

It was under this growth in the industry that Aeneas Coffey's continuous still came onto the scene. During the 1840s the continuous still (also called a patent still) became well established in Scotland, mostly in factory environments. Output rose from under one million gallons in 1840 to over five million by 1850. Four years later, with falling production among pot still distillers and little expansion in demand, patent still output passed that of pot still.

Up until the mid-1800s the Scottish whiskey industry consisted mostly of pot still distilleries, nearly two hundred of them. But the Irish potato famine soon helped convince many alcohol producers of the effectivenes of Coffey's still.

Great Britain struggled to find a solution to feeding the starving inhabitants of Ireland. One solution that was implemented was the repeal of the Corn Laws, an act of 1815 that taxed imported corn so that domestic grain producers in Britain could remain competitive with international imports. Once the Corn Laws were repealed, cheap corn from America flooded into Great Britain. Whiskey producers in both Ireland and Scotland began purchasing the grain, using it to replace the more expensive malted barley.

In the past, it was only through tradition that distillers held to the use of malted barley. While using raw grain was discouraged, it was never illegal to do so. As profit margins became slimmer and production costs soon became part of the distillers' vernacular, suddenly using cheaper ingredients became part of the distilling process. Grain alcohol made from corn soon flowed from the Coffey stills. By 1854, when the output of patent still distilleries passed that of pot, there were thirteen patent still distilleries in Scotland whose combined output was over 7 million gallons. The number of pot still distilleries, which had dwindled to 119, shared an output of 4.75 million gallons. Pot still whiskey was made from malted barley. Coffey still whiskey was made from both corn and barley, giving the traditionalists another reason to act like snobbish twits.

In 1853 the Forbes-Mackenzie Act was passed. It permitted, among other things, the vatting of whiskeys while they were in bond prior to excise having to be paid.

Having a spirit "in bond" means having the spirit stored for a specific reason, whether it's to hold it until duties or taxes on it are paid, or simply to hold it in storage for several years in order to allow the drink to mature and mellow in flavor. Storing whiskey costs money. There's a direct cost of keeping the spirits in a warehouse, via rent or cost of the warehouse, as well as the costs to maintain the spirits and warehouse. Then there are the costs associated with lost (or, more specifically, delayed) revenue. Whiskey sitting in a warehouse cannot bring in money. So putting something in bond is a cost that eventually has to be paid by the consumers.

Vatting is the process of mixing or blending different whiskeys from different charges, or even different stills, in a vat. For someone who was distilling pure grain alcohol from the patent stills, this was a godsend. Now he could cut his more expensive whiskey with a cheaper grain whiskey made at the same distillery, and yet still charge the same price that he always had. It made it cheaper to produce the whiskey he put out in the market.

This is exactly what Andrew Usher did when he introduced Usher's Old Vatted Glenlivet in 1854, Scotland's first vatted whiskey.

Life got even better for the distillers in 1860 with the signing of the Commercial Treaty with France as well as the passing of the Spirits Act. Oh sure, the duty was increased on whiskey and reduced on imported wines and brandies, which led to an increase in consumption of French spirits and a reduced intake of the local brew, but the Commercial Treaty introduced two new concepts to the distillery owners: the power of branding and the power of bottling.

Previously whiskey was sold by the gallon and often only in casks. Newly imported brandies were bottled and labeled showing the area in which the brandy was made. These brandies commanded higher prices than whiskey. This is something that the distillery owners were sure to have noticed. Distilleries soon took advantage of this idea, and started bottling and branding their whiskeys with the iconic imagery that King George IV and Sir Walter Scott had helped popularize a generation earlier.

The Spirits Act of 1860 offered the industry an additional benefit. It permitted the blending of spirits from different distilleries while the spirits were stored in a bonded warehouse.

Blending whiskeys helps mitigate the costs associated with making the spirit. The distillers use untaxed grain alcohol to dilute the aged whiskey, blending it shortly before the whiskey is bottled. Doing this means less overhead costs for the blender, as they have less to pay in both taxes, as well as maintenance costs associated with storing whiskey for years on end. It also meant that making cheap whiskey is a viable business model for some.

The makers of blended whiskey would add 20 percent of an already produced Irish or Scottish pot still whiskey to the grain alcohol. They would bottle the end result, and then ship it off to England, where it would be sold as "Irish Whiskey" or "Scotch Whisky," whichever would bring in higher sales.

An extension of the French Treaty Act in 1863 permitted the granting of "off license," which made it possible for a grocer's shop to sell wine and spirits under their own label on a per-bottle basis. Now it wasn't just the distillers who could make money, but also blending operations found in grocers' and chemists' shops. Names such as Johnnie Walker, Chivas, and Famous Grouse all have their roots, not in distilling, but in the grocers' stores that sold these distinct whiskey blends.

For the second time in a week, we found ourselves trapped in a parking garage.

As we approached the parking garage off Carlton Hill in Edinburgh to get Mackenzie, we saw a large swarm of people, with the crowd getting larger the closer we got to the garage. The ground floor, which housed our car, had been roped off to accommodate a flea market. There, between a flower vendor and a person selling empty bottles, was Mackenzie, trapped.

"What the hell?" asked Krysta.

We both looked around to ascertain the situation: Vendors . . . customers . . . our car . . . more vendors and customers . . . the exit— our exit. It was blocked off.

For a brief moment, we panicked. "Oh come on!" we complained to no one in particular. "How are we supposed to get out?" I said. We scanned the crowd for anyone who might be in a position of authority.

Krysta spotted someone first. She pointed to a man who looked as if he didn't want to buy or sell anything. "Stay here," she said. "I'll take care of it."

I positioned myself where the exit would have been on any other day but this one, while Krysta walked toward the twenty-something Scottish lad and got his attention.

From the distance, I saw her point to the car, then to me, then to the exit. A brief exchange took place, and they both walked toward Mackenzie. He shook his head no.

Krysta's body language changed, and for the first time since I'd known her, I saw her look stressed. She held her temple and rubbed her forehead. She appeared to wipe a tear from her eye, and the young man's hands rose as if both to calm her and to keep her from falling on him. He called to another gentleman, older and more disinterested, who walked over, and all three began assessing the situation.

Then Krysta handed the keys to the older gentleman, and the young man worked to clear a path for the car to leave. Krysta ran back over to me, laughed, and said, "Apparently tears work on Scottish men, too."

Soon we were on the road out of Edinburgh, and on our way to our first distillery tour in Scotland.

Heading to the Glenturret Distillery, home of The Famous Grouse blended whiskey, was . . . if you'll pardon the pun . . . a lark. Krysta and I had intended the day to be only for driving to the Speyside region of Scotland, but as we had spent the previous day whiskey-free, we both thought it best to get some actual work done, if one considers visiting a distillery actual work.

Glenturret is about an hour outside Edinburgh, and an excellent place to start before one heads out to Speyside, as it is almost directly on the way. As an added bonus, it is one of the few distilleries open on a Sunday during the off-season.

I have to admit my own bias against Glenturret's biggest seller, The Famous Grouse. This bias is based on nothing other than my own immaturity. In a world where many brands evoke the imagery of the mighty Scottish Highlands, or significant historical figures of the whiskey world, a whiskey named after a small game bird that can't even be bothered to migrate from areas where it is hunted seems a bit less than imposing. I have the same perspective when it comes to Wild Turkey.

Then there are the commercials, with the anthropomorphic grouse they call Gilbert. The ads are, in a word, cute. But cute is not typically a term I associate with Scotch whiskey. Highland cows? Sure. Baby sheep? Absolutely. Whiskey? Not so much.

So even though The Famous Grouse is available at my local liquor store back in Seattle, I'll pass over it and choose whiskeys with more imposing names.

"Are there any mannequins on the tour?" I asked the counter person who sold us our tour tickets. The question baffled him for a moment before he answered in the negative.

"You will have to dance, though," he added after a pause.

"Wait . . . what?" I said, not believing what I heard.

"The Interactive Experience. It's at the end of the tour. There's a dance in it. We won a BAFTA for it," he said proudly.

I presumed he meant the "Interactive Experience" and not the dance number.

Soon we were on the tour with several other folks wanting to partake in "The Famous Grouse Experience." Our tour guide was an Italian woman named Emanuella, who showed an exceptional amount of energy for the several areas of the distillery open to the public. The problem was that many areas of the distillery were off limits to the public.

On the tour we saw the grain sifter (where no pictures were allowed), the mash tun (where no pictures were allowed), the still room (which we weren't allowed to enter in order to see the stills), and the cask house (which we were only allowed to glance into). We were also discouraged from talking about the bottling, as we weren't allowed to visit the bottling area. In thirty minutes, we had discussed the entire distillation process, and yet seen very little of it.

Despite the lack of depth to the tour, we were encouraged to take a picture of the company's bronze statue of Towser, a feline who had captured and/or killed close to thirty thousand mice while on the job. Towser had better access to the distillery than we mere tourists.

We were then invited to watch, not one, but two videos, counting their BAFTA-winning "Famous Grouse Experience." Our anticipation was less than palpable, it was nonexistent.

They sat us tourists together and turned on the first video. Commercial after commercial appeared in front of our eyes, and a thought occurred to me. I had just paid them money for them to show us these advertisements. While they may be entertaining, they still are only commercials, and I had forked over several pounds for the privilege. A little of me died inside.

Finally, they divided us into two groups of people—those who had paid for the joy of participating in their tasting and BAFTA-winning "Famous Grouse Experience," and those who merely paid for the distillery tour. Those in the latter group were politely dismissed from the group, and we continued without them.

Glasses filled with The Famous Grouse whiskey were placed in front of the remaining guests, and fragrant scratch and sniff cards were placed over the lip of the drinks. I looked down at them both. They were going to ask us to compare the chemically re-created aromas on the cards to the natural ones in the whiskey. I frowned a bit and shot a look at Krysta. She had already scratched her card and was sniffing at it. Others had done the same.

Emanuella gave us a playful admonition for not waiting for her instructions, but most of us had already figured out what she was going to do. We went through each aroma on the card and were asked to name it. Most cheated by looking at the names of the scents, which had been placed on the scratch and sniff cards.

We were then asked to take a sniff of the whiskey. "What do you smell?" asked the tour guide.

"The scratch-and-sniff card!" said someone from the back. I choked on a bit of the drink of whiskey that I had sipped ahead of the class.

Upon tasting, The Famous Grouse was better than I had anticipated, and certainly better than my bias would want me to admit. A little floral, a little more vanilla, and quite light, it was a pleasant little drink. It didn't have the deep characteristics of a classic single malt, but it wasn't designed to be complex. It wasn't offensive in the least.

As an aside, the above paragraph clearly cements my standing

The Famous Grouse
Based out of the Glenturret distillery, and owned by the Highland Distillers Co., The Famous Grouse is their signature blend. It's difficult to say whether this spirit is known more for the quality of the drink or the quality of the commercials.

Nose: I could get a little whiff of the grain, but most of it was covered up by the aromas wafting from the scratch-and-sniff cards that everyone was using.

Taste: A bit of honey, a bit of flowers, and a bit of vanilla.

Finish: It didn't last as long as I wished, but was still consistent with the flavors from the initial taste upon the tongue. Got a tad spicy at the end before disappearing quickly.

Character: The Famous Grouse is the high-school cheerleader everyone was friends with but no one can remember what happened to after graduation. Not overly complicated, and with an eye for self-promotion, she was sweet enough, but you wished she could hold a conversation that had to do with neither her nor the high-school prom queen elections for which she was campaigning.

as the worst marketer in the whiskey world. I can guarantee the folks at The Famous Grouse will never send me a check for the right to use the phrase "The Famous Grouse—not offensive in the least."

That The Famous Grouse is a blend likely had colored at least some of my own bias against the drink, at least aside from the avian moniker. There are many criticisms of blended whiskeys, some earned, others not. But few can deny the effect that blended whiskeys have upon the industry. Simply put, without blended whiskeys and the roughly 90 percent market share they command of all whiskey sales, single malt whiskey would be a novelty in liquors.

Yet it's the single malts, and not the blends, that get the majority of love and attention from various enthusiasts and connoisseurs. The reason for this may be due to the one criticism that might have merit. Many blended whiskeys are made with the mass market in mind, and to attract attention on such a large scale, the whiskeys must not offend. Very few risks are taken to improve the quality of the drink. Any changes in the whiskey process will primarily be those bearing on quantity rather than quality.

This leads to an interesting question for those who want to become interested in whiskeys—should blended whiskeys be dismissed simply based on their mass market appeal?

Before answering, there are three points to consider:

First, there is a tremendous skill involved in blending. A blender has to be able to replicate the same or similar tastes of a label year after year, often with different casks of whiskeys. This is a skill that very few people have.

Second, the history of whiskey could not, and should not, be written without attention to the success of the blends.

Finally, there is a great variety of tastes available even among the blended whiskeys. A Famous Grouse does not taste like a Bushmills, which in turn does not taste like a Johnnie Walker Red. As with any variation in tastes, some will be looked upon with greater favor than others.

It may be difficult or even unfair to compare a blended whiskey to that of a single malt, but it's certainly fair to compare them with each another.

"Can I get you all to line up outside of the door of the 'Experience'? I'm going to let you in soon." Emanuella spoke to us as if we were all five years old. As directed, we lined up without question. This was it. The BAFTA-winning "Famous Grouse Experience."

Soon we found ourselves surrounded by video displays. Above us, beside us, below us, each area had a flickering video monitor upon it. The guide came in and shut the door behind her.

And so we danced. The less said about it, the better.

Where Ireland was a deep green, Scotland seemed more familiar in her winter colors. As we drove to Grantown-on-Spey after the Famous Grouse tour, we found ourselves in a land of long shadows and straw-colored fields, the distinct aroma of cows and sheep surrounding us.

"I think we're losing the radio station," said Krysta, as she turned the car left onto a lesser-traveled road that the GPS told us was a shortcut. Indeed Xfm, the alternative rock station out of Edinburgh, was starting to cut in and out, with the Foo Fighters' lament about being someone's "monkey wrench" being muddled by sudden bursts of white noise. As co-pilot, it was my duty to press the scan button on the radio with the hope of finding something else to keep our attentions.

"Ooo, look. It's starting to snow!" Krysta pointed out as she guided the car up an incline that ran in between two much larger hills. I looked up. As the road crested, a valley opened up before us with rolling hills and mountains visible for miles in the distance, the sun broke through the overcast clouds even as snow still filled the air, and the radio finally found a station, with bagpipe music from BBC Scotland filling the car.

We looked at each other, amazed at the harmonic balance of the moment . . . which we both immediately broke by squealing with delight.

"Oh my God!" I said.

"Was that cool or what?" Krysta added. We both waited for a beat, listening to the bagpipes. We could contain ourselves no longer.

"We're in Scotland!" we said at the same time.

It was one of those moments that occur when traveling, when events conspire with you instead of against you to give you a moment that is near pristine, with even the imperfections adding to the overall quality of the moment. These are the moments that can define a trip, and will always be remembered and cherished. They also often can set the tone for several days afterward. If this was a sign, Scotland promised to be a treasure trove of experiences.

"Look! Pheasants!" Krysta said, pointing to a flock of birds. "Do we have time to stop for a few pictures?"

We had told the hotel that we were going to be there by four, and it was already pushing three-thirty. I told Krysta and she agreed that stopping would mess with our schedule.

We pulled into the parking lot of the small hotel in Grantown-on-

Spey just as the sun was setting. We were a bit on an emotional high from the trip, and found ourselves still reveling in our grand moment.

"Hullo! Hullo!" said the dapper older gentleman who greeted us at the door of the hotel. "You must be Ms. Hopkins," he said as he grabbed our suitcases. "And you must be . . ."—he looked up, clearly trying to remember Krysta's name—". . . Ms. Scharlach."

We exchanged greetings with the host and he walked us to our respective rooms. "Dinner is at seven, and cocktails and hors d'oeuvres are at six thirty."

I thanked him, promising that we would both be there. I plopped down upon the bed and immediately fell asleep.

The hotel was a small affair, with only six rooms available to the public. The place was owned by the host, who had greeted us at the door, technically making him the master of the house. His wife was the chef on site, and responsible for both the dinner and breakfast menus. This was a far cry from the eight-story hotels with hundreds of rooms available that pepper the skyline of downtown Seattle. And I had never been invited to cocktails and hors d'oeurves. Back in the States, we simply called it happy hour, a time when we were expected to drink cheap beer and eat deep-fried vegetables, deep-fried cheese, or, if it was really fancy, deep-fried vegetables with cheese stuffed into them.

I put on my best outfit and met up with Krysta. "What does one wear to cocktail hour?" I asked.

"Does it matter? We are the *only* ones here," she responded. Krysta, with her several tattoos and a wardrobe that would make Johnny Cash proud, was never one to concern herself with other people's perceptions.

We walked downstairs and sat ourselves in the lounge. The host came out. "Splendid! I see you've made it," he said, offering us some cheese and crackers while taking our drink orders. I took him up on his offer of a 12-year-old Cragganmore. After he left, Krysta and I sat in near silence.

"Part of me feels as if I'm at my grandmother's house," I said to

Krysta, pointing out the fine china figurines throughout the room, and the sofas with hand-crocheted blankets tossed upon them for purposes of decor.

She nodded in agreement.

"So, what brings you to Grantown-on-Spey?" said the host, as he came back into the room with our drinks.

"That right there," I said, pointing at the whiskey. "I'm doing some research for a book." I looked over at Krysta and saw that she was about to say the same thing.

"Do you get a lot of that here?" asked Krysta instead.

"Whiskey travelers? All the time. However, we do not get as many book writers. You're here for how long?" He looked up to his right again, trying to recall a piece of information that was hidden in the recesses of his mind. "Three nights, four days?"

I confirmed his memory recall. "Are there any places that you can recommend?"

He thought for a moment. "There's this shop out in Tomintoul.

Cragganmore 12-Year-Old

Cragganmore is another one of Diageo's distilleries, with this one representing the Speyside region. In my opinion, it's the best Scotch whiskey of Diageo's offerings.

Nose: So much going on with this drink. Raisins and honey, a little bit of citrus in the back, and then there's a base floral bouquet on which all of the other aromas sit.

Taste: Lighter than the nose would imply, but still full of fruitiness, with sort of a grapey, green apple kind of flavor. Then it reaches a darker, fuller butterscotch and honey before the grain becomes apparent.

Finish: Where most whiskeys seem to decrescendo, this one seems to crescendo, starting with a subltle vanilla before ratcheting up the spiciness.

Character: Cragganmore seems to me like time in front of the fireplace on a chilly fall evening. No, it's not overly challenging or complex, but it's still a pleasant way to spend one's time. And there are nuances that one can discover, even if it's only about oneself.

I've been there a few times, and the owner there is a bit of a character. I'll see if I can find his address for you. Not that it would be difficult to find. It is the only whiskey shop there."

He guided us to our seats at the dinner table, and we proceeded to have a wonderful meal of chicken breast stuffed with haggis served with a bit of whiskey sauce. It was the third day in a row I had had haggis. Clearly I had found its appeal. After dinner we headed to our separate rooms. Tomorrow—heck, the rest of the week—was to be quite busy.

The Speyside Major

We arrived at the Glen Grant Distillery at ten o'clock in the morning on your typical Scottish spring day—overcast, gray, and damp. There was a bit of mist in the air, and the sky let out a slight drizzle every so often, just enough to ensure that ducks were happy and people were inconvenienced.

Of all of the distilleries in Scotland, Glen Grant is perhaps the one that best exemplifies the distillery of the nineteenth century. Founded in 1840 by John and James Grant, brothers and former illegal whiskey smugglers and distillers, it was situated on then-uncultivated land and what was known as the Black Burn, a stream that fed into the Spey River and provided the water needed for the distilling operation.

After the Grant brothers passed away, the distillery landed in the hands of Major James Grant the younger, who had the good fortune to inherit the place at the start of the whiskey boom, and soon could afford a lifestyle that brought extravagant wealth. An avid hunter, the major went on several safaris into Africa and decorated his massive home with the skins, pelts, and busts of his various trophies.

But the Grants weren't just colorful. They were shrewd and innovative. James Grant the elder ensured that Glen Grant was one of the first distilleries to have access to railways, and his son brought in electricity, added a second distillery almost next door, and found unique ways to get people to visit his site. He had gardens developed on his land where he entertained guests, and greenhouses where rare fruits were grown. The Grants were well respected within the community they called home.

This was the heritage of the place that we were entering, where the founders were mythical, and changed the fortunes of many who lived in the area. But there is also the lesser-known but equally important history of Glen Grant, wherein the great-grandson of the founder had to sell the brand and distillery to Seagram's of Canada in 1978. Through the past few decades, they had found themselves in the hands of Allied Domecq, Pernod Ricard, and Campari, which owns them as of this writing, in March of 2008. This was a company that had seen and survived both the highs and the lows.

As we parked Mackenzie, an older man with a broad smile greeted us at the entrance.

"Do you know where I could meet Dennis Malcolm?" I asked the gentleman.

"Why would you meet with him?" he said. "I heard he's old and a bit out of touch."

An awkward pause fell between us for a second or two until a realization hit.

"Mr. Malcolm?" I said. "It's a pleasure to meet you."

He laughed, patted me on the back, and opened the door. "Nice to meet you, Kate! C'mon in! C'mon in! And who's your friend?"

Krysta introduced herself as we walked up the stairs to their main office. "Ah yes. It's a pleasure. A pleasure!" he said as we took seats at the conference table in his office. "Would you like some coffee or tea?" As we had previously had some diet Red Bull to kickstart our day, we both went for the lesser of the two caffeine choices.

"Grand!" he said, clapping his hands together and heading off to where the tea was located. As we took off our jackets and set down our notebooks and digital voice recorder, he called from the back of the room.

"Do you two consider yourselves modern women?"

Krysta and I looked at each other, unsure if we understood him correctly through his thick Scottish Accent. "Modern women?" I asked. He nodded.

"Yeah. Of course!" we both responded.

"Why don't you help me in the making of some modern tea, then?" he asked good-naturedly.

We both laughed along with him and got up to help him out. After a few quick lessons on how to make tea properly, each of us had a cup of tea and a piece of spice cake in front of us.

"So. Why don't you explain this book you're writing," Dennis said.

I explained to him the basic premise of the book, and how I was hoping to find what made whiskey so special to so many people. I spoke of Mr. Disposable Income, and how he vexed my inner philosopher. I explained that I was hoping his experience in the whiskey world could provide me with some insight.

He sat back in his chair and grew pensive.

"I see," he said, thinking carefully. He paused for a moment, taking a sip of his tea before continuing. "Whiskey is part of my life. A big part. I'm not so sure that many people nowadays can understand this. They just put in the hours at their job and then rush back home. It's their life away from their job that's their focus.

"For me, it's different." He surveyed the room as if he were looking out upon acres and acres of land. "I've been working in the industry since 1960. Started as a cooper, and worked every part of the place. Eventually I became the distillery manager. This. This is my life. I love it. It's . . ."

He trailed off for a moment, and then changed the course of the conversation.

"You've come at an interesting time for Glen Grant. We've just been bought by the Campari folks in Italy. They're investing in the place and things are looking up. We're rebuilding the visitors' center, and we're going to make a coffee and tea shop where people can sit and get a bite to eat . . ."

"Are you going to make them make their own tea?" Krysta said.

Dennis turned a bright red and burst out laughing. "No no," he said. "We'll make it for them proper." Apparently only folks who have been granted interviews have to make tea with Mr. Malcolm.

He soon started regaling us with the story of Glen Grant and the distillery. Going into tour guide mode, he told us of the Grant brothers and their criminal youth, and how they matured into pillars of the community. He talked about the Major and how he once returned with an African child who was found at the side of a road, abandoned by his birth family. Later this child, now named Biawa Makalaga, worked as a butler for the Major and served him until the Major passed away in 1931. Upon his death bed, the Major left Biawa two hundred pounds and asked that any heir who resided on Glen Grant would maintain a servant's position for him so long as he was "obedient, respectful, and willing to remain." Biawa remained at Glen Grant until his death in 1972.

Dennis stood up quickly. "Come with me," he said. "I want to show you something." We grabbed our coats and headed to the distillery. He was in full guide mode now, and showed us all aspects of his distillery. Well, technically it was Campari's distillery, but Dennis was clear as to who initiated the plans to put Glen Grant back on the map in the United Kingdom. He told us the plans for expansion and a variety of promotional ideas that he had as he showed us the mash tuns, the stills, and the warehouse. Every room led his talk in new directions, and he spoke of his goals for each specific area of the plant. Every turn of the corner brought back a memory of how the distillery looked back in the 1950s and 60s.

"That was where the greenhouses were located. I used to sneak onto the land and try to snatch apricots and grapes from the spaces in between the glass."

"Over there was where the mansion used to be. I remember when they tore it down."

But he was at his most exuberant when we headed to the back of the distillery's land. From seemingly out of nowhere, a well-manicured garden began to come into view the further back we walked. As he talked about how hard he worked to bring this garden back he made his passion clear. At some point over the past decades, someone had allowed the garden that the Major had planted to go to seed. Dennis offered no explanation or details of how or when it had happened, let alone who was responsible, but he left no doubt that this was the part of the distillery on which he had left his mark. His vision of the distillery was to bring it back to the glory days of the Major. People would come to the garden and perhaps listen to small concerts on late summer evenings, all the while sipping Glen Grant. This garden was to be Dennis's homage to the Major, a payment for the joy he had received from his forty-odd years in the whiskey industry.

The garden was quite beautiful, even on the cold, overcast day we were there. The lawns were framed ever so carefully with trees and bushes, while paths walked us even further to the back, beside the old Black Burn, now renamed the Glen Grant Burn. The sounds of the rippling stream brought a sense of serenity and an appreciation of a man who was pleased at seeing his dream become a reality.

"How old are you two?" he asked, turning the conversation away from his plans for the future, and waking me from my self-induced trance.

"Thirty," said Krysta without hesitation.

"Really? I would have taken you for twenty-five," he said with a wink. "There's something back here that might be of interest."

We left the garden and followed a path that paralleled the creek. Wooden railings prevented us from falling into the water, but not from being able to reach out and feel just how chilled the stream was. A footbridge took us from the left bank to the right, and another took us back to the left. Soon a small hovel came into view and Dennis stopped us there.

"When the Major wanted to impress someone, he'd take them up this path that you yourselves have just walked, and he stopped them at this point. Here, he would turn to a safe that had been put into the side of the hillside. He'd open the safe and pull out a bottle of his favorite, pour his guest a bit, and then top it off with a bit of water from the burn below."

He entered the hovel and pointed out the safe to us. Opening it, he revealed a bottle of their twenty-five-year-old whiskey, and a tray of glasses. He poured each of us a drink, and then pulled out a large chain with a small cup on the bottom. He leaned over the bridge, threw the cup over the side, and acquired a bit of the water from below. Soon it found its way into our respective whiskeys. "This is for looking as if you're twenty-five years old," Dennis said with a mischievous smile.

In the back of my mind, I shouted to myself: "Take notes! What does the whiskey taste like? You know he does this with all of his guests!"

I told my mind to shut up, and I enjoyed the moment. Here we were, in Scotland, discussing whiskey with a charming Scottish gentleman, enjoying a drink on a cool damp morning, on a footbridge over a babbling creek. It didn't matter how good or bad the whiskey was, or that he had likely done this so often that this was now a ritual. It was beautiful and I couldn't deny it.

I turned to him and said, "I have no idea whether you're a blood relation or not, but it's clear that there's a bit of the Major in you."

He looked at the ground and smiled. "I'm not sure about that, but

Glen Grant 25-Year-Old

Owned by Campari, Glen Grant is looking to improve their sales in parts of the world not named Italy (where they are extremely popular). If they could invite the world to their backyard in order to share a dram, they could accomplish their goal.

Nose: Quite fruity, with apples being dominant. The background oak keeps it from getting too sweet.

Taste: Imagine cream soda mixed with a hint of apple juice with a bit of tannins from the barrel making themselves known, but not excessively so.

Finish: The quintessential "Batman" finish, where it leaves far earlier than anyone expects.

Character: Do you remember the first time you really fell in love? Not the puppy-dog love of the junior-high set, but the nuanced love that occurs when someone sweeps you off your feet for the sake of sweeping you off your feet. For me, this drink will represent the time when I fell in love with whiskey, hard. It is the Don Juan of Scotland's spirit.

I'll tell you something. I've got a bit of the Major in my house. I was able to reclaim these huge doors from his mansion while they were tearing it down. I expanded my home just so I could put them in."

We both laughed. It was clear he loved his job and he loved Glen Grant.

We spent the next hour touring the rest of the grounds, talking about his plans for the future, and examining the new visitors' center. We ended back up at the office, where he gave both Krysta and me a bottle of their whiskey. "For the trip home," he said. We said our good-byes and parted ways. When we got into the car I turned to Krysta.

"I'm not sure," I said as I struggled to pull out a notebook in order to write down the experience, "but I think we were both just on a date."

11

Drinking My Age

No one knows for sure how it got there, but an aphid with a taste and venom for vineyards had found its way into France. What was known was that this insect, now known as *Phylloxera vastatrix*, came from America and by 1863 had been discovered in the province of Languedoc. The wine growers there spoke of the unknown disease afflicting their vines. A vine or two, usually in the center of a vineyard, started to sicken, the leaves yellowing at first, then turning red before drying and falling off the vine. The next year the symptoms worsened on the initial vine and neighboring ones would appear as the original one had the previous year. By year three, the initial vine was dead. Any fruit that did appear on the sickened vines was unusable for wine.

Within fifteen years it had devastated close to 40 percent of the vineyards of France, and 100 percent of wine drinkers. The wine industry nearly collapsed due to the loss of product. Businesses closed, people who lost jobs in the wine areas immigrated to America or Algiers, places of opportunities where their vineyard skills could be used. Various products that had depended upon wine ceased production, including brandies. By the late 1870s or early 1880s, Cognac (a brandy from the Cognac region of France) became nearly impossible to find by the upper class, who had revered the drink. Soon the elite turned to whiskey as their drink of choice. And Scotch whiskey was their primary whiskey of choice.

In the years since King George's visit to Edinburgh in 1822, the English ruling class had looked toward Scotland to fill their romantic notions. Fueled by the stories of Walter Scott, and increasingly accessible due to the burgeoning railroad industry, the Highlands of Scotland became the playground of the rich. In 1852, Queen Victoria and Prince Albert purchased Balmoral Castle in Aberdeenshire. While Victoria's visits became less frequent after Albert's death in 1861, Scotland clearly had the royal family's seal of approval.

The British upper class came to the Highlands to get away from the pressures and gossip of London. The idle rich turned to hunting in the morning, and in the evening they drank the drink of the locals, which increasingly became blended whiskey.

Much to the chagrin of the traditional pot still whiskey makers, the blending business took off during this period, making large profits. There was very little overhead due to both Coffey's patent still and the ability to blend nontaxed whiskey. Further hurting the pot still distilleries was the fact that aged whiskey from the pot stills had to sit in casks for a longer period of time to get the tastes that were deemed palatable. Blending ran contrary to this, as cost-conscious producers could simply mix various whiskeys to get the taste they wanted, and could get to the marketplace sooner. Meanwhile, whiskeys made by pot still makers were stored dormant for years in bonded warehouses, incurring high rental fees, expensive casking, and losses of product through evaporation and by workers who often pilfered a drink or two from barrels when owners and managers weren't looking.

The era saw an explosive amount of growth. New distilleries were built in Scotland to meet the demand of the market, and several Coffey stills even started to appear in Ireland, often alongside pot stills. Practically all of the grain spirit from the patent stills in Ireland was exported, and the pot still whiskey was sold both at home and abroad. Much of the blending was done either by the dealers who sold to the pubs or by owners of markets. It was this era that saw the development of several brands recognizable to us today. Glenlivet, Chivas, Johnnie Walker, Dewar's, and many others all got their start during this golden age, most of them making their money from blends. The success of Glenlivet, the availability of fresh water from the river Spey, and a quick route to markets via railways and steamships encouraged many distilleries to open in the area east and southeast of Inverness called Speyside. It was this rush to the area that created the region revered and honored today as the whiskey capital of the world.

The Dublin distillers, seeing their market share being threatened by these upstarts, did the only thing they could think of: They started a propaganda campaign against the makers of the "silent spirit," so called because the grain whiskey often used as a base in the blended whiskeys had little to no taste and, more importantly to the conservatively run Irish distilleries, no history or tradition.

The traditional distillers of Ireland and Scotland influenced or published a series of pamphlets in the early 1870s, turning a critical eye on the upstart blending companies. Newcomers to the whiskey trade were accused of illicit trading practices. The London *Times* and the *Daily Telegraph* condemned the blends as fraudulent. Even the prominent medical journal warned of consuming "premature spirit of dubious origin."

That isn't to say that their concerns weren't unfounded. Adulteration of spirits had been a common practice in the whiskey world, long before the introduction of the blends. Tobacco juice, tea, or other nefarious products were added to the drink in order to give it an aged look when it truly had never been inside a cask for even a day. The practice was so common that, in 1855, the House of Commons had appointed a select committee to examine the issue, and they concluded that adulteration was nearly a fact of life in the whiskey industry. Whiskey producers were as reputable as a used-car salesman.

Sometimes dealers would add water to a more expensive brand in order to make an extra shilling or two from the cask. Other times sugar, or even pineapple juice was added to help cover up the rougher flavors of the less than quality whiskeys that had made their way to the public. Even more distressing was the use of sulfuric acid, zinc sulfate, and copper sulfates that found their way into the drink.

News reports of these adulterations fostered public debate in which the standard response was essentially: "Yeah? So what? We've known they've screwed with the whiskey for ages."

And yet the blends kept selling.

The Irish whiskey companies also saw increased sales due to the failure of the European vineyards, and many of the larger distilleries saw unprecedented growth. John Jameson's, Power's, even the smallest of the Dublin distilleries, Jones Road, all moved more product. With their additional wealth they sought out influence in parliament to restrict the blended whiskeys from gaining popularity. William O'Sullivan, a member of Parliament who just so happened to be a distiller himself, campaigned against the the blenders in the 1870s. But his influence was limited and no legislation made it into law.

And still the blends kept selling.

The sheer volume purchased by the blending companies soon meant that they could dictate terms to the distilleries providing their whiskey. The Scottish pot distillers became upset when the blenders began purchasing Irish patent still whiskeys and mixing them with malt whiskeys, and the Scottish Malt Distillers Association protested this adulteration of their whiskey. They demanded that the blenders state which spirits went into each blend. The blenders told them, in so many words, to piss off, threatening to purchase their aged whiskey from elsewhere if they kept up their complaining. The malt distillers backed down.

The amount of money that was now being made meant that the larger distilling companies were worried about any new innovation or company that might threaten their income. Rivalries appeared among distilleries near and far. The Irish distillers were suspicious of the Scotch whiskey producers, as they saw the popularity of Scotch whiskey increase and threaten their marketshare. The Scots were annoyed with German distilleries, who were suddenly flooding the British marketplace with a neutral spirit that undercut the cost of British neutral spirits by nearly two thirds. More popular brands migrated toward one another in order to fight off smaller ones.

In 1877 competition forced the Scottish grain whiskey market to join forces and become a cartel. Six of the largest grain distillers, controlling over 75 percent of Britain's grain whiskey industry, joined together to form the Distillers Company Limited (DCL). Robert Stewart, owner of the Kirkliston Distillery, sent out a memorandum to five other distillers outlining the benefits of becoming one united company. These distilleries would give up ownership of their respective companies in exchange for shares of the new one.

In order to compete with the Dublin distillers, who still ruled the world stage, the DCL purchased their own pot still distillery at Phoenix Park in Ireland in order to blend the resulting product into their grain whiskey and label the drink "Irish Whiskey."

However, the patent stills that had popped onto the Irish scene flooded the grain whiskey market in order to undercut the DCL and lessen their hold on the market. The DCL responded by forming the United Kingdom Distillers Association (UKDA), commonly known as the "Whisky Parliament." They forced the Irish patent stills to join with them, under the threat of converting the pot still distillery at Phoenix Park into a patent still, and then flooding the Irish market with cheaper patent alcohol, with the added benefit of undercutting the prices of the Irish patent distillers. The majority of Irish patent distillers joined, but all it would take to make the association fail was one distillery to work outside of the UKDA. Two Irish grain plants refused to join, which encouraged the Cork Distilleries company to withdraw and the UKDA fell apart.

It was a lesson that the DCL would not forget.

The Glenfarclas Distillery was a short drive down from Glen Grant on the A95, through farmland.

"Oooo. Hairy Coos!" Krysta said with excitement. Her left hand pointed at a distant herd of cows, with coats of red hair that seemed to blow in the wind. Krysta's right hand held on to the steering wheel as she asked, "Do we have time to stop for a few pictures?"

I looked at her with skepticism. "Not if we wish to have lunch," I said. She put out her lower lip in a display of faux poutiness. But I was starting to feel like the adult telling the child that she couldn't have candy, ever. The next chance we had to take pictures of exotic Scottish farm animals, I vowed that we would seize it.

After lunch, we arrived at Glenfarclas Distillery and walked into their gift shop. We told the woman behind the counter that we were there to meet George Grant, and after she made a quick phone call, we were told to wait as he made his way across the distillery. Soon he entered and we exchanged greetings.

"So, where have you stopped so far on your trip?" he asked us, continuing the pleasantries.

I ran through the roll call of distilleries we had visited. "And we just came over from Glen Grant, where we talked with Dennis Malcolm."

The woman behind the gift shop counter spoke up. "You were speaking with Dennis, and you were able to get here on time?" she asked in playful mock surprise.

"Did he show you the safe?" asked George.

"Oh yeah."

"Beautiful, wasn't it?"

I agreed, noting that the distilleries in Scotland not only know of each other, but they know of each other's hooks and tricks.

George Grant (not related to the Grants of Glen Grant) was more down-to-earth than Dennis Malcolm, but as he showed us the grounds of his distillery, it became clear that he was equally passionate about the industry and respectful of the heritage surrounding Glenfarclas. Unlike Glenturret or Glen Grant, Glenfarclas was the first distillery in Scotland that we had visited that wasn't owned by an outside corporation.

The Glenfarclas Distillery has been around since at least 1836, when Robert Hay established his whiskey-making business on Rechlerich Farm. Then John Grant purchased the the distillery for a little

over five hundred pounds in 1865, and it has remained in the family
ever since. The George Grant that we were now talking to is part of
the sixth generation of that family.

After the tour, we headed up to the boardroom to talk a bit
more. In the room, on shelves above a bar that was nearly hidden in
the back right corner, was a collection of fifty bottles. Each bottle
came from a different year between 1957 and 2007.

"So . . . what year were you born?" This was the second time that
my age had come up today, and, quite frankly, it was a little worry-
ing. I hesitated.

Krysta had no such hesitation and let him know when she arrived on this planet. He walked to the bottles and pulled out the
bottle from 1977. My brain shifted gears, and instead of lamenting
my lack of youth, I wanted to boast of age. "I'm 1967!" George
laughed and pulled out the appropriate bottle. I was going to be able
to have a taste of forty-year-old scotch. Outwardly, I was able to regain my composure and put on the stoic look of professionalism. In-
wardly, my mind set out to party. I let it.

Glenfarclas (Casked 1967)

An independent distillery situated in the heart of Speyside,
Glenfarclas easily represents both class and promise.

Nose: There's a bit of cola in this, complemented by a bit
of a wine aroma. It has probably been stored in a sherry
cask at some point.

Taste: The cola still seems apparent to me, followed by a sort of woody
chocolate, and then a bit of spice makes itself apparent as well.

Finish: This ends like the finale of the Beatle's "A Day in the Life," with
one final chord that seemingly goes on for longer than one thinks is possible. That chord comes across as a red tea.

Character: I think the Beatles are an apt comparison to this whiskey. Far
more complicated than people give it credit for, the drink is complex, but
also fun (shaped, no doubt, by the novelty of how I came to taste it).

Every year that whiskey stays in a cask, as much as 2 percent of the alcohol can evaporate. So while a spirit can stay in the cask for as long as anyone wants, at some point so much alcohol might have evaporated that it could technically cease to be a whiskey, and instead have the alcohol content of a liqueur. The sixty-three-year-old whiskey that we had at Locke's Distillery in Kilbeggan had to be "fixed" in order for it to have an alcohol content that would make it technically "whiskey-strength."

I looked at my glass and swirled this drink that was as old as I was. It was this kind of whiskey that had made the whiskey world seem so unapproachable. Older whiskeys tend to be higher-cost, making the purchase prohibitive for those with modest paychecks and high credit card debt. When I walk into a liquor store back home, buying a two-hundred-dollar bottle of the stuff is simply out of the question for run-of-the-mill drinking and celebrating. This means that the market for older whiskeys is mostly comprised of either wealthy or obsessive individuals.

Some people have decried the high costs of whiskey, stating that they are "artificially inflated." While the sellers of whiskey are no saints by any means (and not one will try to convince you that he is), there is a logic behind the higher price of the older brands.

Consider a simple cask that has just been filled with spirit and has just started aging. For the sake of simple math, the cask holds one hundred liters, and it has been filled by a spirit that was 70 percent alcohol by volume.

For it to be labeled "scotch" (or "Irish whiskey," for that matter), it has to sit in that cask for three years. So after three years, the cask would be about 96 percent full, some of the alcohol lost to evaporation. After twelve years (the period of time many distillers believe that whiskey needs to age for it to be "ready"), the cask will only be 85 percent full.

If we value the spirit at ten dollars per liter when it was first casked, then after twelve years, the remaining eighty-five liters of whiskey would have to be valued at eleven dollars and seventy-six cents just to ensure that the cask was worth what it was twelve years prior to the spirit's evaporation.

"Yeah, but how do we get from twenty dollars a bottle to two hundred dollars a bottle?" one might ask next. The answer is simple—the law of supply and demand. There are simply more bottles of 12-year-old single malts released into the marketplace than 40-year-old bottles. Whiskey in the warehouse is like a teenager living with his parents. It sits there, not doing anything, and costing the parents a small fortune for annual upkeep. It does not produce any income for the distillery. The sooner the distiller can get it out on the market, the sooner profits will be rolling in. However, since there is demand for 18-, 15-, and 21-year-old whiskeys, some distilleries store an equal amount of whiskey, in order to fulfill the demand. The smaller the supply and the greater the demand, the higher the costs for the consumers.

But where does the demand for older whiskey come from?

I turned my attention back to George, who was conversing with Krysta about America. I interrupted them. "Do you find that it's difficult to sell to both the crowd of folks who just want a whiskey, and don't really care about the subtle differences in flavor, versus those who will go into great detail about how a whiskey tastes?"

George looked thoughtful for a moment. "Well . . . they're both an important part of our market, and they both benefit us." He paused. "Have you ever talked to a whiskey reviewer?"

I shook my head no.

"Most of them are quite nice and easy to get along with, but sometimes they just don't turn off! We were at a function here one night when one started talking to me about the whiskey he was drinking. 'It has a nice nose, and a pleasant caramel taste and sits on the tongue well.' I wanted to say 'Can't you just enjoy it? Can't you just drink it?'"

Throughout our journey so far, we'd run into the dilemma that faces all brands of whiskey: What do you do with the folks who are simply crazy-obsessive about their drink? More than any other factor, it is these folks who make the whiskey world so intimidating to newcomers. If you ask a whiskey professional what's the best way to enjoy the spirit, they're most likely to respond: "Any way you like." Ask a whiskey obsessive the same question, and you're likely to get an answer regarding how much water is proper to add to a specific type of whiskey, and then a lot of detail about how much water to remove for each year that the whiskey has aged. For a newcomer to the spirit, this can be overwhelming. To many, it's simply easier to drink vodka than deal with very explicit instructions on how to drink whiskey. This is exactly what whiskey distillers don't want.

On the positive side, obsessives can bring good word-of-mouth advertising to their products and in some cases can help get their bottles reviewed in various magazines. A good review in *Whisky* magazine or even *Playboy* can help increase demand for a label. And demand for a label increases the chance that the lesser-known distilleries will be able to pay their bills and/or invest in their future.

Demand is often quite amorphous. What causes demand one year may be the reason for lack of demand the next. As near as I can figure out, with whiskey there are three rules of thumb that help influence demand.

One, older whiskeys often have a greater depth of flavor than younger ones. The longer a whiskey can sit in a cask, the more flavor it can extract from the wood of the cask. Sometimes that flavor will be a sweetness from any remnants of the spirit that was in the cask prior to the whiskey. Other times it may be the flavor of the oak cask itself. More likely it's a combination of the two, and some other variables thrown in (as an example, some whiskeys from the west coast of Scotland say that they get their saltiness from maturing next to the sea). Flavors don't evaporate as readily as the alcohol does, meaning that whatever tastes are pulled out of the cask become concentrated over the years the whiskeys sit in the cask. However, a whiskey can be too old. Sit a spirit too long in a cask and it runs a risk of tasting too much like wood, with all the bitterness that comes along with it. What makes whiskey unique is that this changes from location to location, from year to year.

Second, younger whiskeys pay the bills and older whiskeys bring the attention. There's an experiment that I have run on occasion, and its results never cease to amaze me. I've talked with many people about whiskey, and most of them have a passing knowledge of the stuff, but admit to not being experts. Invariably it is these people who want to know more about older whiskeys than the younger ones. It's almost as if there's this presumption of older whiskey being better than younger whiskey. This isn't always the case, nor should it be the default assumption made about the drink. There is a difference in flavors between older and younger whiskeys. As I said earlier, older whiskeys tend to have a fuller flavor while younger ones tend to be lighter. But a deeper, fuller-flavored whiskey is no more a better whiskey over a light one than a pint of porter is better than a glass of pilsner. They are simply different beasts. What makes fuller-flavored whiskeys unique is their rarity. As I also explained above, it's in a distillery's best interest to get their whiskey to market as soon as possible. What this means is that there are more lighter-flavored bottles of whiskey available. Conversely, the fuller-flavored whiskeys are more difficult to come by. What this means is that the pricing of older whiskeys is affected by the law of supply and demand, and the distilleries and companies can raise costs on both ends of the equation. There's also a strong demand for older whiskey due to its unique taste when compared with the more readily available lighter whiskeys, so, again, they can raise prices.

Third, we humans are a shallow lot, as some of us like to own things that define our status. Distilleries understand the pricing surrounding their older whiskeys, so much so that they will and have created limited bottlings, with the sole purpose of getting higher prices for certain releases. While at Glenturret, Krysta purchased a bottle of The Famous Grouse Scottish Oak Finish, an acknowledged rarity. The distillery produced a limited-edition run of just 7,029 bottles, and it comes in a presentation box, complete with a small section of cask made from Scottish oak, and sells for £35, or roughly $70. Glenturret even wood-burns the purchaser's name on the piece of cask, which guarantees the buyer a free tour every time he shows up at the distillery. The company also burns the purchaser's name into a second piece of oak cask and displays it in their visitors' center. As of our visit, Glenturret had sold more than a few bottles of the stuff.

Over the course of the next few years, many of the bottles will be consumed, a few more will be lost to breakage. If the bottle Krysta purchased doesn't get drunk or dropped, it has a strong probability of being worth more five years down the road than what she paid for it. At some point in the next forty to fifty years, there may only be ten or so bottles of this release left. It then will be worth more as a collectible item than a consumable one. When this occurs, it will be worth far more than it will five years from now.

This is the kind of bottle that Mr. Disposable Income came across on that fateful night in Surrey. The hotel didn't own this drink to serve. It owned it to impress. It was one of the last remaining bottles of Dalmore 62 Single Highland Malt Scotch Whisky out there. It was expensive, not because it was an exceptionally good-tasting whiskey, but rather because it was an exceptionally rare bottle.

I muttered a small curse to myself and thought, "I've been going about this all wrong," for all I knew, the whiskey Mr. DI drank could have tasted like tree bark. Rare and expensive tree bark, but tree bark nonetheless.

While Glenturret's release of The Famous Grouse Scottish Oak Finish comes across as a bit of a cynical manipulation of their customers, not all whiskeys that come onto the market arrive with the express purpose of creating a collectible. Sometimes a distillery has found a long-lost cask that had been misplaced in the warehouse. "This happens far more often than anyone would like to admit." George told me on our way back to the visitors' centre. I felt bad. Since he poured me that 40-year-old, I'd been lost in thought, and not given him my full attention. Luckily Krysta had been charming him with stories of recent trips.

Once we entered the center, he took us past the gift shop and into a back room. Incorporated into the room's walls were the original carved oak panels from the *Empress of Australia*'s first-class smoking lounge. The room even had the early-twentieth-century ocean liner's original bar, from which, I'm told, "numerous drams of Glenfarclas have been poured." George directed my gaze upward, and said that when they were looking for a ceiling, they were able to locate the company that had made the original lounge. Not only were they still around, but they still had the plans that allowed them to re-create the ceiling.

I listened with great interest as George bragged about the room, but in the back of my mind a question popped into my head that seemed too rude to ask. What did this have to do with whiskey or the whiskey industry?

While I was trying to suss out the importance of this room by comparing it with our previous experiences at other distilleries, I had a realization. The room was there to impress visitors, to instill a sense of class on both the distillery itself as well as its brand. This was no different than the gardens at Glen Grant, or even Glenturret's boasting of their BAFTA.

I smiled to myself as I looked at the intricacies of the ceiling that George was pointing out. I put aside any more deep thoughts about either whiskey or the distillery. Sometimes it's best to simply enjoy the sales pitch.

12

Castles and Collapses

At breakfast the next morning, Krysta gave me a hard stare.

"What?" I asked after swallowing a piece of potato scone.

"Castles," she deadpanned.

I shook my head, not sure if I had heard her correctly. "What?" I repeated, more than a little confused.

"Castles," she said again. "As in, I want to see one."

"We saw one on Saturday in Edinburgh," I reminded her as I took a bite of the blood pudding that the host had put in front of us.

"Yes, along with fifteen thousand other tourists," she said, sitting back in her chair. "I want one that is rundown and where we don't have to stand in line for forty minutes in order to purchase a twenty-pound ticket."

Over the course of the trip, we discovered two things about castles in Ireland and Scotland. First, they are everywhere. Many are rundown, appearing as nothing more than rubble and rocks. Many are quite small, nothing more than four stone walls and a fifty-foot tower. But they are still, technically, castles.

Secondly, most people in Ireland and Scotland rarely give castles more than a passing thought. The castles are so prevalent in this part of the world that when travelers come, the locals have to remind themselves, "Oh yeah, other people find these hovels *interesting.*"

The host came into the room to pour some coffee into the delicate china cups in front of us. "Are there any castles in the area?" Krysta asked him. "I mean, ones that we can visit."

He thought for a moment. "Most are closed during the off-season. I cannot think of any that might be open today."

Krysta gave me a look that showed her disappointment. I shrugged. "There are castles everywhere. We passed two yesterday. We'll stop at one of those and get some pictures." Just because they might be closed didn't mean we couldn't take pictures of them from the parking lot.

She smiled and clapped her hands excitedly. Appeased, she turned to her breakfast.

"You mentioned a whiskey shop the other day?" I asked the host, hoping it would prompt his memory.

"Ah, yes. I wrote it down this morning." He put down the coffee pot and deftly pulled his glasses out of the front pocket of his trousers and a note from the back pocket. "It's the . . ."

He paused and smiled widely.

". . . Whisky Castle. The owner's name is Mike Drury," he continued. He folded the paper and gave it to me with a smile and a wink.

I shot a look to Krysta. I held the paper up and mouthed, "a castle." She smiled and said nothing.

The Whisky Castle was located in Tomintoul, and getting to there from Grantown-on-Spey required us to drive on several back roads that took us through the heart of the farmlands of the Highlands. In the distance, sheep dotted the hills looking like lint stuck on a sweater, and the wind, blowing at a respectable fifty miles per hour, painted the sky with an ever-changing display of dramatic cloud formations that temporarily hid the bright morning sun.

By the time we parked the car, our nerves were a bit shaken. The wind had tossed the car around fairly regularly, and Krysta had had to struggle to keep it on the road on more than one occasion. When we finally arrived in Tomintoul, we felt as if we had just survived the latest roller coaster at Six Flags.

The door flicked the bell, which in turn announced our presence to the owners of the gift shop that connected to the whiskey store. A woman behind the counter smiled and greeted us with a big "Hello!" Krysta and I both returned her greeting, and I pointed to the room that held the many bottles of drink and said plaintively, "Whiskey."

"Of course, of course," she responded, nodding. "Mike, two heading your way," she yelled down the hallway.

"Aye!" came the response from a wild-haired man who seemed to be attached to the telephone. Rather than interrupt him, we both started looking at the bottles that filled his shop.

Much like the gift shop in Edinburgh, there were dozens of brands on display that covered the full spectrum of Scotch whiskey brands. Many of the more popular single malts were available. But unlike the gift shop, non-Scottish brands of whiskey were also available, as well as private bottlings, which are marketed by the many independent bottlers of single malt Scotch whiskey.

Independent bottlers play a unique role in the Scotch whiskey industry. They buy individual casks from distilleries and other sources and then they decide how and when the whiskey should be aged, finished, and bottled. For example, they may decide to keep the whiskey in its cask longer than the original company would have, or finish the whiskey in a different cask than the one in which it was stored. In short, they offer different whiskeys than those offered by the distilleries.

It is also quite rare to come across an independent bottling via the typical sources in the United States. Thus I was staring at several bottles of whiskey that I had never seen before.

"What can I do for you two fine ladies this morning?" said the deep, booming voice of Mike.

Startled to the point of forgetting why I was there, I asked simply, "Is there any whiskey that you can recommend?"

"Sure, sure," he said. "Blackadder Single Malt from Highland Park, ten years old."

"Really?" I asked. "Why is that?"

"Because I got to clear them off my shelf so I can put other bottles up," he said, patting my shoulders before chuckling at his own punch line. I stood there, dumbfounded, unsure whether he thought the Blackadder was a good whiskey or not.

"To ask me for my recommendation is not really a good way to choose whiskey," he said, turning back to the security of his counter.

"Why is that?" I asked.

"Because," he returned, his grizzled looks containing a bit of a grin. "I am not you. And though others have tried, you cannot be me."

"So you can't tell me what whiskey is better than another?"

"Ah, but that is not what you asked now, is it?" he smiled. As I replayed the brief conversation, I wondered if he treated all of his customers like this.

"I was hoping you could provide me some insight into whiskey," I said. His eyes looked up from the legal pad in front of him.

"Oh really. What sort of insight?" he said, the bemused look on his face never leaving.

"Well, for one, what would make a person spend thirty-five thousand pounds on a bottle of whiskey?"

He squinted behind his glasses. "Are you a reporter?" he asked.

"No, no. I'm writing a book. About whiskey. I'm trying to figure out folks' passion for it," I said.

He lumbered like a bear out to a different position behind his counter. "Ah, I see." From seemingly nowhere, he pulled out a bottle of something that had no label. "So you're a writer?" He opened the bottle and placed it upon the counter.

"Something like that," I said. Krysta came over, her red hair bouncing as she was nearly jumping up and down in excitement. In her hands was the bottle of Blackadder that Mike had pointed out to me a mere moment before. "Kate, look. Blackadder. I wonder if there's a bottle of Baldrick around here," she pondered, referencing the classic British sitcom.

"Is she your friend?" asked Mike, pointing at Krysta.

I nodded. "Of course."

He smiled again, and pulled out three small tasting glasses. He poured a bit of drink into each glass, followed by a capful of water.

"So . . . Kate," he said lifting a glass and indicating that both Krysta and I should do the same. We both obliged.

"There's not much I can offer you here in the way of advice. When it comes to whiskey, there are but few things that I know for sure."

He paused to ensure we were both ready to receive his words of wisdom.

"People spend thirty-five thousand pounds on bottles of whiskey because they can. You should always drink what you like. And the Diageos of the world will always find ways to arse up the drinks that you like. Sláinte!" He took a nip from his glass and let the whiskey do its magic. Krysta and I followed suit.

Krysta's face flushed. "Mmmm. What kind of whiskey is this?" she asked.

"Oh no. You don't get to find out," he said in an amicable tone.

"Oh c'mon. You can tell me," she protested as the phone in the store rang.

Mike, seeing his opportunity for a gracious exit, smiled and pointed to the phone. "That's for me," he said. "Cath!" he shouted back to the gift shop.

"Yeah, yeah. I'm comin'," came the response from the woman in the shop. Mike excused himself and picked up the phone. I returned to stare at the bottles, while Krysta went to talk to the woman who had made her way to the counter.

What was that all about? I thought to myself as I looked over the various bottles of whiskey both familiar and rare. Forget the answers to the questions he provided, I wondered what the heck he was doing offering us whiskey after less than five minutes in his shop. Was this a common tradition in Scottish whiskey shops, or were his actions meant to be friendly yet keep me from asking more questions? Or was my American cynicism showing through again, making it difficult to accept a friendly drink and words of advice?

I picked out three different bottles of whiskey, an independent bottling of a ten-year-old Strathisla from Signatory Vintage, an 8-year-old from Braeval that was aged in a sherry cask, and a bottle of Penderyn, a Welsh whiskey that I was picking up for a co-worker back home. All the while, Mike's booming voice dominated the room while he was on the phone, his deep, guttural Scottish diction making it all the more difficult for a Yankee like me to ignore. I paid for the whiskey at the counter, where Krysta was talking with the woman. Considering the £100-plus cost for three bottles, both the Whisky Castle and I had profited from the transaction.

We left the store, with heavier luggage but lighter pocketbooks, to head out to the Glenfidich Distillery. Unknowingly, we were in the midst of the unofficial "Grant" arm of the tour of Speyside. As

Unknown Scotch Given to Me at the Whisky Castle

As Lew Bryson, editor of the magazine *Malt Advocate*, wrote to me in an e-mail: "The secret to learning what you really enjoy in whiskey is found in just two words: Blind. Tasting. Stop thinking about how much the whiskey cost, and where you got it, and who else likes it, and what Jim Murray rated it, and what medals it won, and what distillery you're supposed to like . . . and just taste the whiskey. If you can get a friend to set up four whiskeys for you, without you knowing what they are, and you taste them and write down just some simple descriptions of what you like or don't like about all of them . . . you'll learn a lot about your taste in whiskey, which is the most important thing in enjoying it."

Nose: Floral at first, sweet, and then the peat manifests with the caress of a velvet glove.

Taste: Interesting mouthfeel, chewy, kind of oily, but not to its detriment. Briny, with a bit of sweetness in the back.

Finish: Long. Exquisitely long. Vanillas flow through with a nice crunch of oak in the back before a hint of sherry pops up.

Character: A one-night stand where you both know it could never work out in the long run. But oh, what fun was had! Too bad you never got the person's name or phone number.

we have seen, Glen Grant was founded by James and John Grant. Glenfarclas has been owned by a series of George Grants since 1870, and now we had discovered that Glenfiddich was founded by William Grant. Add in the fact that our hotel is in GRANTown-on-Spey and I realized that to have the surname Grant in Scotland must carry a small bit of a whiskey reputation with it.

I had chosen Glenfiddich for two very interesting reasons. They were risk takers, and they were still independently operated.

In the late 1960s, they looked to break their dependency on blended whiskey and started setting aside additional casks for single malts. The end result was that as the demand for single malts increased, Glenfiddich had enough whiskey on hand to make a fair amount of money, and soon found themselves as the largest seller of single malts in the world.

One would think that being in this position would mean that they were owned by one of the major conglomerates, such as Diageo or Pernod Ricard. In fact, Glenfiddich is one of the more successful independents in the world.

All of this was put forth to us by our tour guide, Brian, a kilted Englishman with a dry sense of humor and limited tolerance for what can best be termed "whiskey nonsense." Such nonsense would include such items as "The Famous Grouse Experience," whiskey connoisseurs who have limited sense of business, and critics of caramel coloring. This last item may need some explaining.

In continuing with this schism between whiskey obsessives and whiskey producers, the topic of coloring whiskey is one that separates the two groups the furthest. The producers of whiskey willingly add caramel coloring to their product in order to achieve a uniformity of product. This ensures that their drink looks the same from year to year, and doesn't raise the eyebrows of their regular customers. Whiskey obsessives claim that adding the coloring changes the drink and cheapens the product's natural flavor. It's difficult to say who's right in this debate, as there is little evidence to support either side of the argument, which means it's more of philosophical argument than one about whiskey quality. The only support to the obsessive's point of view are the handful of Scotch distilleries who do not add coloring and proudly state so on their labels. From what I could tell, these distilleries receive a little more respect than the makers of mass-produced drinks, but any claims that these are better-tasting whiskeys are still subjective.

Thanks to arriving in Scotland during the off-season, we found that we had Brian to ourselves. Quickly surmising that we had the basics of the distilling process pretty much committed to memory after eight previous tours, we spent most of the time talking about the industry rather than touching upon the joys of gristing and the pleasures of the still room. Beneath everything Brian told us about Glenfiddich there was a strong sense of pride, firmly partnered with an air of arrogance.

"Did you see Glenfarclas's computer controls of their process?" I told him I had.

"We still keep people on site to do that sort of work. We believe that only a person can truly tell us when it's right to put the mash into the still."

"Did you see how many stills they had at Glen Grant?" he asked later as we entered the still room.

"Yeah, about eight, I believe."

"Here's eight . . . ," he paused dramatically ". . . of twenty-four."

Later: "Here's a cask warehouse. It's one of forty-four." I had to force myself not to roll my eyes. While his boasting may have been annoying, I couldn't help but think that Glenfiddich had a look about it that Glenturret, Glen Grant, and Glenfarclas didn't. It looked busy. According to Iain Slinn in *Whisky Miscellany*, the Scapa Distillery on the island of Orkney has only three permanent employees. The rest of the work is taken care of by part-time staff and automation. Here at Glenfiddich, there are close to two hundred people working full time. While the insinuation by our tour guide was that Glenfiddich owes its success to their personal attention to detail, an argument could also be made that because they are so successful they can afford to have so many people on staff. What I couldn't argue, and didn't want to, was that they had an impressive operation.

"I have a treat for you," said Brian, as he ushered us into a minivan after we had finished our tour. "There's something I want to show you." We exited the parking lot of the distillery and took a right, driving down toward a second, smaller plant. He parked the van and introduced us to the Balvenie Distillery, owned by the same folks who own Glenfiddich. Purchased as a mansion in 1892, William Grant turned the mansion into yet another distillery, ensuring that only his brands had access to the source of water in the area.

As Balvenie's Web site states, "The basement was to become a bonded store for maturing whisky, the first storey a malt floor, whilst the upper two floors were to be used as grain lofts." Over the next few decades, Grant and his descendants expanded upon their second distillery. In the early 1920s the old mansion was leveled to the basement floor and the stone blocks were used to build a new malt barn and kiln. The old malt kiln was converted into malt bins, electric lights were installed, and the number of stills was increased. Later still, warehouses and offices were added. It was a warehouse that Brian was keen to show us.

After climbing up a set of stairs, we found ourselves looking out upon Balvenie's cooperage, with ten or so men working on casks in various states of repair. With a nod of acknowledgment, one of the workers on the floor went to a radio and turned down the music. The rest of the team never even looked up. Under the bright fluorescent lights, they continued with their hammering, sanding, and charring of their respective casks.

"This is my favorite place at these distilleries," said Brian. We stood for a moment to watch the work going on down below us.

The cooperage at Balvenie/Glenfiddich is another example of how the company seeks to control every aspect of the operation. Having one on distillery grounds is a bit of a luxury nowadays, one that most can't afford. The lack of cask makers at most distilleries was a bit surprising to me, especially when most everyone involved in the production of whiskey will state that anywhere from 60 to 80 percent of the flavor one gets in a dram comes directly from the cask. To outsource that sort of control seemed like a massive oversight.

For the most part, distilleries buy casks from America that were previously used in the aging of bourbon. This again is mostly due to cost, as there are ample empty Bourbon casks to be had. American regulations state that for a whiskey to be called bourbon it must be aged in "charred new oak containers." The word "new" has more than likely ticked off more than a few bourbon executives, as they only get one use out of a cask, while the Irish and Scots get three or four uses.

As always with Scotch whiskey, there are exceptions. The folks at Macallan create their whiskey by maturing it in oak sherry casks from Jerez, Spain. Balvenie has released a 17-year-old whiskey aged entirely in a new cask. More recently, distilleries have taken to aging their whiskey in one barrel for a specific period of time, and then "finishing" it in a completely different barrel for a shorter period. Now there are whiskeys (both Scotch and Irish) that were aged for 10 or 12 years in a bourbon cask, and then a year or so in a Madeira or port cask.

The choice of which casks to age the whiskey in is only one of the factors that add to the flavors insinuated into the spirit. Factors as seemingly unimportant as the geographic location of the warehouse and even where the barrel is stored within the warehouse are assumed to play their part. We have seen that Scotch whiskey aged in warehouses on the islands is said to taste a bit "salty" because the casks there are exposed to the aerated mist of the sea. It is said that warehouses with earthen floors provide the best results, as they maintain a higher humidity level. In a humid warehouse, the loss of spirit to the "Angel's Share" will materialize as a decrease of alcohol, which may help in obtaining a higher-quality whiskey. In a drier warehouse, this loss will materialize through a diminution of overall volume, resulting in a rising of the alcoholic strength, and will deliver a drier spirit.

Most of this information was put forth as a matter of fact by various tour guides, but little was offered in the way of hard proof to back up these claims. Many instead used stories to illustrate their point. My favorite is one that I've heard from more than one distillery.

The story roughly goes that a long-retired worker comes back to visit his old haunts, and a decade or two has passed since he last set foot in the distillery. The place has changed owners more than a few times, and his co-workers had long since been replaced. When he is asked about what year of whiskey had the best taste, he responds that he can't speak to that, but that he knew that he could always find a good drink from any barrel stored in the southwest corner of the cask house, and he admits to having taken more than his fair share of illicit sips from casks in that location. Embarrassed, he states that he had never confessed his tastings to anyone before. As he is escorted throughout the distillery by a tour guide, he comes across the old warehouse, and he and the guide make their way to the southwest corner. And it is there that they happen upon several current employees, taking illicit drinks from one of the casks. When asked why they are taking drinks from that cask, they respond, "The drinks are always better here in this part of the building."

The story itself is probably false, but there may be some truth to the science behind it. During this maturation process the whiskey "breathes" in the barrel, and how much it does so can depend upon the variation in temperatures and levels of humidity in the building. As many of the Scotch whiskey warehouses are several dozen years old, they are often unevenly ventilated, and the odds of environmental variation between one area of a warehouse and another are quite high.

After ten minutes of watching the coopers without so much as sharing one word among ourselves, Brian directed us back out of the warehouse, and pointed us to yet another building. "I've got another surprise for you," he said, trying to hide a grin.

As we walked through the door, Krysta said "Cool!" Before us, spread out on a floor that was thirty yards deep to seventy yards across, was barley that was waiting to be roasted. Two workers were there, spreading and rotating the barley in order to keep the grains at a consistent temperature and moisture level.

"Ah, I see you brought us some help," said one of the workmen to Brian. Our tour guide looked at both of us, prompting us to volunteer.

"Ooo. I'll do it," said Krysta excitedly. Giving her a wooden shovel, they demonstrated to her how to throw the barley, and then spread it evenly upon the ground. After she returned the tool to the workman, all she could do was hold her shoulder and say "Ow!"

That pain she felt is an affliction common to those who work the grain on a regular basis, sort of a whiskey maker's version of tennis elbow, except that they call it monkey shoulder. Not so coincidentally, Brian used this as an opportunity to let us know of their new brand of whiskey called exactly that: Monkey Shoulder.

We thanked the workmen for their time and went up to the second level, where we walked along the walkways in the rafters before Brian opened yet another door. This one led into the room where they dry the barley with smoke from their peat. It was a smaller room, maybe fifty feet by fifty feet, and the grain looked like piles of snow. Brian encouraged us to take a walk through the hills of grain, a luxury moment in which both Krysta and I were happy to indulge.

Riding back the half mile to Glenfiddich, Krysta nudged me from behind. "Is that a castle?" she asked.

"That is Balvenie Castle," said Brian as he pulled up next to the building that housed Glenfiddich's offices. "It's closed at this time of year."

Krysta's lower lip jutted out in a mock pout similar to the one she had given at breakfast. "Let's explore," I said, to which she applauded.

We said our good-byes to Brian, thanked him for his time, got into our rental car, and drove as close to the castle as the road would allow. From there we got out and took a handful of pictures, both of the castle, which had been abandoned since 1720, and of the entirety of the Glenfiddich Distillery.

"Uh, Krysta?"

"Yeah?"

"You might want to look behind the castle," I said to her, looking at the farmland that sat next to where we were taking pictures.

Behind us, no more than twenty feet away, stood five hairy cows, each doing a fair bit of chewing of cud, and each quite interested in what we were up to.

"Hairy coos!" Krysta squealed. She turned her attention to them and continued taking pictures.

Krysta got her castle and cows, and I got my second straight day of whiskey-filled goodness. As I looked at the rubble of the land, I felt for certain that I got the better deal.

We folk who live in the modern age have the benefit of recent events to know what happens when an industry shows an exceptional amount of exuberance. With the dot-com bubble burst of 2000 and the subprime mortgage crash seven years later, anyone with even a modicum of experience with the market knows that what goes up with irrational exuberance will come down, often in direct correlation to how high the high was.

With the whiskey market at the end of the nineteenth century, the heights were majestic. The subsequent crash left the Irish whiskey industry almost completely destroyed. The cause of the crash could not be attributed to one specific event but rather several, which, when combined, meant millions of pounds lost and dozens of distilleries closed.

There were some rough parts to the industry as the world suffered a depression in the early 1880s. A few distilleries closed, and others were purchased by larger, more established firms, and then either brought into the firm's stable of brands or shut down outright. But after the depression, the grain whiskey market rebounded, and soon whiskey was being marketed heavily and sold to the higher classes overseas. Bottling, introduced to the whiskey producers the generation before, became more ingrained in production, making smaller sales possible to individuals rather than to the taverns and inns that were the staples of the sales previously. Brands such as Dewar's, Jameson's, Power's, Haig's, and Johnnie Walker all became ensconced in the public's consciousness thanks to heavy advertising and public relations activities.

The whiskey crash started in 1898, when a Scottish blending firm called Pattison's went bust in an Enron-style crash. The Pattison brothers had a small operation, selling only three brands, two Scotch whiskeys and an Irish whiskey. But they were most efficient at producing greed. But they continually purchased their own stock in order to artificially inflate its worth. Then, using the faux worth of the company as collateral, they were able to gain credit, which they spent on their operation and to purchase more stock. Eventually the market caught up with them when a creditor came looking for Pattison's half a million pounds of debt. When they were unable to pay, the company went bankrupt. Public trust in the industry tanked and the price of whiskey soon followed. Distilleries that had thrived as recently as two years prior were now fighting for their existence. Banks began calling in their lines of credit, and the ability to expand became severely crippled.

The Distillers Company Limited, which had avoided the larger risks that some of their competitors had taken, saw their opportunity to strike. In 1902 they began purchasing distilleries that were in financial straits. Once they purchased a troubled distillery, it was soon closed. It was the most efficient way of eliminating the DCL's competition. It was also the most efficient way of looking like a heartless cad.

The DCL threw a lifeline into Ireland as well. In 1902, Archibald Walker, who had distilleries in Scotland, England, and Ireland, sold to the DCL and became a board member. His distillery in Limerick was closed soon afterward. Soon the DCL became more feared than respected, and to get a call from them likely meant that it was the end of one's livelihood. Within a generation, the DCL became a near-monopoly. As Peter Mulryan writes in *The Whiskeys of Ireland,* "In 1900 there were fifteen patent-still distilleries in Scotland; by 1922 DCL had bought all except one."

The DCL had made their fortune off the Coffey still and had changed the whiskey industry. No longer did the independently produced pot still whiskey rule supreme. The marketplace was demanding cheaper whiskey, if they demanded it at all.

To make matters worse, the technology had outpaced the legislation. No government body could figure out just what the hell "whiskey" was supposed to mean.

It was an argument that had been going on since the complaints of adulteration in the 1870s. In response to the threat of various practices of food adulteration, the government had come up with the Food and Drug Act of 1875, which addressed the complaints of adulteration of product, but still never clarified what "whiskey" actually was. *The Lancet,* a medical journal that had advocated for purity, offered this suggestion in 1904: "We have pointed out again and again that the terms 'brandy' and 'whiskey' had specific meanings, these terms being used to distinguish in the former case a spirit derived exclusively from wine and in the latter case a spirit derived from barley malt."

In 1890, the Select Committee on British and Foreign Spirits produced a baseline definition: "Whiskey is certainly a spirit consisting of alcohol and water." But this was not sufficient, because even vodka fits into this definition. But it did work to curtail those who were using more nefarious and toxic ingredients in their mix. It became safer to drink whiskey, yet still no one could determine what whiskey was. Those in the patent still business became more aggressive in pushing the boundaries of the traditional definition.

Apparently they pushed too far, because in 1905, in a court in the London borough of Islington, it was proved that two tavern owners had acted fraudulently by selling a bottle of whiskey containing 91 percent alcohol. The magistrate's judgment stated "that by Irish or Scotch Whisky is now meant a spirit obtained in the same methods by the aid of the form of still known as the pot still."

Overnight the million-pound blending industry was found to be illegal. Those who held to the traditional definitions of pot still whiskey were ecstatic; the DCL, who were making their money via the blends and the patent stills, less so.

The DCL went into survival mode after the Islington ruling, and lobbied Parliament for a royal commission of inquiry, which would negate the Islington court finding, and allow the DCL to return to their money-grubbing ways unimpeded.

In February of 1908, the commission sat for the first time and proceeded to debate the issue for eighteen months, yet they could not come up with a single answer. They did say that they were "unable to recommend that the use of the word whiskey should be restricted to spirit manufactured by the pot still process." The DCL and other patent still producers breathed a tremendous sigh of relief. The commission's answer was a victory for the patent stills—the commission could not say that whiskey could only come from pot stills. The DCL could blend grain alcohol into any amount of aged whiskey that they wished. The pot distillers in Ireland now had competition from patent distillers in Scotland. The Scottish distillers could produce whiskey both cheaper and faster, and the government had ruled that it was the same thing as the whiskey from Ireland.

The golden age of whiskey had been over for almost a dozen years. The wine industry started to rebound, thanks in large part to the practice of grafting the roots of the surviving French grapevines onto the roots of American grapevines. As wine became more plentiful, so did brandy and its status as the drink of the social elite. Whiskey became the second choice of drink for the wealthy.

Meanwhile, the heavily marketed scotches made their ways into the home of Britain's middle classes. Soon, more Scotch whiskey was being sold than Irish. Blended whiskeys dominated the marketplace. Pot still distilleries began showing even more signs of stumbles and failures. And when the pot still distilleries showed any sign of financial insecurity, the DCL would come in, purchase the brand and company, and then shut it down. One by one the Irish distilleries were closed.

The outbreak of war in 1914 only saw an increase in restrictions by the British government. The supply of barley was disrupted and grain delivery to the distilleries soon became of lower priority. Some distilleries converted their production from whiskey to that of industrial alcohol. The whiskey industry was seeing no help from the government.

This lack of help was somewhat intentional. The chancellor of the exchequer, David Lloyd George, was an obsessive anti-drinker with a temperance movement background and a firm stick up his tuckus, and looked to implement the prohibition of alcohol for the duration of the war. "Drink is doing more damage in the war than all of the German submarines put together," he stated in a speech in February 1915. He then upped the ante by proposing at various times the abolition of spirits, the nationalization of the licensed trade, and the imposition of double duties. Any of these would have crippled or decimated the whiskey industry. As might be imagined, this met with considerable public hostility, and since the government was not strong enough to force through these measures without the support of the Irish, Lloyd George had to compromise.

The compromise was reached between the distillers and the future prime minister. The agreement was shaped by James Stevenson, a director of Johnnie Walker who had been appointed by Lloyd George to run the Ministry of Munitions. It was he who pointed out to Lloyd George that a ban on distilling would mean no alcohol for high explosives, no constituents for anesthetics, and no yeast for baking bread. By appealing to the commonsense needs of a country at war, he was able to convince Lloyd George that closing down the distilleries was the last thing that the country needed. But Lloyd George had to have something to show the public that he stood by his words of temperance.

It was from this that the Immature Spirits (Restriction) Act of 1915 was created. It required that whiskey be bonded for at least two years; if not, the chancellor's punitive duty would apply. In 1916, the amount of time in bond was increased to three years. It was the belief that it was the younger, more raw whiskeys that were causing all the problems, and that the aged whiskeys simply subdued the consumers. Additionally, whiskey could no longer be sold directly from the still, and it had to be sold at a minimum alcoholic strength. While the distilleries who sold higher-quality drinks had already implemented these practices, those who hadn't were facing financial crisis.

By 1917, distilling for whiskey was suspended throughout Great Britain in order to have enough food for the islands. The distilleries wouldn't open again until 1919. These disruptions made life difficult, but not impossible. But by 1920, two very different events coincided to shut down a majority of the remaining Irish distilleries.

First, Prohibition in America, implemented in 1920 by religious zealots and amateur social scientists, shut off a vital market to the Irish distillers, and a vast amount of income dried up overnight.

Second, the Irish War of Independence and subsequent civil war had left the economy of the Irish Free State decimated. When the distilleries were foundering, there were neither the financial nor political resources available to keep them afloat. Additionally, trade with the Great Britain market was now more difficult due to import and export laws. The distilleries that had been failing during the Great War now had to close. By 1932, there were only five distilleries left in Ireland, and two of them were being mothballed until the market looked ready to improve. In Northern Ireland, the DCL had closed (directly or indirectly) all but three small, nearly insignificant pot distilleries—Coleraine, Upper Comber, and Bushmills. Today only Bushmills remains—the last distillery in Northern Ireland.

It was during this time that the DCL announced that "Ireland had become an irrelevance." From a whiskey point of view, they were right.

13

Rain and Peat

As we headed toward Inverness and eventually the A82, which would take Krysta and me to the west coast of Scotland, a sense of foreboding washed over me. Coming up was the one area of Scotch whiskey where my knowledge was weakest, the islands. Island whiskey is Scotch whiskey made on any of the outer isles, from Orkney in to the north to the southernmost of the Inner Hebridean Islands, located off the west coast. It's also the type of whiskey that most enthusiasts equate with smoke . . . peat smoke, more specifically.

While planning my trip to Scotland, it quickly became apparent that my time was limited, and I could either go to Speyside, the region with the greatest number of distilleries in Scotland, or to Islay, the island with the greatest number of distilleries. I could not do both. I chose to do Speyside. When I announced this on my Web site, I was immediately told that I had made the wrong decision. One island blog wrote that "the Accidental Hedonist . . . will unfortunately/stupidly miss out on Islay during their current Ireland and Scotland trip." It was clear that many people believed that Scotch whiskey . . . true Scotch whiskey . . . is the deep, smoky, peaty whiskey, and that the rest of the bottles that Scotland provides are merely some form of corporate propaganda.

So instead of heading to the islands, I had settled upon the city of Oban, and their one distillery. Additionally, I had purchased an "Islay Gift Pack" at the Scotch Whisky Heritage Centre back in Edinburgh, and made Krysta promise to drink each bottle with me. As a fallback position, it was a rather weak one. Perhaps we could sneak out for a quick, unplanned day trip.

As we passed through the town of Fort William on our way to Oban, a distinct aroma filled the car.

"What's that smell?" I asked.

"I'm not sure, but I think it's peat," Krysta said.

Sure enough, as we looked at the various houses we were driving by, an excessive amount of smoke was rising from several chimneys.

"Great," I thought to myself. "Even Scotland is mocking my choice."

We made it into Oban and checked into our hotel, a popular seaside resort that was surprisingly chock-full of people in what I thought was the off-season. After dinner I headed to the front desk.

"Pardon me," I said to the young woman behind the counter. "If I wanted to take a day trip to Islay tomorrow, what would that entail?"

She looked at me as if I had asked her what flavor of dog she would like to have for dinner.

"You want to go to Islay?"

"Yes," I said.

"Tomorrow?"

"Yes."

"Stay the night there?" she continued to ask with an air of incredulity.

"No. I would want to make a day trip of it. I'd like to see a distillery if possible."

"Can't be done."

Somehow, I had known that this was going to be the answer.

"What if we stayed the night?" I responded.

She looked down and rummaged through some folders on her

desk, looking for something. Finding a sheet of paper, she glanced at it and then turned back to me.

"Sorry. No."

"The piece of paper told you that?" I asked.

She turned the paper around and showed me. As I leaned in to read the typing on it, she turned it back around and summarized it for me.

"Tomorrow night, a storm is expected off the Atlantic with wind gusts up to eighty miles per hour. The next day, there's more storms and wind, with it finally breaking up by late afternoon. You'd be stuck there for two nights."

I noted her choice of the word "stuck." I got the impression that Islay may provide some of the more interesting whiskeys on the planet, but that's only because there's not much else to do there.

"What's the weather going to be tonight here in Oban?" I asked her.

She looked back down at her sheet of paper. "Rain with gale-force winds up to seventy miles per hour."

I shouldn't have felt so pleased with myself, for now we were stuck, not just in Oban, but at this hotel. I thanked her and went up to our room. When I opened the door, Krysta held out the gift pack. "We're not going anywhere tonight," she said.

I nodded. "Gale-force winds. Shall we do half tonight and half tomorrow?"

"Only if there's something on TV." We settled in and got out some glasses. I pulled out the bottles of Bunnahabhain, Bowmore, and Jura, as they were lighter in their smoky flavor. I knew that the Ardberg and Laphroaig were the heavier, peatier drinks, and saved them for tomorrow. I had no idea where the Tobermory fit on the peat scale, so I saved it for the next night, on the assumption that it would be better to have it later. The next two days would be all about the peat.

Peat is an organic material that forms in bogs and other similar environments that are waterlogged, sterile, and acidic. These conditions favor the growth of a variety of mosses. For those who've forgotten their high-school biology, mosses are bryophytes, or nonvascular plants that are fairly small, at least as far as plants go. Their tiny bodies (0.4–4 inches tall, on average) grow close together in clumps or mats in the damp areas that bogs provide. And, as plants, they die. However, they do not decompose. Instead, the dead organic matter is laid down and remains as other organic life forms above it, again most often moss, and the life/death/layering cycle begins again and is repeated. It slowly accumulates as peat because the lack of oxygen and the acidic conditions in the bog prevent any decomposition, and the weight of the organic matter above compresses the nondecomposed matter below. What remains is basically smooshed carbon matter that is the earliest stage in the formation of coal.

Peat is soft and easily compressed. Once cut from the land, the peat would be stacked on other blocks of peat, forming a peat stack, called storrows. There it would dry, as the upper part of the storrows would weigh heavily upon the lower part, forcing the water out. After drying, peat can be used as a fuel. It has industrial importance as a fuel in some countries, such as Ireland and Finland, where it is harvested on an industrial scale. In many countries, including Ireland and Scotland, where trees are often scarce, peat is used domestically, for cooking and heating. Distilleries prefer to use the upper part of the storrows, as they are wetter, rootier, and provide more smoke when aflame.

So as whiskey was becoming more popular in Ireland and Scotland during the sixteenth and seventeenth centuries, what fuel source was likely used to not just dry any grain used, but to light the fires beneath all stills great and small?

Inferred in the above rhetorical question is the fact that traditional Irish whiskey, at least that distilled way back when, also contained the same smoky flavor often associated with the Scotch whiskeys of today. This runs contrary to today's conventional wisdom that, with few exceptions, Scotch whiskey is peated, and Irish whiskey is not. Historically speaking, they would both have had some measure of smoky flavor.

It's the drying of the malted barley with smoke from a fire fueled by peat that really imparts the smoky flavor to the spirit. There were (and are) other practical applications for this practice. Certainly dried malted barley had a longer shelf life than any that remained damp, but peat smoke also makes the barley more resistant to bacterial infection. While farmers would not have known this back in the 1600s, they would have noticed that peated, malted barley lasted longer than the moist, and might have noted that people who consumed it were sick less often than those who had not.

How does the barley gain the smoky flavor? The process of smoking the grain dry results in an increase of a group of aromatic chemical compounds called phenols. As the peat is burned and the malted barley dries, phenolic compounds, in the form of phenols, cresols, xylenols, ethylphenols, and guaiacols, travel as part of the smoke and land on water molecules of the wet barley. As the water evaporates, the phenolic compounds stay behind.

We can measure how many phenolic compounds stay behind by determining how many molecules can be found out of a sampling of a million. This is often written as parts per million, or ppm. Heavily peated single malts are produced from barley containing phenolic compounds of more than 30 ppm. Medium-peated malts come from barley of about 20 ppm, and anything with less than 15 ppm is considered a lightly peated whiskey. However, even "unpeated" barley contains phenols, but at a low level, between .5 ppm and 3 ppm. Our nose can detect the peatiness of anything as low as .1 ppm.

As the peated barley goes through the whiskey-making process, it does lose some phenols over the course of hanging out in the mash tun, fermenting, and distillation. Laphroaig's barley is 40 ppm. But when the spirit comes out of the still for the second time, it's down to 25 ppm. After it has been aged in the cask for 10 years, it's down to between 8 ppm and 10 ppm. By the time the 30-year-old is released, it will be as low as 6 ppm.

Of course, most drinkers don't concern themselves with phenolic compounds, preferring instead to remain blissfully unaware of the science behind the tastes. The same could be said of Krysta and me as we started our drinking excursion to the islands. We took drinks of the whiskey with a bit more ignorance than either one of us was willing to admit.

"Whew!" said Krysta, taking a sniff from the bottle of Isle of Jura. "That smells mediciney. I'm not sure if I like it."

I took the bottle as she handed it to me, catching a waft of the aroma. Having had some experiences with island whiskey before, I had a more restrained response."Yeah. I think it's an iodine smell."

"Yeah, well, I hope it tastes better than it smells." She poured the whiskey into two glasses with a perfect eye, each of us getting an equal amount. We then tossed in a bit of water as had been demonstrated to us several times during the trip.

That medicinal smell found in peated whiskeys comes from the cresol phenol. But if there's only a small amount of cresol within the spirit, one is more likely to smell it than to taste it. This was aptly demonstrated by the Jura, which tasted more like the guaiacol phenol, which carries the flavor of . . .

"Smoke," I said pulling the glass away from my lips. "Not a lot, but it's there." I examined the glass as I concentrated on the taste. "It's a little sweet, too."

Krysta was not impressed. She switched on the television and settled on an episode of *Torchwood*. "It's . . . okay," she finally said. She also looked down at her glass. "I mean, it's good. It's just not what I like."

I empathized with her. I had, at several points in my life, sworn off peated whiskeys, as whatever subtlety they had was lost on me. Yet often I would come back years after the last one, seeing if my tastes had changed as I had gotten older. Then a few years ago I tried a high-grade lapsang souchong, a tea that has been dried over cedar or pine

---

Isle of Jura Single Malt Whisky 10 Year-Old
Jura is the perfect introduction to peated malts, as they use peat as a flavor rather than a dare.
Nose: Aside from the medicinal smell, there was a bit of nuttiness, like almonds. There was also a floral sweetness.
Taste: The smoke is there, to be sure, but it's mostly about the grain.
Finish: Long and mostly smoke-filled, if that's your thing.
Character: This drink is the progressive rock band of the whisky world. Either someone gets it, or they don't. And sometimes even a progressive rock band isn't above a standard love song done with three chords and a 4/4 tempo.

smoke. Ever since, I've had no problems with peated whiskeys. It was as if the tea had kick-started my sense of appreciation for all smoky beverages.

We finished a glass each of the Bowmore and the Bunnahabhain as Captain Jack Harkness fired lasers at some evildoer on the TV. There was a connection here between this science fiction show and these smokier, peatier whiskeys. Each had a passionate fan base, each had its own mythology, and each was successful but owed a fair amount of its success to other institutions. Torchwood owed itself to the *Doctor Who* series, Scotch whiskeys owed a debt to Irish whiskey.

I turned to give this theory a test-drive on Krysta, but my head gave me an internal warning, complete with Klaxons and sirens. "Warning!" I said to myself "You've had three glasses of whiskey in an hour. Do not take any of your ideas with any degree of seriousness. Warning!"

I took an inventory of my circumstances. I was trapped in a hotel room that was about the size of a Mini Cooper, on the west coast of Scotland, with floors so old that we could hear every footstep taken in the room above us. A storm wailed outside our window, and threatened to keep shouting for the rest of the evening. For entertainment, we were drinking and watching sci-fi shows.

Yes. It was best not to think too hard about whiskey under those circumstances.

The next day we headed into town amid weather that was sunny and dreary at the same time. How Scotland manages to have sunny skies one moment, and then be overcast and pouring down rain the next, is a paranormal event so disconcerting that I wondered if a space-time continuum was wavering around me. Clearly I had watched too much science fiction the night before.

The Oban Distillery was an odd beast. Every other distillery we had been to thus far had been situated a mile or two from a local town or tucked into a side street off the main thoroughfare. In Oban, the distillery was smack in the middle of downtown, huddled next to restaurants and souvenir shops. This was unsurprising when I considered that the town of Oban grew around the distillery as it was founded in 1796, probably as an illegal distillery and probably popular due to immediate access to transportation. The bay was less than one hundred yards from the front door.

Krysta and I walked into the Oban Distillery as tourists, as I had scheduled no meetings or interviews with anyone associated with the brand. By this time, we knew the drill, now defined as a six-step dance.

Step one: Purchase tour ticket and hang out in the visitors' center until tour starts.

Step two: Start tour, talk about barley, malting.

Step three: Head to the mash tun and talk about mash and fermentation.

Step four: Head to the still room and talk about distillation and the spirit safe.

Step five: Step into a room with casks or cask facsimiles, and talk about aging.

Step six: Have a drink, there's the gift shop, please buy our stuff, thank-you-bye-bye.

In this regard, Oban didn't disappoint in the least. The tour guide was a pixie-sized forty-year-old woman who threatened a couple from Spain due to her own allegiance to the Celtic Football Club and a yet-to-be-played match with Barcelona.

The problem for us was that, after several previous whiskey stops, we were somewhat well versed in steps one through five. As far as step six was concerned, both Krysta and I were running out of space in our luggage, and any purchases would have to be weighed against the value of any future purchases that might be made in Glasgow, our next stop.

But we trudged through the tour, dutifully noting the slight nuances that made it different from the other ones, the best one being the threat of explosions in the still room if anyone took flash photographs. I thought that while it would not be optimal if a distillery blew up in a small downtown area, several other tours had shown no concern with the camera.

Tours and visitors' centers have been around since 1969, when Glenfiddich had found that there was enough interest in their operations to support first a tour and then a gift shop. Other distilleries eventually followed suit, and now a large percentage of distilleries offer some activities for tourists. Tastings became part of the tour and gift shops evolved into visitors' centers with the addition of on-site restaurants, bars, and exhibits. Not all distilleries offer such activities, but enough of them do that one could have a two-week vacation in Scotland, visit a distillery every day, and still have places to visit on any subsequent trips. So prevalent are the distillery tours now that the Scotch Whisky Heritage Centre in Edinburgh has printed up a brochure that lists every place that one can visit.

The problem with this is that there is some anecdotal evidence that, at least in the short term, having a visitor center causes the distillery to lose money. The benefit is not from gathering the tourist's dollar, pound, or euro, but as a marketing tool. Every T-shirt sold and every gift purchased is essentially their version of viral marketing. A visitor will head home to Japan, Greece, or America and search out bottles and brands from the distillery he has visited.

For those who have the problem of being too popular, the issue is that the tours become less intimate. Tours are run on the hour, every hour. Time for questions is limited, and quite often the tour becomes a means to get people to spend money in restaurants, bars, and gift shops. Rather than showing visitors intricate details of the whiskey-making process, they instead become another stream of income. At this point the distilleries run the risk of alienating their fans rather than encouraging the passion for their brand.

This is exactly what happened at Oban, thanks in large part to our friendly yet explosive tour guide.

"You're from America, are ya?" she asked.

We nodded.

"I'm surprised to see you here, what with the exchange rate."

"Yeah, it's been killing us over here," I said. Krysta and I looked at each other. Both of us had, at several points in this trip, put back items we wanted to purchase because we couldn't afford the cost in

American dollars. "It works both ways," Krysta said to the tour guide. "You'd probably get killer deals over in the States."

"Don't I know it! I'm heading to New York in the fall. I'm packing a piece of luggage within a piece of luggage just so I can have one for the things I'm gonna purchase." Both Krysta and I grimaced.

"Well. At least you give away a free glass on your tour. It'll give me something to remind me of this place," I said with a hint of irony.

Not picking up on the sarcasm, the tour guide said without thinking. "Ooh. We have some nice things in our shop if you're interested. You can pick up some whiskies here you can't get in the States. Have you seen the distillery reserve?"

Krysta and I left without purchasing anything.

For the second night in a row, we spent our time sequestered in our hotel room due to the second storm. We finished off the island whiskeys, with Krysta still turning up her nose at the medicinal aro-

---

 Oban 14-Year-Old
Oban is another Scotch whiskey owned by the Diageo corporation, as part of their "a single malt for every taste" strategy. While peated, it's not as peated as the island whiskies, and can be considered a good place to get acquainted with smoky Scotch whiskey without being overwhelmed.

Nose: There's a fair amount of fruit, with both citrus and pears making themselves known. There are also some savory aromas, coming from a small bit of smokiness of the peat.

Taste: The fruitiness from the aroma makes itself known in the taste as well, with a lemon-orange flavor holding firm, and the bite of the oak and the smoke playing in the back. Very bright and full on the palate.

Finish: Average, not extensively long or curiously short. The fruit follows through into the finish with a bit of spice before disappearing.

Character: This is the character actor whose face you always seem to recognize in the movies but whose name you can never recall. Y'know. It's that guy. It's good, but not exceptional. Recognizable, but not memorable.

mas they produced, and me writing down her responses as if I were a psychologist. She was my patient, lamenting the fact she was unable to connect with her whiskey emotionally.

"What did you like about the Laphroaig?" I asked.

"That it tastes better than it smells," Krysta responded.

"Mmm-hmmm, mmm-hmmm. And how did that make you feel?"

We were also lamenting/celebrating the fact that we were near the end of the overseas portion of our trip. Tomorrow we were to be heading to our last city, our last hotel, and our last distillery. While we were looking forward to heading home, we were cognizant of the fact that we would have to return to our lives. Over the past two weeks, we had been adventurers, exploring as many nooks and crannies of Ireland and Scotland as we could fit into our schedule. Each area we had come across had the aura of uniqueness that can only be noticed when experiencing wanderlust. Over here on the British Isles, hills and mountains were aspects of the beautiful scenery that contributed to the mysteriousness of the region. Back in the States, hills and mountains were part of the background, to be taken for granted and ignored. Whiskey had allowed us to see these lands and to view them through uncynical eyes.

"To whiskey!" I raised my glass.

"To Scotland!" Krysta responded.

"To Ireland!" I finished. We clinked our glasses and drank. We turned in and shut out the lights. Outside the storm rattled our window and deluged the town of Oban.

The next morning we headed down the A82 to Glasgow, which we soon deemed "the city of perpetual damp." Not only did the city experience the same schizophrenic weather that had been so prevalent in Oban the day before, it seemed that no matter where we were, every place seemed some measure of wet. The hotel, the restaurants, the club where we went to see a band, all were oddly moist.

Auchentoshan is situated a mere ten miles from Glasgow's downtown, and was the perfect "last distillery" to visit on our trip. It was relatively easy to find, thanks in large part to Emma. We were there at ten o'clock in the morning, the first and only visitors waiting for a tour.

Laphroaig 10-Year-Old
Pronounced la-FROYG, this is the whiskey I think of when I hear the word "Islay." It is owned by Fortune Brands, which also owns Jim Beam and Canadian Club.

Nose: The medicinal smell hits very, very hard, but there is a nice hint of oak underneath it, teasing me.

Taste: Peat, and then a hint of barley, then a little more peat, with whispers of salt, and then more peat.

Finish: The finish lasts seemingly forever, with the peat still making itself known, but evolves and decrescendos into a sweet/savory taste on the roof of my mouth.

Character: There are two ways to approach this.

If you are new to whiskey: If you ever had a teacher slam a yardstick on your desk to snap you out of your daydreaming, that slam is Laphroaig. It will either make you very annoyed or force you to sit up straight and pay attention.

If you are familiar with peat: Strong and yet still holding complexity beneath it all, this Scotch whiskey is akin to the many honorable generals who have earned their reputation on the battlefield. Bold, cunning, and due all levels of respect, there's much more to them than what they show to the laymen of the world. But unless you're a soldier, you just won't get it.

They let us in, and soon we found ourselves the only guests of Sean, the tour guide.

Even though this had been our sixth scotch distillery tour in as many days, we found ourselves engrossed. The tour turned into a personal conversation. As we looked at the still, we talked about football. As we looked in the storage houses, we talked about the music scene in Glasgow. Every so often, Sean would bring up a fact about Auchentoshan, but this seemed more a professional courtesy than line upon line of company-speak.

From what he did say, we found out that Auchentoshan, meaning "corner of the field" in Gaelic, is a unique beast in the Scotch whiskey catalog. It's one of the few remaining Lowland distilleries in Scotland. As the market tends to favor the Highland brands and distilleries, Auchentoshan and other whiskeys of the Lowland region are sometimes a bit of an afterthought.

They also use only unpeated barley for their mash, and triple distill their product, making it more of a modern Irish whiskey than a Scotch whiskey. As with nearly every whiskey region in the world, there are exceptions to the regional traditions that make it difficult to say things such as "Only Scotch whiskeys use peated barley" or "Only Irish whiskeys are triple distilled." The fact is, the only guidelines that the whiskey companies have to follow are the regulations written by the governments of the nations in which they are located. Bourbons do not have to be aged for three years, Irish whiskeys do not need to be triple distilled, and Scotch whiskeys do not need to have the taste of peat within them.

What was missing from the tour was any reference to Suntory, the owner of the distillery. Suntory Limited is a Japanese brewing and distilling company. Established in 1899, it is one of the oldest companies in the distribution of alcoholic beverages in Japan, and touted by Bill Murray's character in *Lost in Translation*. It is also not Scottish, an obvious fact, to be certain, but an important one. What with the great emphasis on heritage and history, bringing up a non-Scottish ownership group would run contrary to the image that the marketing of the past tries to accomplish.

We walked back into the visitors' center with Sean, about fifteen minutes later than most tours run, and he led us to the bar in the corner of the gift shop. This is what the trip was all about. Sunlight streamed into the room as he seemed to go into his rehearsed spiel.

Nothing came out of his mouth, as he searched for something to say.

"You've probably heard your share of hype, eh?" he eventually said, looking at the several bottles he had placed on the bar.

It was true. Truth be told, every time we had been offered a tasting, it had been almost nothing but hype, be it Jameson's pleading to make themselves better than their competition, or the romance over the stream at Glen Grant.

"Then I'll try to avoid giving you any more, and tell you instead what I like."

He walked us through the several different bottles that Auchentoshan produces, each light and interesting. The novelty of this distillery had been growing upon me over the course of our time there.

"And this is my favorite," Sean said, pouring us each a glass of Three Wood. This whiskey is matured in three different cask types—American bourbon, Spanish Oloroso sherry, and Pedro Ximenez sherry—"producing a rich, complex whisky with incredible toffee and sherry oak flavors," said Sean in mock enthusiasm. He smiled and winked. "I had to give you a little hype."

Auchentoshan Three Wood

As much as the folks at Auchentoshan are hesitant to admit it, you should think "Irish whiskey" when you see this whiskey in your local store. Triple distilled and not one iota of peat used to dry the malt, this whiskey would be as at home on the Emerald Isle as it is in the Lowlands of Scotland.

Nose: Very fruity, but more of a dried fruit, like raisins mixed with brown sugar. Deep and rich.

Taste: Thick and chewy, with dark flavors like burnt caramel and molasses mixed with the oak from the barrels. The sherry flavor makes itself known in very subtle ways.

Finish: The finish lasted long after we had gotten into our car, with the warm oak and spice remaining long after the party had finished.

Character: Christmastime is when we drink and eat items we would never consider consuming the rest of the year. Egg nog, figgy pudding, and roasted chestnuts are all items that we desire, due mostly to the novelty of the season, but which we can't find any other time. This whiskey reminds me of these foods. There's a bit of novelty to it, and I'd drink it more often if there seemed a good time to do so. But for the life of me, I can't think of a good enough time.

That night, Krysta and I celebrated our last night in Scotland in a small Italian restaurant, going over what we had accomplished.

"We barely scratched the surface of Scotland," I said, in a tone of frustration and astonishment.

Krysta winked. "Yeah. It gives us a good reason to come back, right?"

I laughed. But yet I still felt as if I didn't have a full grasp of the world of Scotch whiskey. There were so many places we didn't go, and so many people we didn't talk to.

Krysta must have noticed my mood. "There's no way we could have covered the entire industry."

I nodded. But I wanted to cover the entire industry. "This has been the trip of a lifetime, and I am not looking forward to its coming to an end," I said.

"We still have America and Canada to go though. Our North American tour."

I lifted a piece of Scottish-Italian gnocchi to my mouth, smiling a bit. Again I nodded.

She said, "And we're off to Pittsburgh next, right?"

"Yup."

"Okay. I have just one question about that."

I looked at her, letting her know she could ask.

"Why?"

PART II

The Left Side of the Atlantic

1

Whiskey Rebellion

After a brief stopover in our respective hometowns, Krysta and I agreed to meet to continue our journey back in the United States, specifically in Pittsburgh. I was dreading the trip for several reasons. One, after the awesomeness of Ireland and Scotland, it would be difficult for the areas in North America to compete. Two, there is simply less to do, whiskey-wise, on this side of the Atlantic when compared to the hundreds of distilleries one can explore in Scotland. Finally, Pittsburgh is my hometown, and coming home always depresses me. Outside of Allegheny County, it reeks of what once was, not what is. The steel industry is a shadow of its former self, its status as a frontier town had been lost centuries ago, and the whiskey industry that the area helped create is now nonexistent. The trip here would promise to have a shadow of former glory cast upon it.

This area of western Pennsylvania had not always seemed so chock-full o' angst. It once offered people, immigrants mostly, the opportunity to start over. This is exactly how the Scots felt about the area in the early and mid-1700s. The reasons they came over were numerous. Escaping religious persecution was one factor, looking to

avoid starvation was another; others simply wanted to start anew.
Some came as indentured servants to Boston and Philadelphia, soon
leaving the service of their employers to strike out on their own.
Waves of Scots came to North America in 1717 and then again in
1720.

The Ulster Scots, those who had been living in what is now Northern Ireland, were also part of the mix, bringing with them their strict
Calvinist upbringing and their disdain for authority. Known here in
America as the Scotch-Irish, they affected and influenced every region
of North America in which they settled. Western Pennsylvania, Nova
Scotia, Ontario, Philadelphia, even the Carolinas all have been affected by the immigration of the Scots and the Scotch-Irish.

The Scotch-Irish settlements began pushing the frontier farther
and deeper into the Appalachians. They did not expect an easy time
of their migration. Prepared for the worst, they carved a new life for
themselves out of the wilderness, taking land from neighbors and na-
tives when it suited their purpose. The habits of colonizing Ireland
and seizing the arable lands from Catholic enemies carried over to
the New World. Their desire for land, the willingness to fight and die
to keep it, and their distrust of any governmental authority laid the
foundation of the frontier mentality of the American West. In the
mid 1700s, this included anything west of the Appalachian Mountains.

With the Scots came their farming techniques, which included
the use of grains to make whiskey, and their rebelliousness, which
often resulted from the excessive use the aforementioned whiskey.

What the new landowners and farmers soon found out was that
barley, the crop they used to make whiskey back in the British Isles,
was not the most efficient grain when compared with other options
available. The immigrants discovered that other grains did better in
the fertile soils of the regions with longer growing seasons. Wheat
was certainly tilled, as was rye. But the first settlers found that wheat
was difficult to produce in their newfound fields, and when they
could produce wheat, many communities lacked a mill to grind it.
But corn thrived in the New World. It could be planted in early May
with the most minimal of effort, and by July a full crop would be

available. If they waited until October to harvest the corn, the farmers were almost always assured of a yield three or four times that of wheat. It was the use of corn by Native Americans that had the biggest effect on the farmers of the colonies.

I don't mean corn as in the generic term that was ascribed to the grain by many Europeans. I mean *Zea mays*, or maize, as the Land O'Lakes commercial used to call it. Native to the Balsas River valley of southern Mexico, it is said to have been domesticated as early as 1500 BC, and it began to spread widely and rapidly throughout the Americas. As it was introduced to new cultures, new uses were developed and new varieties selected to better serve in those preparations. Maize was a major staple of most pre-Columbian North American, Mesoamerican, South American, and Caribbean cultures. By the eighteenth century it had already found its way to Kentucky, where it was cultivated by the Shawnee. Later still, it would be overproduced by American farms, but I believe that's a different book.

Grain grown on the frontier was difficult to ship back to the East Coast markets. The roads between the settlements west of the Appalachians were few, and those that did exist were often too poor to transport an excessive amount of crop. Pioneers who did make the trip across the mountains with their crops found that much of them rotted. As their ancestors and relatives in Europe had done, the farmers turned to distilling their excess crops into whiskey. Whiskey lasted longer, brought in larger profits, and was far easier to transport to the high-paying markets of Philadelphia. In Pennsylvania the whiskeys produced were primarily rye whiskeys; farther to the west and south, corn whiskeys predominated. By the end of the American War of Independence in 1784, the first commercial distilleries had been established in what was then the western Virginia county of Kentucky. From the start they produced corn-based whiskeys.

By the end of the Revolutionary War, it could be said the residents of western Pennsylvania had a bit of a problem with most authorities. They gladly took up against the British during the Revolutionary War, as many of them either remembered or heard stories of the injustices that the Brits had inflicted upon their family back in the Old World.

But they weren't too keen on the new government. Whether it was due to the lack of resources provided to the local militias during the revolution or lack of confidence that the new American army instilled when they did show up, there was some talk of a separate state for western Pennsylvania, or even seceding from the young United States altogether.

The government didn't help its cause when it decided to institute a federal law requiring that all stills in the nation be registered and that seven cents' tax per gallon of whiskey be paid on the capacity of the still. This further compounded the locals' perception that they were being unjustly taxed. Due to the discrepancy between the cost of whiskey in western Pennsylvania and eastern Pennsylvania, the western whiskey was taxed at a higher rate than the cheaper varieties made in the East.

The grain farmers also did not appreciate the fact that having a duty based on the output of the still meant that they had to pay tax on the whiskey they consumed themselves. To the farmers of western Pennsylvania, they felt that they government was treating them in the same way a cat treats a litter box.

This dissatisfaction with the government grew to the point where even if a local farmer wanted to register his still, the tax opponents made it difficult for him to do so. The locals of western Pennsylvania began shirking their duties to the new government, and refused to open a tax office in the coincidentally named Washington County. If any of the farmers in the area wished to register their stills, they had to travel to one of the neighboring counties.

When someone was convicted of an excise violation, he had to travel across the state to Philadelphia, a trip that not only took weeks but cost a fair amount of money. Time spent traveling to court meant time spent not farming and not earning an income.

With all available options seemingly untenable, the residents responded with measures unerringly similar to those taken at the beginning of the Revolutionary War. They started attacking the taxman. Many attempts at enforcing the excise resulted in violence and humiliation.

Robert Johnson was one victim of such violence. A party of men, armed and disguised, attacked him at Pigeon Creek, where they tarred and feathered him, cut off his hair, and stole his horse, necessitating a long and painful walk forty miles back to his residence.

General John Neville, a revolutionary hero, was an inspector of revenue under the new excise laws, and he also faced the rebels' wrath. Shots were fired at Neville and a U.S. marshal he was escorting through the area to summon farmers who had not paid the tax to the court. On July 16, 1794, a group of men surrounded the Neville mansion demanding to see the U.S. marshal. The confrontation led to Neville's shooting of one of the protesters. The next day, over 500 people surrounded the home. At least one more protester died, and Neville's home was burned to the ground.

In response to the escalation, David Bradford, a successful attorney, businessman, and deputy attorney general, assumed leadership of the whiskey rebels.

Bradford and his group sent a letter to the local militias requesting a gathering on Aug 1, 1794, on a nearby field to begin a possible four-day military excursion. Seven thousand troops showed up to provide their support. Hugh Henry Brackenridge, a moderate voice within the rebellion, convinced Bradford to warn Pittsburgh to "banish all obnoxious characters within eight days or face destruction." In other words, the tax collectors should leave as soon as possible. In other words, the tax collectors needed to get out of town, unless they wanted to have a really, really bad day.

In what must have been a march more for show than of substance, the farmers and militia marched through Pittsburgh in protest without problems or conflict. The relative peace of the march was influenced by the 379 residents of Pittsburgh supplying the "invading army," as many easterners termed the whiskey rebels, with food and whiskey. The only damage done by the rebels was when they crossed the Monongahela and torched the barn of Major Kirkpatrick, an army regular assigned to the Pittsburgh garrison.

Word of an assembled army was enough to force the government's hand. By August 7, 1794, George Washington invoked the Militia Law of 1792 and began mobilizing roughly 13,000 troops from eastern Pennsylvania, Virginia, Maryland, and New Jersey. Washington

himself took command, and shared leadership duties with General
Henry "Lighthorse Harry" Lee, governor of Virginia and the father of
Robert E. Lee.

Amnesty was initially offered to those involved in the various
acts of defiance by a presidential commission on August 21, 1794.
Many of the rebels refused the amnesty offer, either as an admission
of guilt for actions they didn't believe criminal, or because they dis-
liked the federal government and its threat of force.

Washington and his troops marched to what is now Monongahela, Pennsylvania. Over two months, the army rounded up suspects, working quickly to suppress the revolt. Most of the rebels had
escaped by hiding with nearby relatives. Others had left the area and
sought new homes in other parts of the country. David Bradford escaped and fled to a location near what is today called St. Francisville,
Louisiana, about one hundred miles from New Orleans.

But twenty of the rebels had been captured.

After ensuring that there would be no more attacks by the rebels,
most of the army began the trek home on November 19, with the
suspects and their guards following six days later. Suspects and wit-
nesses together, many of them barefoot and lacking winter clothing,
were then marched to Philadelphia to stand trial.

The men were imprisoned, where one died, and two were convicted of treason and sentenced to death by hanging. Washington,
convinced that the central government's power to enforce laws had
been proven, pardoned them both.

The suppression of the Whiskey Rebellion had the unintended
consequence of encouraging the small farmers of western Pennsylvania to relocate to the then-frontier lands of Kentucky and Tennessee,
which were outside the sphere of federal control for many years. In
these frontier areas, they found people were already making whiskey,
as the area was good corn-growing country and the water filtered
through the limestone layer found deep below the Kentucky soil was
fresh and clean.

Other folks moved north into Canada, and helped pave the way
for the Canadian whiskey tradition. The Whiskey Rebellion was the
impetus for two very different approaches to whiskey making. One

approach gave birth to an American icon; the other nearly took over America when Prohibition came into affect.

But the majority of people stayed behind. Thomas Jefferson finally repealed the much-hated tax in 1802, as it had never been collected with much success. The farmers took what they knew of making whiskey, and began selling it exclusively. The farmers of western Pennsylvania laid the foundation of the American whiskey industry.

It was another sixty years before anyone would consider the idea of collecting revenue from alcohol. This freedom of production allowed the American spirits industry to flourish at the beginning of the nineteenth century. It also gave me a good reason to visit my hometown of Pittsburgh under the pretext of "research."

2

Riding the Coattails

Pennsylvania is one of those states that is difficult to explain to any-one who hasn't lived there. While Texas and California have certain stereotypes that seem to apply across their respective states, Penn-sylvania isn't burdened with such a problem. So let me set the record straight: Subtract Pittsburgh and Philadelphia from the Key-stone State, and one is left with Alabama. My hope is that residents of Alabama see this as a compliment, and residents of Pennsylvania take this as a wake-up call.

I can make this statement because I've lived in Pennsylvania, ex-periencing both city and country living at one point or another during the first twenty-three years of my life. When one lives here, it becomes apparent, regardless of age, that rural and urban may be only sepa-rated by thirty miles in distance, but culturally they are separated by thirty years.

I tried to make this distinction to Krysta as we drove into down-town Pittsburgh in a green Pontiac that we had christened "Franco Harris," after a local football hero from a generation back.

"Outside of Allegheny County, once you get away from the river towns, it's quite rural. More than most people realize," I told her. "Two hundred fifty years ago, before the Industrial Revolution hit and steel and coal became the primary industries, this was all farmland, peppered with immigrants from Scotland and Ireland."

"And they brought their stills with them?" she asked.

"Yup."

"Which is why we're here rather than starting in Kentucky," she deduced.

"Kind of. There was other stuff going on as well."

By this point, I was close to following her lead. In the time since we'd parted at Glasgow, Krysta had caught up on the history of whiskey in western Pennsylvania. It was she, and not I, who had arranged for the two stops we were to make relating to Pittsburgh's whiskey heritage.

"I was thinking we could go to Woodville, John Neville's house, check that out, and then head over to West Overton to look at an old distillery," she said as I was parking the car.

"Oh. Ummm, okay . . . sure," I said.

"Did you have something else planned?"

"No. No," I said. "That sounds great."

Actually, I was lying. I did have a plan, but it was a little difficult to explain to someone who had planned something far more productive than I had. What I wanted to do was find a specific bottle of whiskey that was a bit of a legend in Pittsburgh. Regarded only a little higher than window cleaner, this was a whiskey that promised a near instant hangover; just add sixty minutes and stir. This was the brand called Imperial.

Imperial whiskey at one point represented the post-Prohibition bar culture in blue-collar Pittsburgh. After prohibition, the once popular and prevalent whiskey industry that had been located in Pittsburgh was completely destroyed. The workers who put in hours at the steel mills searched for a replacement in their favorite bars and taverns. They settled on a small brand offered by Hiram Walker out of Windsor, Canada: Imperial whiskey.

By the time I was born, drinking an Imperial was as common as people ordering Jack Daniel's today. An "Imp 'n' Irn" (a shot of

Imperial dropped in a glass of Iron City, a local beer) was a standard order in many locations across the city. The whiskey had ingrained itself into local lore in less than a generation.

Yet, just as quickly, it disappeared and was replaced by larger, more heavily marketed brands of bourbon and Canadian whiskey. As its popularity waned, the folks who owned Hiram Walker (Allied Domecq) gave up on the brand and sold it off. To whom I did not know. All I knew was that it still existed, but it was damn difficult to find.

Imperial whiskey had become a representation of how I envisioned Pittsburgh, circa 1960. It became, from my point of view, an icon of the era of my father's youth. Upon my return to Pittsburgh, I vowed to find a bottle, even if I had to scour flea markets for empty ones.

But how was I to explain to Krysta that all I wanted to do during our thirty-six hours in the Steel City was find evidence of a sub-par bottle of whiskey? I had failed to mention this lapse into sentimentality to her, and she had arranged a more reasonable itinerary, at least from an historical aspect.

We checked into the William Penn Hotel and found ourselves in a room that was so large it had its own weather patterns.

"Jesus Christ!" we both said in awe. We could fit two hotel rooms from Oban into this room.

We unpacked, and Krysta went to take a shower. Ensuring that the water was running, I picked up the phone and called a liquor store.

"Uh . . . hi. I was wondering. Do you stock Imperial whiskey?"

"Yessssss," they answered with a hint of suspicion in their tone. I had expected this. Asking for Imperial whiskey was akin to stating a preference for driving used Yugos.

"Great!" I said, and I hung up the phone. Victory. When Krysta came out of the shower, I told her of the addition to the itinerary. She looked at me skeptically.

"So you want a whiskey that doesn't taste any good?" she asked when I explained everything.

"Yes."

She shrugged as if to say, "It's your money."

The next day we headed out to John Neville's House in Bridgeville. We were traveling down State Route 50 when we saw a middle-aged man dressed in eighteenth-century garb standing by the side of the road. He was waving his arms, trying to get the attention of passersby.

"Do you think this is the place?" I asked, as I turned the car into the parking lot that he had directed us to when he saw that he had caught our attention.

"If not, he really needs to explain his outfit," responded Krysta.

He ran over to our car as we stopped.

"Ahoy. Ahoy! Are ye here to speak to Master Neville?" he asked as Krysta rolled down her window so we could hear him verbally accost us.

"Oh. Dear. Lord," I said under my breath. A quick and painless punch to my arm from Krysta told me that I was to behave myself and keep my cynicism in check. She yelled back to the gentleman.

"We are. We wish to know about the rebellion."

"Oh." He looked a bit sheepish. "Ah . . . the gentleman . . . the one who is usually here to talk about the Whiskey Rebellion . . . hasn't showed up for work today," he said, breaking character.

We paused. Krysta looked at me as if to ask, "Should we go on?" I shrugged and got out of the car. Krysta followed suit.

"So what brings you here on a Sunday?" he asked, as he guided us to the entrance of a two-story house that overlooked both a creek and a major roadway. The noise of the cars passing by did little to increase the imagery that his outfit was trying to create.

"She's writing a book on whiskey," Krysta said, pointing at me, playing up her role as my public relations representative, as she dug out her camera. Over the course of the past few weeks, we had both learned that this magical phrase made people open up, and often their demeanor changed. Mr. Creative Anachronism was no different.

"Oh really?" he asked. We entered the house and saw two middle-aged women sitting in a side room. "Margaret, these two ladies are here doing research on a whiskey book!" said the man.

"Wonderful!" said the older lady. "You certainly came to the right place. Are you here for the tour?"

Krysta and I nodded.

"Wonderful!" she repeated. "The docent is just finishing up with another tour, and we'll get you started. You can look over our gift shop while you wait." She pointed at a table that had a few books and pamphlets on it. I said nothing of the fact that one table of outdated pamphlets does not a gift shop make.

"Would you like to see the still house?" asked the man.

"Still house?" I thought to myself. "Oh yes!" I said. "That'd be great."

"It's no longer a still house, though. We use it for storage." He pointed at a shingled shack painted brick red.

"Is there a still in there today?"

"Ah . . . no," he admitted. "It used to be where the tutor had to sleep," he offered as recompense.

"Oh, um, great!" I said. With no still, or even a re-creation of a still, we'd essentially be looking at boxes of the pamphlets found on the table.

The younger woman spoke up. "Don't we have some bottles that we found on the site?"

"Oh yes!" said the man. "I'll see if I can locate them." He headed back outside.

The door opened, and an older woman appeared wearing what looked to be Martha Washington's hand-me-downs. "Ah, here she is," said Margaret. We were introduced to the tour guide. "They're here doing some research on whiskey," she offered.

"Oh, that's wonderful!" said the guide.

I started to get a Stepford wives/Stephen King vibe, with a little bit of Williamsburg thrown in, as we followed the docent into the first part of the house.

The tour took us around the entire house, through the dining room, the downstairs bedrooms, the living rooms, the kitchen, with the docent telling us how hard they worked to get an authentic look to the house, ensuring it looked like it could have back at the turn of the nineteenth century. Little was discussed of John Neville, who was the sole reason we were there to begin with.

As we watched another woman in period costume cut some lemons in the re-created kitchen, I took Krysta aside. "Have you noticed the distinct lack of anything having to do with whiskey?" I asked. She nodded.

"Did they mention the Whiskey Rebellion specifically on their Web site?"

Krysta nodded again, and we verified by looking at the pamphlet for the mansion, which referred to the Whiskey Rebellion. I spoke up.

"What role did this house play in the Whiskey Rebellion?" I asked.

"Well, by the time of the rebellion, the general had moved out of this house, and into his new mansion on Bower Hill." She continued with her historical explanation of Woodville's place in the Whiskey Rebellion, but I suddenly knew what she was going to say. General John Neville didn't live here at the time of the rebellion; his son did. It was the general's new house that the rebels had burned down. The only role Woodville played was that it was the place where the general stayed afterwards. This place had as much to do with the Whiskey Rebellion as a green room has to do with a talk show. I groaned a bit inside.

It was great that they had such pride in the house, and as an archaeological site, it was quite interesting. They did give some insight into the time period. But it had almost nothing to do with whiskey or the Whiskey Rebellion.

That did not stop them from trying to placate us. Near the end of the tour, the younger woman approached us with a box. "Here are the bottles we had found in the area," she offered helpfully.

I looked through the box. Indeed, there were several bits and pieces of old glass bottles, aged by time. I hadn't the heart to tell her that the bottles were likely from the late nineteenth century, if not later. Bottle making on a mass scale was the result of the Industrial Revolution. It was improbable that they would have been of John

Neville's time. Not unless they made them on site. I didn't broach the subject, for fear of insulting them and belittling the time they had taken to provide me with any bit of whiskey information they could find.

After taking a few pictures, Krysta and I headed back to the car. An awkward silence sat between us.

"Well," she started. "That was interesting . . ."

I nodded. It was . . . kinda. But part of me was spooked by the experience. I wasn't used to helpful people. Nor was I thrilled that they had inferred a solid relationship with a moment of history when that connection was minimal.

"Bah!" I said. "Let's go to a liquor store. I want to pick up that bottle of Imperial."

Pennsylvania is known for having rather draconian liquor laws, remnants of their return from Prohibition. The state has full control of what is sold, where it's sold, and when it can be sold. Only 5 to 10 percent of the liquor stores are open on Sunday, and I had to have this bottle. We continued our drive down State Route 50 and found a Shop 'n' Save grocery store, with a liquor store located inside.

In the two rows of liquor sold in the store, Imperial stood on the bottom shelf, priced at a cheap nine dollars and some odd cents. A sense of relief came over me. I had my bottle. I looked at it. No longer made by Hiram Walker, I saw at the bottom of the bottle, "Blended by Barton Distilling Company. Bardstown, Kentucky."

Pittsburgh's legendary favorite Canadian whiskey was now made in Kentucky.

"What's wrong?" asked Krysta.

I couldn't put words to my disappointment. It was sort of akin to finding out that your American flag was made in Korea. I wasn't sure if non-Pittsburghers would understand.

"Nothing," I lied. "Let's head to West Overton."

An hour later we turned off Route 119 and drove into West Overton. Almost immediately we came upon a six-story barn made of brick, and a recently painted sign that read "Old Farm—Pure Rye."

"I think this is it," I said. Krysta nodded.

We got out of the car and started walking the grounds. It was now late afternoon, the shadows were becoming long, and a chill began to make itself known. We were alone. Krysta pulled out her camera and started taking pictures.

Several other brick buildings surrounded the barn, all clearly related to the distilling company that was here until the fear of Prohibition forced it to shut down in 1919. I pulled out my own camera and shot a handful of pictures, mostly to give me something to do.

Much like other similar places in western Pennsylvania, West Overton likely started as a milling place for the grains grown in the area. As in Scotland and Ireland, where a mill was found a still would be close by, as the grain could be converted into profitable whiskey in short order. On the Internet I had discovered that the distillery on this site was owned and run by Abraham Overholt, for which the currently available rye whiskey Old Overholt is named. As far as I know, Old Overholt was never distilled here in West Overton. What was made here was a brand called Old Farm. From what evidence I could find, they were somewhat successful at it. When they went from a farm-based distillery to a commercial one, they increased their production from eight gallons a day to over two hundred and, by most accounts, sold all of it.

I looked at the surroundings. Here was rural western Pennsylvania, quiet and serene. Every once in a while, a truck, be it pickup or eighteen wheeler, drove by, breaking the silence. The rolling hills kept the sounds of the area deep within its valleys.

It was in places such as this that rye whiskey was made and sold throughout America. I thought of the places that must have sold the ryes of western Pennsylvania. Certainly New York, Boston, and Philadelphia had a penchant for it. Cleveland and Cincinnati sold the whiskey. Chicago was probable. The farther west, the less likely, as transportation costs would have made it prohibitive, especially when sold against the distilleriea west of Ohio. It was likely sold as Old Monongahela whiskey, or just Monongahela, much in the same way that all whiskey from northern Kentucky was to be called "Bourbon"—after the markings left on the barrels showing its port

of origin as it was shipped down the river to Pittsburgh, and later in
the port towns of the Ohio and possibly even the Mississippi Rivers.

How popular was Old Monongahela? In *Moby-Dick*, published
in 1851, the character Stubb lists the whiskeys of the day: "Would
now, it were old Orleans whiskey, or old Ohio, or unspeakable old
Monongahela!"

Krysta yelled from the front door, breaking my stream of thought.
"They make quilts here!" she yelled at me from a distance.

"Cool!" I yelled back, faking enthusiasm.

We took as many pictures as we could of the building, and several of the surrounding ones as well. We hypothesized on what part
of the whiskey-making process took place in which building.

"Do you think they stored the casks here?" I asked.

"Could be," said Krysta. "I think they stored the grain in the
large barn there."

"That makes sense. The windows would help aerate the grain,
and alleviate the fire hazard." It was clear that we had learned a lot
of the industry over the past few weeks.

But there was only so much one could glean from a distillery that
has been closed for nearly ninety years, especially when there was no
one there to tell the tales of the past. After twenty-five minutes, I
had my fill.

"Let's get out of here," I said. "We have an early flight tomorrow."

As we drove back to Pittsburgh, I sat in relative silence, thinking
about the history of my hometown. I compared the reverence that
the Scots have for their whiskey with the near ignorance most people
in America have of western Pennsylvania's place in whiskey history.

I had known that this trip was going to be different from our adventures in Ireland and Scotland. Heritage was a focus of the whiskey
industries of the British Isles, but here in North America, Prohibition
had nearly wiped out everything. America's whiskey heritage, pre-
Prohibition, has all but been erased. Today's bourbon industry has
seen this lack of heritage as an opportunity; its product is marketed as
America's whiskey. Michael Veach, an ex-archivist for United Distillers, put it to me this way: "The biggest misconception about the in-

dustry is that people tend to believe their marketing. [For example,] 'Beam has been doing [distilling] the same way for two hundred years.' Okay, show me Jacob Beam's column still and hybrid grains. Things like this give the consumer a distorted view about the industry."

I found his sentiment both accurate and depressing, especially when trying to compare our history to that of Ireland and Scotland. As we look for evidence of the industry before 1920, disappointment would be with us as an unwelcome travel partner, making reconstructing an accurate portrait nearly impossible. I knew this before even the wheels of my airplane touched down the day before. And yet, here I was not twenty-four hours into the start of our North American leg of the journey, and I was saddened. Lip service to the Whiskey Rebellion was all that was given at one site, and the best-preserved distillery in the area was looking to become a quilt museum.

Canada did not look to be much better. If scotch is the Bob Dylan of the whiskey world, then many of the products released by the mega-Canadian distilleries could be seen as mere Boy Bands, covered with gloss and sheen, prepackaged to the point of removing any hint of character. While Prohibition had removed a fair amount of whiskey heritage here in the States, my fear was that greed had sanitized Canada's history to the point of being unrecognizable.

But we had to go to Canada next, for there is very little in the way of whiskey sites to be found in the United States that are older than seventy years. If I am to keep our travels in parallel with whiskey history, there's simply no place to visit in America that can effectively tell the story of whiskey in the 1800s. For that, we had to head to Toronto.

I shook my head in frustration. This is the state of our whiskey heritage, and I wasn't going to change it with only forty hours in Pittsburgh. It would have to remain sad and unfortunate, because such is the state of Pennsylvania's whiskey history.

When we got back to the hotel room, I sat at the table and looked at the bottle of Imperial. As an icon for western Pennsylvania whiskey, it was nearly perfect—mostly forgotten and produced in Kentucky.

If you look at a map, there is one common variable that connects every area that became a force in whiskey: access to waterways. By the beginning of the nineteenth century, America was just starting

Imperial Whiskey
The long-lost staple of both Windsor and Pittsburgh.
Nose: What aromas does Windex carry?
Taste: Astringent acne cleaner with a hint of corn.
Flavored chemically.
Finish: Thank God it ended quickly. It tasted like Dow Corning on a
bender.
Character: It's the spammer, the late-night commercial, and the con
artist all rolled into one. Its goal is to make money in the short term,
quality be damned.

its expansion to the west, and had not developed common paths and
roads equal to what Great Britain had. The quickest and most cost-
effective way of shipping goods around the country was via rivers,
lakes, and canals. As grist mills popped up in the New World, and
soon afterward the stills, whiskey makers began to ship their products to the marketplaces where they could return the highest profits.
Rivers like the Delaware, Ohio, Monongahela, Allegheny, even the
Mississippi all had whiskey transported on them for various people
and from various farms and distilleries.

By 1810, when distilling was concentrated in upstate New York,
western Pennsylvania, Ohio, and Kentucky, those four states produced more than half the nation's grain and fruit spirits. An important element in making the western frontier the center of the whiskey
distilling industry was the fact that it was separated from the east
by the Appalachian Mountains. The success of the distilleries would
have been dependent upon the ability to get their whiskeys to large
markets. The farms and distilleries of eastern Pennsylvania, as an example, likely had no problem in getting their product to the markets
and ports of Philadelphia, where they could be purchased for local
consumption or put on a boat and sold in a port to either the north or
south.

Meanwhile, those who made whiskey west of the Appalachians

had no problem in putting their whiskeys on a boat, and then dropping them off at any and every city that allowed them. Those on the
west side of the mountains were mostly out of touch with the seaboard
and the ports that fostered trade. They were isolated and cut off from
the East and they were forced to develop their own resources, products, markets, and, in some areas within the newly formed country, currency. Land transportation across the mountains was expensive and
impractical. But rivers and canals offered all sorts of opportunities. A
whiskey made near the Monongahela could be put on a boat and find
itself in Pittsburgh, or pick up the Ohio River and be dropped off in
Cincinnati or Louisville, and then head north on the Wabash, or even
make it to the Mississippi and hit any one of the hundreds of small settlements that were popping up seemingly every day.

There was no lack of customers for the drink, as the young
American nation had such a predilection for drink that it would
eventually lead to such things as the career of W. C. Fields, the
bankroll of John F. Kennedy, and Saturday nights on Fraternity
Rows throughout the country. Rum, the spirit of choice during the
Revolutionary War, fell out of favor, and whiskey stepped in quickly
to take its place. It became the popular spirit of the day. Like Great
Britain, the New World was a land largely without clean drinking
water. Alcoholic beverages were a common way to deliver hydration
to the human body without making the consumer sick. Whiskey was
an extension of this mindset. Whiskey was drunk on a daily basis, as
a means to start the day or complete a deal, or even as prescribed
medicine.

The demand for whiskey increased because it was also used as
currency in areas of the nation that had limited or no access to the
money established by the new government. As dollars and cents
would have been difficult to come by, whiskey was readily available
and was often used to conduct transactions. This was a practice that
lasted throughout America's expansion to the West Coast.

At the turn of the 1800s, the whiskey sold would have been gotten
to the market as quickly as possible. Commercial distilleries had yet to
be established as their own industry, so the majority of the whiskey
on the market would have been made by local farmers looking for a

quick profit in order to pay for other crops or to expand their own lands. So the spirit would have primarily been unaged, white spirit, distilled from rye, with a little corn thrown in (if from Pennsylvania) or distilled from corn, with a little rye thrown in (if from Kentucky.)

George Washington made whiskey, a clear spirit with both rye and corn used to get the quickest return possible on the grains not needed to feed the family, neighbors, and any livestock on hand. The first president, at the suggestion of his Scottish plantation manager, began producing his own whiskey at Mt. Vernon. By the time of his death he was making eleven thousand gallons of the stuff every year, and was turning a tidy profit. This is a fact that the Daughters of the American Revolution would probably not like to be advertised to a great extent.

It's important to repeat that aging whiskeys in casks was a known process. By the start of the nineteenth century, the Irish and Scots both were aware of the technique, as were the brandy producers in France. What prevented most whiskey producers in North America from aging their whiskeys was the need for quick money or bartered goods, and the immediate demand for the spirit.

The only aged whiskeys available would have been those that traveled a long way in their casks, such as Old Monongahela or Bourbon. Soon it became apparent that the whiskey that had sat in the barrels for an extended period of time took on certain characteristics of the cask that many thought made it taste better than the white liquor. As early as 1793, people began advertising "old whiskey," alerting the well-read consumer that their whiskey wasn't that clear stuff but the smoother, more palatable aged version. Old Monongahela and Old Kentucky weren't rustic affectations but rather an indicator of aged whiskey being sold. It was likely that this was the period of time during which some of the makers of whiskey who had an eye on future, long-term profits began to intentionally store their product. Barrels were charred to effectively clean out anything that may have been stored in the cask previously, and from there, aged whiskey became an established commodity.

As farming processes matured and businesses developed in the early part of the nineteenth century, so did whiskey markets. The great majority of whiskey consumed in America was produced in Pennsylvania and would have been a sort of rye blend, with a heavy emphasis on the rye. Rye whiskey would have been the default choice of the whiskey drinker. In 1810, Kentucky produced a little over two million barrels of whiskey. Pennsylvania produced and sold three times as much. Soon, other whiskey producers in the country began copying the business plans of the more successful Pennsylvania distilleries, and rye whiskeys became the default choice of the whiskey maker throughout most of the country.

Production increased as technological improvements from Great Britain made their ways across the Atlantic. The stills that had been developed to produce whiskey quickly found their way into the farms of America and Canada. The flat, shallow still of small capacity heated so quickly that a distiller could run off a batch in as little as three minutes. Soon another design came along that limited both labor and fuel requirements, and producing whiskey became even more profitable. Finally the American distillers got the patent still. Producing whiskey became quick, continuous, and inexpensive. The profit margins from whiskey increased substantially and the output exponentially. This introduction of Coffey's still brought North American whiskey production from farms to industrial environments.

Poor economic conditions only increased the demand for alcohol. The country suffered from a depression between 1814 and 1817, and one of the few stable jobs one could have was making and selling alcoholic drinks. While wages were low and unemployment in the cities fairly high, the per capita consumption of whiskey, beer, and wine kept moving upward each year. The reasons? An increase in the median age of people, and thus the number of people who were of "drinking age"; and the tens of thousands of immigrant adults who had come to America. The booming population filled in the demand for the drink, and immigrants to North America sought out beverages similar to those of their homelands.

3

Blame Canada

To the north of the United States, in the British colonies of Canada, settlers from Ireland and Scotland began to set up farms and communities. With the farms came the stills. By 1827—twelve years after the first settlers had arrived to clear the land and establish farms in the Bathurst District—the government had already licensed two dozen stills in the small villages of the area.

The problem in Canada was that it had a smaller population than the rebel nation to the south, and soon farmers in Ontario found themselves with too much grain and not enough purchasers. In 1794, John Graves Simcoe, the first lieutenant governor of Upper Canada, said: "From the quantity of grain produced for which a market cannot readily be found, the inhabitants have been induced in many places to set up stills." Whiskey soon became the first drink of Canadians, and England, never missing a chance to bring in more money to their government, set upon taxing production of the whiskey. The loyalists of Upper Canada accepted the tax without the resistance that their neighbors to the south had shown.

The immigrants of the great white north had the same issues as those in the United States a generation before. Both money and time were limitations that prevented setting up malt houses that would provide a place to dry and germinate the grains they used in their homeland. Canada's first distillers used anything they could get their hands on—oats, rye, wheat, corn, even potatoes and peas.

Much like the United States, the pioneers of Canada drank a lot. With whiskey costing twenty to thirty cents a gallon, it ended up being the preferred drink. Farmers took drinks with them into the fields. Factory workers had breaks that included a shot of rum or whiskey. Even children were sent to school fortified with a glass of the stuff being the equivalent to us giving our kids a shot of DayQuil before getting on a school bus.

Besides, what else was there to drink? Fresh water was rare, milk didn't keep, and coffee and tea were expensive. Whiskey and beer, for many, were the best options.

This was the environment in which Molson's was founded.

In 1786, an Englishman named John Molson arrived in Lower Canada, Montreal, with little money, and an idea to start brewing. He created his brew house, and presumably found a moderate amount of success. By 1801, he purchased a copper still, placed it on his property, and started distilling whiskey, likely as a low priority, because three years later he demolished his still house to add a stable to help with his increasing brewery fortunes. He purchased another still in 1811, but it sat mostly unused.

It was his son Thomas who took up the whiskey mantle and looked to take advantage of the English markets.

In order to prove himself as capable a businessman as his father, Thomas bought the distilling business and, sensing an opportunity, traveled back to England to learn about the craft of whiskey making. When he returned to Canada in 1831, he opened up his own distillery on the shores of Lake Ontario, in a small town called Kingston.

By 1832, he had produced almost one thousand gallons. The following year he produced over five times as much. He purchased new stills and soon controlled 18 percent of Upper Canada's total distilling capacity.

Family problems in the business required Thomas to move back to Lower Canada in 1834, but this time his distillery venture was welcomed back in Montreal with open arms.

As new towns and villages in both Lower and Upper Canada became settled, inns and taverns were often one of the first buildings to go up. And Thomas Molson was there, telling the new tavern owners and innkeepers how cheap his product was.

While other buildings were being constructed, meetings of all sorts were held at the inns. Political meetings, court sessions, even church services. As roads connected these new villages, travelers would often arrive exhausted, and end up at the inn to recuperate. Whiskey would have been the first choice on the menu. Many inns offered coach drivers a free drink or two if they arrived at their location rather than a competitor's down the road, or even in a different town.

This trend of giving away free drinks of whiskey continued on in both America's and Canada's expansion west. General stores were known for having a cask of open whiskey to offer their customers a drink while they shopped. They figured out that customers tended to buy more when tipsy. If only the store owners had potato chips and jalapeno poppers for sale, they would have made a killing.

By 1839, the Molson Distillery was producing 150,000 gallons of whiskey per year, making it the largest producer of whiskey in North America. Their next largest Canadian competitor was Gooderham & Worts Distillery, of Toronto, which had an output of 28,234 gallons.

But the Molson Distillery failed to keep up with the technology, and their ties to tradition were similar to that of many of the Irish distilleries of the same period. They soon found themselves being surpassed by the distilleries in Upper Canada that had employed the patent still. By 1861, Hiram Walker & Sons in Windsor was producing 400,000 gallons and Gooderham & Worts in Toronto had become the largest distilling operation in Canada, with 1.25 million gallons of spirits in production. By 1896, they got out of the whiskey business and focused on beer. It was Gooderham & Worts that became the preeminent whiskey seller from North America.

We arrived in Toronto with the goal of visiting the Gooderham & Worts Distillery site. Canada, much like the United States, has a lack of historical sites dealing with their place in the whiskey world, and any place advertised as "whiskey-related" was good enough for me.

In doing my prep and research before coming to Toronto, the old distillery site stood out, partly because of the significance of the place. Gooderham & Worts, located in what is now known as the Distillery District, was *the* place in Canada for whiskey. Their legacy helped set the foundation for the Canadian industry today. What also drew me to the site was the fact that it was in Toronto, the largest and arguably most cosmopolitan of all Canadian cities.

But really what attracted me to the place? They had a kick-ass Web site. I have always been a sucker for the bright, shiny object that is the Internet.

With the Web site containing such phrases as "Did you know the Distillery District was once home to the largest distillery in the British Empire?" and "Our Mission is to develop The Distillery as Canada's premier arts, culture and heritage precinct" and—the one that got me most excited—"this facility has played an important role in the growth and wealth of both the city and nation," I found myself inordinately excited about visiting Gooderham & Worts. Here was a location that knew its place in Canadian history. I had to see this distillery for myself.

"Look, they have a Segway tour of the distillery," I pointed out to Krysta as we drove from the airport to downtown in a car we called "Hiro Nakamura," a blue Pontiac that we had named after one of the characters from the superhero television series *Heroes*.

"How much?"

"You can't put a price on history!" I objected. "You can't put a price on education!"

"How much?" she insisted.

"Seventy dollars," I said.

"Jesus!" she said, keeping her eyes on the road.

". . . per person."

There was an awkward pause as she digested this information.

"Is there a non-Segway tour?" she asked.

I frowned. "Yes," I said, like a child who had been caught trying to hide her report card. "There's a walking tour."

"How much is that?"

"Fifteen dollars per person," I said.

"Yeah. We're walking," she said as we made our way into the Distillery District. I pouted silently.

James Wort arrived in Canada in 1831 from the east coast of England, and established a grist mill at the mouth of the Don River just outside of York, Ontario (later to be renamed Toronto). William Gooderham, a successful miller from Suffolk, England, and James's brother-in-law, followed and showed up on James's doorstep with fifty-four people and £3,000 to invest in Wort's milling company. The partnership of Gooderham & Worts was born and with it came one of the more successful business stories of nineteenth-century Canada.

James soon died, but the company lived on, with his son assuming partnership in 1845. But it was William who had the foresight to install the distillery on the location in 1837. While many other smaller distilleries were closing due to increases on taxes, Gooderham, who had the capital to establish his product, was able to create cheaper, "common" whiskey, aged for only a few months, and found a market for people who wanted cheap whiskey by selling it in the new general stores that were popping up all over Upper Canada. He soon was successful enough to expand his market to other areas of Canada by providing different whiskey-based products.

Unlike his competitors, William treated whiskey as an industrial product rather than an agricultural one. This allowed him to keep an eye on expansion as well as different alcohol-based opportunities. He added rectifying equipment, which allowed the distillery to produce the high-proof spirits needed for medicinal and industrial alcohols. He made aged rye whiskey. He added patent stills before anyone else in Canada.

By 1861, Gooderham & Worts's success required that they expand. They built a five-story distillery, with storehouses, elevators, and a private wharf, on the shores of Lake Ontario. They were producing two and a half million gallons of whiskey per year. By 1875, they produced one third of all of the spirits in Canada, and paid over one and a half million dollars in taxes. Of all of the distilleries in countries under British influence in the late 1800s, Gooderham & Worts was the most successful.

We had arranged to show up at the distillery at eleven o'clock. That would give us a half hour to explore the site before the eleven thirty walking tour that Krysta was so adamant about attending. I was still sulking over the lack of funds required to do the Segway tour, but I was also satisfied in knowing that were going to be shown the intricacies and nuances of the distillery.

"Imagine how much quicker this walk would be if we had Segways," I said to Krysta as we inhaled the exhaust fumes of a nearby bus. She shot me a look of disapproval. I noted that I shouldn't bring up the issue any further.

From a distance, the distillery site appeared as a vast industrial complex that was slowly being converted into a young urban professional's wet dream. Condominiums were being developed and huge billboards sat three stories off the ground asking for future residents to take a look. As we walked into the district proper, art studios and restaurants with thirty-dollar entrées stood side by side. The brick roads were being reinstalled to create an air of authenticity. It was postmodern development at its finest. It was industrial gentrification without the messy conflict of having to deal with the lower class.

It also covered the equivalent of three city blocks. We had a lot to explore.

Much like the older and much smaller Old Farm Distillery in West Overton, certain aspects of the complex were immediately recognizable to both of us. The place where the grain would have been stored was apparent, as were the cask houses in the eastern part of the complex. Other times we had to guess at what the buildings would have been used for. And yet still others confused us, specifically the cannery. Neither of us could recall a distillery that had, at one time or another, canned its product.

"We should head to the tour," Krysta mentioned, looking at her cell phone for the time. "Where's the tour office?"

This was a fine question. In our twenty minutes of exploring, neither one of us had seen anything resembling a visitors' center or a tour office. We flagged down the men adding the bricks to the roadway, and they pointed us to the far end of the complex. Once we got there, we were greeted by a sign that said that the company responsible for the tour had moved to "Building 32."

"Where the hell is building thirty-two?" I asked no one in particular. We quickly walked back to the main thoroughfare and looked at a map. We had passed it twice in the process of looking for the office.

We walked to what we believed was where the map was pointing us, and we walked into a graphic design office.

"Umm," I said to the receptionist. "You wouldn't happen to be the people offering the walking tours of the distillery site?"

She smiled as if she dealt with this question all the time. "Oh no. That's downstairs." We apologized and headed downstairs, and saw nothing resembling an office, but we could see into a closed room holding several Segways. Nobody was there to unlock the doors to let us in. The time was exactly eleven thirty.

"Is this it?" Krysta asked. I shrugged, and tried the door. Locked.

"What the . . . ?" My patience was running thin, and I pulled on the locked doors with a little more energy. Krysta, who was well versed in dealing with my tantrums, went to look for someone, anyone, who might be in charge.

There were close to fifty buildings on the site. And, this being a Tuesday morning, there were few people around. Yet Krysta almost immediately found the office that oversaw the management of the site. As I was stumbling around coffee houses and restaurants, looking for people who might know, she found me and pulled me to the office. There we were greeted by a receptionist who was busy taking care of twenty-eight phone calls. When she had a spare moment, she looked at me, and then at Krysta.

"You're the whiskey writer?" she asked me. Krysta had filled her in.

"Yeah," I responded. "Do you know if the tour office is closed today? We're here for the walking tour."

"Umm. They're not really our responsibility. We're not associated with them."

"But you do manage their site, right?"

"Yes."

"Could you tell me where they are supposed to be located then? Your maps outside say that they're in building nine, but there's a sign saying they moved . . ."

"They're not in nine anymore?" she asked me, as if I were the one running the place.

"Uh. No," I said. "Look, do you have any press materials, or anything that can tell me about the history of the site?"

She looked to a glass-enclosed conference room, where a woman sat, writing on a legal pad.

"Nancy here," the receptionist said pointing to the woman, "is our historian. Would she help?"

My heart skipped a beat. "Yeah! Yes!"

She went to Nancy and told her what was going on. Nancy looked up at me and headed out to the lobby where Krysta and I stood.

"Hi," she said, extending her hand. "I hear you're having some bad luck getting information about the distillery."

We nodded.

"Have you visited our Web site?"

"You mean the one that states that there's a walking tour at eleven thirty?" I said.

"Well . . . yes. There's a link to the history site there."

"But you don't know of anyone who can tell us about this site, or Gooderham and Worts?" I asked.

"Just the tour group." She paused. "I'll tell you what. Let me run off a copy of our brochure," and she headed back into the office. A moment later she returned.

"Ahh. Our printer is down," she said. Of course it was.

I told her that was okay, and that we would explore the site ourselves, and I would do extra research myself. I offered my hand and a word of thanks.

Krysta piped up. "Could I take a picture of the old bottles of whiskey you have there in your office?" She pointed to the office beyond the receptionist's desk, where there was a shelf of bottles that must have been at least one hundred years old.

"Ooo. Ummm. No, not really. Unless you want to take the picture from here." She pointed to the reception area in which we were already standing. This would have given Krysta a distance of about twenty feet. Krysta took her pictures and thanked Nancy. I suggested to Krysta that we finish the tour ourselves, and we left the office.

I was frustrated. I wanted to pout and stamp my feet. I wanted to go on that tour or, at the very least, get some direction from someone in authority about the place that this magnificent distillery had in the history of whiskey, Canada, and even Great Britain. I remained petulant as we continued walking around the site, and Krysta tried to offer suggestions that might get me out of my mood.

"Hey, have you seen the menu for this place?" she asked as we walked by a bistro/restaurant.

"Meh," I replied, full of disdain. We kept walking.

"Ooo . . . a microbrewery!" she said five minutes later as we walked by a retrofitted brew house.

"Feh!" I said. Beer wouldn't be able to pull me out of my immaturity, I thought to myself. We continued to walk.

"Chocolate?" Krysta prompted, as we discovered a chocolatier.

I paused for a moment before resigning myself to my needs. "Okay. Chocolate."

Five minutes later, I had downed four truffles, one of which was laced with a shot of whiskey. My mood had improved.

A few hours later we had lunch with a pair of friends, Matthew and Catharine, who both were well acquainted with Toronto. We discussed the distillery.

"When you told me you were going to tour the site, I wanted to warn you," Catharine said, taking a bite from her salad.

"About what?" I asked.

"Well. It's kind of like an amusement park that no one goes to."

I nodded. "It seemed like an apt metaphor for the Canadian whiskey industry as whole," I said. Corporate-run, manufactured to look engaging and interesting, and yet still somehow inaccessible.

This wasn't just an observation I was making about the industry. As the popularity of the aged spirit has increased over the past decade, only the Canadian whiskeys have failed to see any of the spoils come their way. Sales of Irish whiskeys, scotch, and bourbon have all seen increases, while Canadian whiskeys have remained mostly stagnant, with few exceptions. From my perspective, the new whiskey drinkers could not find anything in the Canadian whiskeys that they could gravitate toward. Bourbons sell their southern heritage. Scotches sell their dominance and their place as market leaders. Irish whiskeys seem charming and an exotic alternative to the dominant Scotch whiskey. What does Canadian whiskey have? What could they market? The charm of industry? The fact that they were available during Prohibition to those willing to break the law? Canadian whiskey seems to be a pragmatist in a room full of romantics, and it is being ignored because of it.

4

Westward, Ho!

During the 1800s, whiskey was the drink of the North American West. As American and Canadian pioneers journeyed across the continent, whiskey came along with them for all sorts of reasons. It provided income, entertainment, and could be used as currency. It was easy to make, easier to carry, and easier still to drink.

Until the rise of the temperance movement, American citizen soldiers marched and fought on alcoholic liquors that were issued to them as part of their rations. Rum and whiskey fueled the soldiers during the Revolutionary War. In the War of 1812, soldiers were issued meat, bread, vinegar, soap, and whiskey.

While Andrew Jackson removed spirits from army rations, whiskey capitalists and entrepreneurs soon found out that young men of the armed forces were the means to make an easy profit. Black markets and saloons often quickly appeared next to the forts that were now populating the American and Canadian territories. By 1840, smuggling whiskey to the army was called "running the mail." These "mail runners" were the type of folks usually associated with the black market, being either criminal or profiteers, oftentimes both. They sold low-quality whiskey to the army and were able to demand top money, sometimes as much as thirty-five dollars a gallon.

Kenneth McKenzie was a perfect example of one of these whiskey traders. A Scotsman who immigrated to Upper Canada at a young age, he soon found himself working for the Columbia Fur Company, based out of St. Louis, Missouri. From there he carved an empire of trade and marketing that encompassed a territory larger than many European nations. As the forts went up throughout the West, fur traders like McKenzie were able to set up their own outposts—as part of already established forts, or by building close by. In 1828, McKenzie built Fort Union at the confluence of the Missouri and Yellowstone Rivers. From there, he looked for buyers for his furs. What he soon found out was that his potential customers would be more keen to purchase or trade if they had been plied with a drink or two. With the help of whiskey, he made a fortune selling beaver and buffalo pelts, not just to white settlers, but to Native Americans, who had little or no experience with alcohol.

Between 1832 and 1834, Congress implemented increasingly punitive laws in order to prohibit people using any liquor, but especially whiskey, as a product to be traded with Native Americans. The fur traders worked to lobby against it. They failed, but soon found ways around it. When it became illegal to sell alcohol to Indians, the traders simply gave away watered-down whiskey, doctored with tobacco, pepper, molasses, and anything else that gave it a kick. On days where trading was to occur, nonalcoholic versions of the fake whiskey were sold. So prevalent was the use of whiskey in trading that many traders formed their own distilleries.

McKenzie was no different, and had founded his own on the Missouri River. One day he showed off his distillery to two fellow traders, looking to impress them. When they suggested that all three should go into business together, McKenzie responded with an emphatic "no." They left a little pissed at McKenzie, and responded by the only means they had available. They snitched. When they found themselves at Fort Leavenworth, they reported McKenzie to the authorities.

The result? On June 30, 1834, Congress prohibited distilleries in Native American territory—a law that is still on the books today.

Another life that was typical of the way that whiskey influenced people in the 1800s was that of Abraham Lincoln. In 1811, the Lincoln family moved ten miles from Sinking Spring, Kentucky, to a similar place on Knob Creek. "My earliest recollection is of the Knob Creek place," Lincoln wrote of his childhood home in Kentucky. He lived there for five years, until he was seven years old. When he wasn't tending the family farm, Lincoln's father, Thomas, worked at a distillery run by Charles Boone (a relative of Daniel Boone's) located at the confluence of Knob Creek and Rolling Fork Creek. Thomas Lincoln's duties probably included barrel making and other related carpentry.

It is for this tie to Lincoln that Jim Beam Brands today sells a bourbon called Knob Creek.

The Lincolns moved to Indiana when they had difficulties proving the deed status of their land, and Thomas used whiskey as part of the down payment on their home in Perry County.

In 1832, Abraham Lincoln ran for the Illinois state legislature. After he lost that election, he and two partners applied to the state for a retail liquor license and opened a tavern in New Salem, Illinois. Lincoln lived in the back room. Among other things, his liquor license prohibited him from selling whiskey to "Negroes, Indians, or children." He later, along with one William Berry, opened two more taverns, and ran these operations (charitably called general stores) until 1837. So with Washington making whiskey and Lincoln selling it, it would appear as if we Americans should have had no problem with the drink.

As the Industrial Revolution took hold in North America, the established whiskey distilleries back east soon began to reap the benefits. By the 1850s, improvements in distilling technology, brought over from Ireland and Scotland, increased the distance between those producing whiskeys on a large scale and the farmer/small-scale distiller. A growing network of railroads eliminated the necessity of making whiskey near markets in order to be sold locally, or waterways in order to be sold in distant cities. Names such as Hiram Walker and Seagram's became widely known in Upper Canada, and Schenley and Moore & Sinnott dominated the American markets, with all of the major whiskey producers in North America either doing business with one another or trying to put competing brands out of business.

The railroads provided quick and reliable shipment to distant marketplaces on a regularly scheduled basis. Those companies that took advantage of this newfound accessibility to distant cities and towns soon found themselves making a fair amount of money. And as the populations of Canada and America increased, so did the size of the marketplace. Larger distilleries found themselves with increased demand and also had to deal with the relatively new concept of brand recognition.

The growing temperance movement in the United States also made Canada, with its comparatively lax laws, look attractive to American entrepreneurs, such as Hiram Walker and J. P. Wiser, both of whom founded distilleries in Ontario within eyesight of the American border. With lower costs for land, and high-yield return on crops, they soon found themselves able to produce an impressive amount of whiskey, and there was increased demand for it.

Once America headed into the Civil War, the whiskey distilling business of the South was hampered by lack of access to the major cities of the North, as well as later by the destruction of the Confederacy's infrastructure. While the distillers of Kentucky and Tennessee languished in the fog of war, the distilleries of the North, especially those in western Pennsylvania, thrived. The Canadian distillers also hit the proverbial jackpot as the reduced stocks of food and beverages in the United States created new export opportunities. With both Walker and Wiser having near-immediate access to the American border (with Walker across the Detroit River in Windsor, Ontario, and Wiser in Prescott, right across the St. Lawrence River from Ogdensburg, New York), import access was both convenient (if one wanted to export into America legally) and profitable (especially if one wanted to ignore export/import tariffs and simply smuggle the whiskey into the United States).

Finally, the divide between small and large-scale distillers was increased as additional pressures from raised taxes levied by the government made legal distilling unprofitable for those with smaller operations. By the 1870s the era of industrial whiskey making was in full swing.

Farther west in the Territory of Montana and the future province of Alberta, the business practices started by the likes of Kenneth McKenzie were still in use by others in the fur trade.

In 1869, Montana authorities began stamping out the illicit sale of liquor. The American law passed in 1832 that made it illegal to sell liquor to Indians was technically still in effect, but in vast territories of the North, enforcement was limited, and difficult to prosecute in areas that weren't technically part of the United States.

But as Montana began to make overtures to Washington, D.C., about statehood, they established a territorial government. Laws once thought of as irrelevant began to be enforced, and the fur traders began to see their profits fall, and a few within their ranks were fined or jailed.

In search of new markets with lax law enforcement, frontier entrepreneurs John J. Healy and Alfred B. Hamilton, obtained a permit from American authorities to cross the Blackfeet Reservation and head north. Once granted, this permit had the effect of opening trading in British North America (now southern Alberta, Canada).

Healy and Hamilton soon moved their operations to Alberta, and found what they were looking for—to be out of the reach of the American lawmen. They saw the region as an untapped market. It supported a large native population that traded for alcohol. The men established Fort Hamilton, a small trading post, only twenty kilometers from present-day Lethbridge, Alberta. Soon the fur trade became of secondary importance, as the major business of "Fort Whoop-Up" was selling whiskey.

Once others saw the success of Healy and Hamilton, they followed suit. Over the next several years, numerous other whiskey posts sprang up throughout the region, along what became known as the Whoop-Up Trail. One such fort was erected on the Elbow River, located where the present city limits of Calgary have grown. Wherever the whiskey posts showed up, crime increased, as did other disruptive influences that surround people involved in illicit trade.

For the newly formed Canadian government, it was their first test with America. The government had settlement plans that involved neither America nor any trade that could lead to instability of the region. Eradicating the whiskey posts was of utmost concern.

The Canadian government acted in 1873 by forming the North-West Mounted Police (NWMP), their frontier version of a regional police force. A side benefit of the NWMP was an assertion of Canadian sovereignty over the lands now being populated by traders from the neighboring country to the south.

The NWMP, distinguished by their bright red uniforms, were called to Fort Whoop-Up in October 1874 with the task of establishing Canadian control in the territory and control of the alcohol trade. Their first strike on the alcohol traders had come after a native complained at Fort MacLeod about a group of traders who had sold him overpriced whiskey. Expecting a battle, they set up field artillery pointed directly at the trading post. They then shouted at those inside to come on out without a fight.

There was no response from inside.

When a member of the NWMP walked to the front gate and knocked, one, and only one, trader opened the door. He invited the police in and offered them some dinner. The rest of the traders had heard of them coming and fled in fear. Shortly after, the North-West Mounted Police caught and fined the perpetrators at a location several miles away.

Once Canadian law enforcement was established in Alberta, the whiskey traders again found their business in jeopardy. Some traders were arrested by the police. Most, however, either moved on to places where their trade could proceed unencumbered or changed their occupation.

As for the NWMP? It later became better known as the Royal Canadian Mounted Police.

It wasn't long before whiskey companies in North America were asking the same questions as those in Great Britain—namely, just what defined "whiskey." But before they could say what whiskey was, they had to say what it wasn't.

As larger distillers established their brands, copycat distilleries would often pop up, selling adulterated whiskey. Sometimes they would name their brands so as to intentionally confuse the product with established brands; other times, they would simply undercut established prices. As in Scotland, whiskey throughout America was adulterated with iodine, tobacco, and other substances, mostly to make the spirit look more expensive than it actually was. The whiskey companies who saw these practices as a threat began lobbying their respective governments for help.

The result of this lobbying was the American Bottled-in-Bond Act of 1897, which stated that, for a whiskey to be taxed as whiskey, it had to be aged and bottled according to a set of legal stipulations contained in the United States government's Standards of Identity for Distilled Spirits. If a product didn't meet the stipulations, it could still be taxed, but it could not classify itself officially as whiskey.

The stipulations were pretty straightforward. To be labeled as "Bottled-in-Bond" or "Bonded," the whiskey would need to have been straight whiskey that was the product of one distillation season and one distiller at one distillery. Then it must have been stored, and thus aged, in a federally bonded warehouse for four years, and bottled at 100 proof. Finally, the bottle's label had to identify the locations where the whiskey was both distilled and bottled.

What this act did was put the authenticity of whiskey directly in the government's hands. People who purchased "Bottled-in-Bond" whiskey knew that they were getting aged whiskey, instead of spirits made to look as if they had been aged. Whiskey that didn't meet the standards would be considered to be inauthentic, illegal, or oftentimes both.

As the Bottled-in-Bond Act took hold, American distillers saw their sales grow. They figured out that there was a benefit in excluding certain blended brands from being called whiskey. As Canada was the largest provider of blended whiskeys into the United States, the American distillers saw their opportunity to displace the Canadians from the top of the whiskey world. In 1906, after the United States Congress passed a Pure Food Law, American distillers lobbied Washington to have straight whiskey recognized as the only whiskey. In other words, products that blended neutral spirits with aged whiskeys—that is, the whiskeys of Canada—should be deprived of recognition as a pure food in the United States and hence be outlawed.

Most of this was a response to the inroads Canadian distillers had made into the United States. By the beginning of the twentieth century, Hiram Walker and Gooderham & Worts had established a strong presence in the American market. Various American distilleries, at least those not doing business with the Canadian brands, wanted to cut the Canadian distilleries off at the knees. They did this by claiming that the Canadian brands were less than pure alcohol.

A government chemist and the solicitor general of the United States agreed with the American distillers' argument, and blended whiskeys were decreed less than pure and, according the Pure Food Law, had to be prevented from reaching American consumers. In 1908, Canadian Club and other types of blended Canadian whiskey were refused entry into the United States. Existing stocks were seized by authorities and removed from shelves.

Hiram Walker & Sons appealed to the United States Supreme Court. A temporary injunction was granted, and a complete inquiry into the whiskey controversy began. In 1910, President William Howard Taft quoted from the inquiry report in handing down his decision:

> Whiskey, for more than one hundred years, had been the most general and comprehensive term applied to liquor distilled from grain. . . . Its flavor and color have varied with the changes in the process of its manufacture in the United States, Ireland, Scotland, and England. . . . The efforts of those engaged in the manufacture were directed toward the reduction of the amount of Fusel oil in the product. . . .
>
> It was supposed for a long time that by aging of Straight Whiskey in a charred wood a chemical change took place which rid the liquor of Fusel oil. . . . It now appears by chem-

ical analysis that this is untrue; that the effect of the aging is only to dissipate the odor, and to modify the raw, unpleasant flavor, but to leave the Fusel oil still in the Straight Whiskey. . . .

After an examination of all the evidence, it seems to me overwhelmingly established that for a hundred years the term Whiskey in the trade and among the customers, has included all potable liquor distilled from grain.

Taft's decision made it clear: whiskey was whiskey, whether blended or straight. The Canadian brands could export their drinks into America with no fear of being labeled "impure."

5

Capone's Cash Cow

After driving the length of Ireland, and then throughout the most scenic areas of Scotland, poor Ontario never had a chance. It's a four-hour drive from Toronto to Windsor, a time frame that seemed easily accomplished in the planning phases. But Highway 401, which connects the two cities, suffers from the fact that it's neither Ireland nor Scotland. In fact, it's much like the drive from Buffalo to Toledo. Any idea of deep, lush Canadian farmland had been beaten to a pulp and then buried in a tar pit by the scenic reality of places whose best redeeming feature were that they had a Tim Hortons donut shop AND a Boston Pizza.

By the time we entered Windsor proper, Krysta and I were both suffering from Severe Annoyance and Sarcasm Syndrome, also known as SASS.

"Oh look!" I said, as we entered the city. "A Best Buy! How exotic!"

"Oooo. A Pizza Hut! We can't get those back home!" Krysta added.

"Should we get some Canadian cuisine for dinner?" I asked.

"Great idea! Let's stop into any diner and ask for something deep-fried."

Clearly Canada wasn't living up to our expectations. What we didn't want to admit was that the fault was entirely our own. Toronto did nothing for us, aside from introducing us to some unsavvy whiskey historians. The reality of the situation was that everyone we had met in the Great White North had been friendly, outgoing, and willing to help us with any reasonable request that we had.

Every time I head to Canada, I feel as if I'm visiting my better-behaved, over-achieving relatives. Whereas America feels like one of those families where there's an excessive amount of shouting at the dinner table and fighting over even the most irrelevant of slights, Canada feels like the family where they keep their house tidy and the shouting to a minimum. Every time I leave Canada, my eyes tear up as I look at the border from the back window, wondering if I've been adopted by America and Canada is my real family. Thus Krysta's and my own slights toward the country were really nothing more than a gleeful acknowledgment that sometimes, just sometimes, Canada isn't perfect.

Of course, by the time we arrived at our hotel in Windsor and had an exceptionally helpful receptionist check us in and an exceptionally nice custodian lug a mini-refrigerator into our room on the fourteenth floor, Krysta and I were cowed into realizing that, once again, we were really just another group of loud, obnoxious Americans.

We were in Windsor to visit the folks at Hiram Walker, producers of Canadian Club Whisky.

Canadian Club held a special place in my heart. As a youth growing up in the blue-collar parts of Pittsburgh, it was this brand that held sway over a great many people. As the local Pittsburgh distilleries failed to reopen after Prohibition, and bourbon had yet to hit its stride, it was the Canadian whiskeys that won over the workers looking for a quick tipple or three after work. I can still recall the giant four-liter bottles of Canadian Club that peppered people's home bars without a single trace of irony. Nothing says commitment to a brand more than having four liters of a company's whiskey in the basement.

Canadian Club and Hiram Walker served Pittsburgh after World War II. I felt an odd kinship with the brand.

We were greeted by Meghan at the front door of the visitors' center. The inside was downright palatial.

"Hello! Hello! I'm glad to see you could make it!" she said to us as she ushered us into the foyer. Both Krysta and I looked around in awe. The room was lined in oak, and had vaulted ceilings and chandeliers.

As Meghan took us on a tour of the place, she told us that it had been built in the 1890s, and it was based on a palace located in Italy. All evidence pointed to the fact that Walker had no problem in selling his whiskey.

The tiniest of ringing sounds entered into the room.

We looked around to see where it was coming from. At floor level was a gray-white cat with bright yellow eyes, working to avoid eye contact with us interlopers.

"That'd be C. C.," said a male voice. "She's our house cat." The man introduced himself as Dan Tullio, director of the Canadian Club brand.

"We picked her up to be a mouser, but soon found out that she would set off the motion sensors at night. So we had to put a bell on her, so we can find her and place her in a room that has no sensors before we go home for the night."

". . . and the bell prevents her from being a mouser," I finished.

"Exactly. And she's too cute to get rid of," he joked, as he led us down the hallway to his office.

"I'm a dog person myself," Meghan said to me as we noted C. C. following us.

The cat followed us wherever we went. As we explored and were told of the historical significance of each room, the sound of "ting-a-ling" followed. Upstairs in the video room, or the downstairs in the office, the cat was there, never acknowledging us, but still making sure that we were available in case we were needed.

"Did you get a chance to see the neighborhood?" asked Dan, as we placed our coats on the chairs of the conference table.

"No. Not Walkerville itself," I admitted.

Walkerville was the company town that Hiram Walker founded to house his workers, the whiskey version of Hershey, Pennsylvania. Hiram had purchased several holdings surrounding his distillery, to both control and profit from the surrounding businesses that the distillery created. By 1867, he had not only his whiskey operation but a hotel, a store, and several homes that he leased out to workers.

By the 1880s, the village had grown to a population of roughly 600 people. The area had its own police and fire departments and a church (St. Mary's, named after Walker's wife, who died in 1872). It was all financed by Hiram Walker. The city officially incorporated in 1890, and existed until it amalgamated with the city of Windsor just after American Prohibition.

Canadian Club is the perfect whiskey if you want to discuss Prohibition, as so much of its history is steeped in the movement. Hiram Walker, an American to the end (maintaining residence across the river in Detroit until his death), moved his distillery to Canada in order to avoid the influence of the temperance movement that was taking hold in the United States. Prohibition forced the sale of the family-run company to someone who wasn't American. The end of Prohibition saw their sales increase, as there were only a handful of distilleries with aged product on hand to sell to the now legal American market. The Hiram Walker distillery is as tied to the issue of temperance and Prohibition as Martin Luther is tied to Catholicism.

"Wanna see something cool?" Dan asked, as we headed into the basement of the visitor center. I nodded. He led us into a brick room that was located below the offices.

"This is Hiram Walker's speakeasy. This was where Hiram's sons had their meetings with the mobsters from Detroit and Chicago. Look here." He pointed at a small dimple in the wall. "A bullet hole." My attention was distinctly caught.

I walked up close and put my finger into the hole, examining it with a fair bit of joy. "Do you know the circumstance surrounding this?" I asked.

Dan laughed. "Oh sure. Some guy had a slight disagreement with another guy." He directed us to the pictures on the wall, each one a black-and-white photograph of some form of smuggling operation. In one picture were several cars driving across the ice. In another, a picture of boats at the docks that were once immediately outside of the visitors' center. In still another, a woman wearing an altered dress showing how she was able to put six bottles of whiskey on her person. Two things became immediately apparent to me.

First, the Hiram Walker Distillery was on the front lines of the black market of whiskey that was smuggled into America by the likes of Johnny Torrio and Al Capone. Secondly, the current owners of Canadian Club, Fortune Brands, had clearly decided that this tie to gangsters and the Prohibition era was a marketing tool, albeit one used mostly on the site of the visitors' center.

I loved it. Marketing aspect or no, it was refreshing to see a company acknowledge the seamier part of their history. This was something that was new to me in my explorations of distilleries.

"I wanna show you something else." said Dan. "Follow me." Krysta, Meghan, and I dutifully complied, following him through a maze of hallways that turned left and right, accompanied by the ever-present "ting-a-ling, ting-a-ling" from the cat.

Soon we came into a room painted a bright blue. "This is our pool room. Beneath the flooring here is a swimming pool. However, we have converted it into more of an archive library."

I stared out at the shelves that lined the walls. Old bottles, papers, and unfiled folders were sitting waiting to be discovered.

"We're going through these when we have the time, but we don't have a full-time employee on them," he said, nearly apologetically. He went over to a box on the table and pulled out several papers. "Take a look at this."

I looked at what appeared to be coded telegrams that had been decoded.

"It tells the story of one Mr. Carleoni out of Montreal. It says here that he's behind on his payments."

I looked at the date of the missive. The late twenties.

"And this . . . ," he said, showing me the second piece of paper. ". . . this is a report about the death of Mr. Carleoni, who accidentally fell into a furnace."

"Jesus!" Krysta said.

"Cool!" I said. What did I care? He had been gone for over eighty years. The historical significance of these papers was far more interesting than the horrible way in which he had been murdered.

Dan looked at the shelves like a child showing off his comic book collection. "There's all sorts of stuff in here like that throughout our collection," he said, smiling.

"You mean your unarchived, uncataloged collection," I corrected, staring at a sheet of paper that explained how to decode the codes that the smugglers used. Dan laughed and acknowledged that a fair amount of gold had yet to be panned.

My eyes continued moving up and down the shelves. There were old advertising campaigns, forged bottles of faked Canadian Club, there was . . .

There was a four-liter bottle!

"Oh my God!" I said. "This . . . this takes me back to my childhood!" I pointed at the gargantuan bottle. My mind flashed back to the personal bars of several of my neighbors, each of whom had had

Canadian Club 6-Year-Old

Canada's most popular blended whiskey, and possibly the oldest whiskey brand from North America. It's owned by Fortune Brands.

Nose: A hint of anise wafts below the grains of the drink, and a fair amount of spice is present as well.

Taste: Cola was the first taste I could place, with a bit of pepper along for the ride.

Finish: Short and dry, with a bit of a metal taste in my mouth afterward.

Character: When I was in college, there was a bar band that played every weekend. They weren't risqué, and, as their set list consisted mostly of cover tunes, they rarely offered music that was innovative or original. But they were dependable, and could entertain the packed bar to the point where everyone was having fun. That's who I thought of when I drank Canadian Club 6-year-old.

one. Suddenly I was back in the basement of my hometown friends, playing Monopoly with them next to the neon beer signs and bottles of liquor that distinguished their parents' collections.

"Do you want one?" Dan asked.

"Oh, I couldn't!"

"No, really. I insist," he said.

I paused and bit my lip, thinking about how to explain this to the customs officials. "Yes. I want one." We shook hands, and arrangements were soon made for me to be the proud owner of an empty four-liter Canadian Club bottle.

I briefly thought of journalistic ethics. My id gleefully reminded me of the several bottles of whiskey that had been given to me. I was already a stooge of the whiskey companies. But now? Now I was a stooge with a giant Canadian Club bottle. I considered that I came out even.

6

To Kentucky and Prohibition

The trip had turned into a firsthand experience of every air travel cliché. If it wasn't the kid kicking the back of my seat on the way to Ireland, it was Northwest Airlines deciding that it was in their best interest not to let anyone know that their airplane would be grounded. As we had to get to Louisville via Detroit, this was a bit of a problem.

It was relatively early, and Krysta and I were sitting at the gate, groggily waiting for the privilege of being shoehorned into a vehicle that is only slightly more accommodating than a Greyhound Bus. The only difference between an airplane and a bus, as far as I can tell, is instead of having a bus driver telling you to not step over the line between the passenger seats and the steps, airlines have attendants who tell you that the first-class area, and thus the first-class latrine, is strictly off-limits to those who have neither the money nor the air miles to upgrade. Luckily, airlines sell tiny bottles of liquor to help soften the blow of class distinction.

For me, the boarding area is a bizarre netherworld, where time stands still, no one seems to age, and everyone accepts all of the abuses that come with the airport. Everyone, that is, but Krysta. The time to board the plane came and went. Soon we were a half hour late. Then an hour. No news of the delay was communicated to any of us at the boarding gate. By the time the morning's Bloody Mary had worn off, Krysta decided to take action. She got out of her seat and headed toward the counter, the other passengers looking at her as if she were Oliver Twist having the audacity to ask for enough to eat.

"Could you tell us what's the delay? We were supposed to board the plane an hour ago," she asked the woman at the counter.

"There's a bit of technical difficulty with a minor component of the plane relating to the inboard restrooms. Once that's taken care of, we should be able to board you with no difficulty."

"So there's no need for us to be transferred to another flight?" said Krysta, looking out the window over the boarding attendant's shoulder.

"Not at all," she responded. "You should be in the air in less than forty-five minutes."

"Then why are they taking the luggage off of the plane?"

Krysta pointed to the airplane outside the window. Sure enough, the luggage was being pulled off the plane.

"Isn't that a sign that there's something serious happening to the plane?" Krysta asked, already knowing the answer.

"Son of a bitch!" said the diminutive woman, picking up the phone. "Ray . . . what the hell is going on?" She held up a finger, indicating to Krysta that she should wait.

Soon afterward, Krysta walked back to me, with two new tickets on a different airline. We would still be heading into Louisville, but only after a transfer in Charlotte, and six hours behind our schedule. "Ladies and gentlemen, it seems as if the problems with the airplane are more serious than initially stated," said the attendant into the PA system, at long last. "If you would please come to the counter, I will find a way to get you to your final destination."

A herd of people ran to the counter as we walked away. When we last looked, the line was several dozen people deep.

I had been to Louisville the previous year, so I felt relatively secure in knowing what to expect once we landed. We'd get our hotel room, head out to dinner, and then head back to hotel, where we would get our beauty sleep for the big day tomorrow.

Alas, the hotel proved to be a tad . . . unsettling. Once we made it out of the Louisville Airport, we were happy to find the hotel was a mere mile from the terminal. However, there was a distinct Scooby-Doo/Haunted Mansion aspect to the place that left us feeling uneasy.

The floor was a muddled forest green, with dark stains left over from the years of wear. The aroma was a distinct lemony-bleach cleaning product that only covered the smell of . . .

"Is that the stench of failure?" Krysta asked. "I mean, underneath the lemony fresh smell."

"It's not an aroma normally associated with joy and bliss, that's for sure," I added, as we walked down the hall. Our eyes darted back and forth, looking for ghosts or perverts around each corner.

"What an odd shade of yellow," I mentioned to Krysta as we walked down the hallway to the check-in desk.

"Kate, I don't think that's intentionally yellow. I think these walls were once white. That's the yellow you get from years of smoking," Krysta said.

"Oh. Ew . . . EWW!" I felt almost sick to my stomach, and thanked whatever higher spirit out there that allowed alcohol to be my vice rather than nicotine. I made sure to stick to the center of the hallway, as far away from either wall as logistics would allow.

We checked in and headed to our room. By the time we figured out that the air-conditioning unit ticked like a time bomb that was never able to go off, we felt as if we needed to do something.

"As far as I can tell, we can do one of two things at this point," I said. "One, we could spend the rest of the night looking for another room or hotel. Or two, we could find a place to drink."

"Did you get insurance on the car?" asked Krysta.

"Yes."

"Then I say, 'Let's drink,'" she responded.

I nodded. We programmed the local taxi company's phone number into our respective cell phones, in case we became too intoxicated to drive back to the hotel. I then dialed the cellular modem of my laptop into the Internet and looked for a place to eat. We packed ourselves into the rental car and headed into downtown Louisville.

After the flight delay, and the spooky hotel of the damned, getting into some semblance of normalcy was of utmost importance.

As with any city that caters to tourism, there are areas and places that year-round residents simply do not go. They know where the great places to eat are, and they know where the cheap places are. Places that cater to tourists rarely contain such qualities. This is Kate's Law of finding good places to eat—Ignore places that cater to tourists.

I was aware of this law at this time, but I intentionally sought to ignore it. This was the decision that led us to Maker's Mark Bourbon House and Lounge, found right in the heart of "4th Street Live!," an area of downtown draped in neon and laden with stores and restaurants often found at a local mall. That they call this their "premier dining" area tells me that the folks at the Louisville tourism board don't get out that often. Either that, or they wish to keep the better places in Derby City free from out-of-town crowds.

Maker's Mark Bourbon House and Lounge is the famous whiskey's attempt at cross-marketing appeal, and is one of the few places in 4th Street Live! that can't be found in other cities. As far as I could figure out, this is a recent trend, where owners of the various brands are looking to find ways of making money off their whiskeys without actually focusing on the spirit. Krysta and I tossed around a few ideas for cross-promotion as we sat in a dining room with hardwood floors, dark earth-tone colors on the walls, and lighting seemingly provided by nothing more than a multitude of 20-watt lightbulbs and candles.

"How about a Jim Beam Bed and Breakfast?" I offered.

"Oooo . . . I got it! The Canadian Club Club, for those who like their whiskey, and keeping their car safe!" she responded.

"Well then, they have to make the Johnnie Walker Walker, for those senior citizens who want to show their love while dealing with their arthritic hips."

We laughed and toasted each other with the water that had been provided to us.

The waiter came and went with our orders. I had desired a small fillet of beef, and Krysta ordered some buttermilk fried chicken. But more importantly, I had ordered a glass of Maker's Mark, with water back, and Krysta and I had decided upon a tasting tray of bourbon: Knob Creek, one of Jim Beam's small batch offerings; Old Rip Van Winkle, a label now produced by the folks out of Buffalo Trace; and a glass of Russell's Reserve, named after the master distiller at Wild Turkey.

"Wow, your food looks good."

Krysta and I looked over at the fifty-something man who was having dinner with his wife.

"I'm sorry. What?" asked Krysta.

"Is that chicken? We were just talking about ordering the chicken, weren't we?" The man looked at his wife for confirmation that they had indeed just been talking about the buttermilk fried chicken. She nodded in the affirmative, seemingly taken aback by her husband's forthrightness.

We were also a little taken aback. I am from the West Coast and Krysta from the East. These are places in which wide berths are given to fellow diners, who are allowed their own "bubbles" in which to operate and discuss whatever intimate details they may wish to talk about in public. Very rarely is a fellow dinner acknowledged, let alone consulted about his dinner choice. We approached this breach of etiquette as an exotic cultural difference, even if this was a culture a mere 474 miles from the East Coast.

"It's quite good," said Krysta, looking at me briefly before turning her attention to the couple at her right. "I would definitely recommend it."

The man smiled. "You see, I told you you should have ordered it."

His wife reminded him gently, "Yes, but you know that I'm avoiding fried foods." She paused. "It does look pretty good, though."

The man leaned in close to me, as if he wanted to share a secret. "I keep telling her that sometimes she needs to indulge herself."

His wife rolled her eyes as the server approached our table with the four bourbons.

"Lord! It's clear you have no plans tomorrow," the man said to me, laughing.

"Well, you know, I figured that since I was in Kentucky, I should start acting like it." I realized too late that this comment either didn't make any sense or would come across as me thinking that citizens of Kentucky did nothing but drink four bourbons at every meal. I tried to change the subject.

"Are you a bourbon fan?" I asked the man.

"Oh, it's okay. I prefer Jack myself. But there are a few bourbons I like. You going to see some of the distilleries down here?" he said.

"We are."

"Oh, you're going to learn a lot," he added, taking a bite of his own meal, which had just arrived. "Which ones are you going to?" he asked after swallowing.

"Buffalo Trace, Heaven Hill, a few others," I said, taking a bite of my own meal, and chasing it back with a sip of the Maker's Mark.

"That's great. That's really great. We went to the Maker's Mark tour last year, didn't we?" he asked his wife.

She nodded, before returning to the conversation that she and Krysta were having, which had seemingly deviated from the path that my conversation was on with this man.

"Did you know that they make beer down there?" he said to me.

"Really?" was all I could muster, as my mind tried to interpret what he said. He can't mean that they actually produce and sell beer there, can he? Perhaps he's referring to the mash. I've heard some people call it a beer before.

"Oh yeah! That's what they said when we were there a few years back. We learned a whole lot about how they make whiskey," he said.

"Have you been on other tours?" I asked.

He nodded, as his mouth was preoccupied with a recent bite from his plate. After he finished swallowing, he added, "We went to Jack Daniel's last year. Beautiful place, really. And of course we've been to Jim Beam."

"Of course," I added for no apparent reason. I nodded over at Krysta, still engrossed in a conversation with the man's wife. "We recently went to Ireland and Scotland to a few of their distilleries over there."

"I never could get a handle on scotch," he said, wiping his mouth with his napkin.

Over the course of the following hour, we took part in what I've since learned is a common ritual when whiskey fans meet up: the taste comparison. This occurs when two people who know little of one another but share a passion for whiskey try to find common ground or engage in a subtle game of one-upmanship. Various types and brands are discussed and compared. If distilleries or tastings are thrown into the mix, they are brought up solely as a means to establish a level of credibility.

For example, say two people are discussing Jim Beam, and between the two of them, this is the only whiskey that they have ever consumed. If person A has visited the Jim Beam Distillery while person B has not, the implication is that person A has more whiskey experience as a whole. When the discussion involves several dozen companies, brands, and distilleries, it becomes a highly nuanced discussion, with people withholding information until necessary to trump their conversation partner. Of course, the trumped participant can dismiss the experiences of the other by saying things such as "I could never get a handle on scotch," thereby negating any perceived gains from the status card thrown.

As it was, our dinner conversationalists weren't strictly status seeking, as they were looking for common events to discuss. But as they had been to several distilleries that we had yet to visit, we looked to them for information on what to expect. Every time Krysta and I brought up our recent trip overseas, a dismissive sentence was soon to follow.

But that was okay by me. The next few days were filled with a bit of uncertainty. The Scottish and the Irish have a more sophisticated outlook toward, not just whiskey, but alcohol in general. I did not know if that translated to the whiskey professionals on this side of the ocean.

Our newfound dining companions helped fill in enough of the

picture that I could set reasonable expectations—primarily that Kentucky exemplified the American whiskey industry, with emphasis on the word "industry." I shouldn't expect the smaller, scenic operations that we had come across in the British Isles.

In return for their help, I offered the only currency I had available to me—drinks from the bourbons on our tasting trays. We each had a sip from all three glasses, with the consensus being that Russell's Reserve had the best flavor, with me being the lone "against" vote, finding its finish a bit quick for my liking. I was more keen on the Old Rip Van Winkle, which I found both sweet and spicy, and which had a finish that seemed to last long past when I swallowed the drink.

For a moment, I felt a bit lucky that we had run into people with their own joy for whiskey, and that we were able to share a moment with them. It wasn't until later that I understood that finding a whiskey fan at a restaurant that was leveraging a known whiskey brand in the restaurant's name to pull in customers was as lucky as finding a music fan at a concert. It would have been more notable had we run into someone who hated the spirit.

The end of dinner also brought forth the end of the moment. When the waitstaff delivered our respective checks, it was as if we both realized that we were talking to complete strangers. Where a moment before we couldn't stop talking about whiskey, suddenly we couldn't find any common ground. As we got up to leave, we said a cordial but uncomfortable good-bye and went our separate ways. Fifteen minutes later, Krysta and I ran into the couple again in the gift shop of the local Hard Rock Cafe. We barely acknowledged one another.

As I was driving back to our hotel, sober yet sated, I asked Krysta, "Did you catch their names? I don't think that ever came up."

She shook her head no. We had all just started talking, and then spent an hour or so simply sharing the moment.

In order to understand how bourbon came to be America's whiskey of choice, one has to understand the affect that Prohibition had on the country. To do that, knowledge of the law helps.

Maker's Mark with the Red Wax Seal
There are a few varieties of Maker's Mark. The one with the red wax seal is the most common. With their recipe containing wheat instead of rye (in addition to the required corn and the standard barley), the drink is bit unique when compared with most bourbons out there.

Nose: A bit of oak, a bit of honey, a lot of fruit and a lot of spice. A very deep quality about it.

Taste: Chewy, with a somewhat oily consistency (in a good way); a sweet toffee taste runs underneath a nutty, woody flavor.

Finish: Lasts longer than other, more popular bourbons, with more of the toffeeness balancing out against the flavor of the barrel.

Character: Maker's Mark is like that blue-collar genius people run into from time to time. Sure, he follows Zen philosophy, and can discuss the intricacies of Nietzsche and Rousseau. But really? He prefers to be in his garage, working on his car.

The amendment to the United States Constitution reads as follows:

Section 1. After one year from the ratification of this article the manufacture, sale, or transportation of intoxicating liquors within, the importation thereof into, or the exportation thereof from the United States and all territory subject to the jurisdiction thereof for beverage purposes is hereby prohibited.

Section 2. The Congress and the several States shall have concurrent power to enforce this article by appropriate legislation.

Section 3. This article shall be inoperative unless it shall have been ratified as an amendment to the Constitution by the legislatures of the several States, as provided in the Constitution, within seven years from the date of the submission hereof to the States by the Congress.

The United States Congress passed the article on December 18, 1917. The amendment was ratified on January 16, 1919, having been approved by thirty-six states. It went into effect one year later on January 17, 1920. It was the first amendment to the American Constitution that had taken away freedoms rather than ensuring them.

The amendment had a devastating affect on the American whiskey industries. Well established multimillion-dollar companies shut their doors, in many cases never to reopen.

How did it get to this? How did a farm product earn the ire of a small segment of the population to the point where the government made all drink illegal?

America had been founded on the farm, and the products that resulted. This included ale and whiskey. Drinking in colonial times started early in the morning and continued throughout the rest of the day, well into the evening. It was so ingrained into the culture that it is easy to understand how it and the drunkenness that resulted raised eyebrows and had more than a few folks lamenting the loss of our moral culture.

In 1789, the first temperance society was created by two hundred farmers of Litchfield County, Connecticut. From there, the idea took hold and spread to other areas of the country, with moderate effect. The early years of the Industrial Revolution sparked the founding of the Sober Society in Allentown, New Jersey, and the Union Temperance Society in Saratoga County, New York.

One of the more effective attempts to moderate the drinking habits of Americans was the American Temperance Society, established in 1826. The American organization was dominated by young Evangelical Presbyterians and Congregationalists from New England, products of the "Second Great Awakening," the religious revival that swept the country between the 1790s and 1830s. The largest group were clergymen, though doctors and businessmen were both well represented.

The American Temperance Society aimed its propaganda not at the drunkard, whom it considered beyond redemption, but at the affluent moderate drinker. It is this group and this approach that influenced

the Irish Temperance Movement; first the Protestant groups of
Dublin and Belfast, and eventually Father Mathew and his flock.

In 1840, the "Washingtonians" were launched in Baltimore by
six men while drinking at Chase's Tavern. As a matter of amusement, two of the six had gone to attend a temperance lecture at a
nearby church in order to mock and heckle. Instead, they were convinced by the speakers. They returned to the tavern, told their
friends, and the six of them vowed then and there to live a life of abstinence.

Abstinence is the key word there, as many of these societies eschewed "tempering" of drinking habits and encouraged out-and-out
prohibition of alcohol. So even though many of these groups had
"Temperance" within their name, many of them rejected that idea
outright, demanding that drink of any sort was a sin. So while they
may have had a handle on what they believed to be moral, they had
less of a grasp of how to look up words in Webster's Dictionary.

The Prohibition movement was a force in local politics in varying
degrees throughout the mid- to late 1800s. But it was not until after
the Civil War, when the National Prohibition Party and the Women's
Christian Temperance Movement (WCTU) were organized, that it
was seen as a national movement. By the time the Anti-Saloon League
was formed in 1893, all pretense of getting people to reduce the
amount of alcohol consumed each day had been dropped. With the
expansion of the Anti-Saloon League into virtually every state in
America and various provinces throughout Canada, the WCTU, and
the enlistment of the clergy of many church denominations, the fight
to achieve prohibition took on new dimensions. Where previous Temperance Societies were satisfied to secure enactments of "local option
laws"—which enabled local governments, counties, cities, townships,
and even states to prohibit the sale of alcohol—these new societies
wanted nothing less than national prohibition.

The WCTU had its first national victory in Canada, helping influence the passage of the Dunkin Act of 1864, which gave counties
and municipalities the right to enact prohibition laws into local ordi-
nances. This was followed by the Canadian Prohibition Act of 1878,
which allowed any community to opt into prohibition by a simple

vote. By the start of the twentieth century, many areas of Canada had gone dry. The notable exception was Quebec, which had a long tradition of wine drinking, and took exception to anyone telling them that they had to put their wine away.

The Prohibitionists, sensing that the Canadian national attitude would be in their favor, decided to push the regional option into a national law in 1898. The prime minister, aware of Quebec's position, chose not to introduce a federal bill, instead opting for a non-binding federal referendum. The referendum passed, 51.3 percent to 48.7 percent, in favor of national prohibition.

The result of this was that Prohibition in Canada was instituted on a provincial level instead of a national one. With different provincial priorities, as well as differing ideas on what exactly constituted prohibition, provinces enacted alcohol restrictions according to their own timeline. Prince Edward Island was the first to enact it in 1900, while Quebec waited until 1919, and then quickly repealed it, realizing that Prohibition included breaking up their love affair with wine.

The provincial temperance acts varied, but in general they closed legal drinking establishments and forbade the sale of alcohol for beverage purposes and its possession and consumption except in a private dwelling; in some provinces native wines were exempt. Alcohol could be purchased through government dispensaries for industrial, scientific, mechanical, artistic, sacramental, and medicinal uses. The exemption that would have the largest effect on America was the decision by regional governments to allow distillers and others properly licensed to sell outside the province. It was common for many distilleries to make millions of dollars exporting around the world, and not sell a drop of whiskey within the province that they called home.

The prohibition movement was also picking up steam in the United States. Carrie A. Nation, a member of the Anti-Saloon League, had begun attacking taverns, throwing rocks at and taking hatchets to various bars and drinking establishments across the Midwest. While many in the temperance movement eschewed her tactics, it became an effective way of getting her story into newspapers across the country. Many more people were exposed to the temperance movement, and as a political movement, it swelled. The political forces involved were mostly religious in nature. Prohibition was demanded by the "Drys," which consisted mostly of people of the conservative Protestant denominations, those who were to evolve into the Evangelical Christian movement and influence politics in America through the early twenty-first century.

The Drys identified saloons as dens of the politically corrupt and held to the belief that drinking was a personal sin. They were opposed by the "Wets," made up of more liberal Protestants (such as German Lutherans) and even conservative Roman Catholics, who believed that the government should not define morality, let alone codify it. Of course their position came from one of jealousy, as the church felt that only they had that right.

The difficulty the Wets had was that the Drys had other issues that they were involved in. Many of the Drys were also carrying the banner of women's suffrage. African American labor activists believed that prohibition could help the workers of the lower classes with regard to civil rights. Even tea merchants and soda fountain manufacturers generally supported prohibition, thinking a ban on alcohol would increase sales of their products.

As a group, they Drys became a political force not to be ignored. They did not discover lawmaking, but they were certainly experts in the process.

From the mid 1870s until 1919, the Drys crafted their message, first by asking folks to limit their intake of drink and making statements along the lines of "Drinking ale and beer is okay, but hard liquor is out." Soon they were pushing the local option, saying it was a city/county/state's right to prohibit the sale and production of any sort of alcohol.

When they couldn't get a politician to see their point of view, they stocked various councils, legislatures, and state houses with those who did advocate temperance and later prohibition to counter the opposing position. The issue became a rural versus urban debate, with city politicians being painted as elite sophisticates, unable to see the evil they were defending. Debates soon devolved into issues involving morality, and in-depth discussion about alcoholism and alcohol abuse were lost in the din. Many states became dry, not because the majority of citizens preferred it, but because the Dry minority controlled the state congress. Alabama, Arkansas, Georgia, Idaho, New Hampshire, Texas, Utah, Mississippi, and Tennessee were voted dry without putting the issue to a popular vote. Iowa became the first state to have the legislators vote the state dry, while the citizens voted against prohibition in a separate referendum vote.

It was a costly half century for the supporters of the hundred or so temperance unions that peppered the land. A conservative estimate of the contributions made by church groups and individuals in support of temperance and prohibition during this period places the amount at roughly $50,000,000.

But the laws and drinking habits of the people of America were miles apart. For example, in 1870, fifty years before Prohibition, 35.5 million Americans had a per capita consumption of alcohol (beer, wine, and liquor) of 7.7 gallons annually. By 1914, 100 million Americans were drinking 22.5 gallons annually. The words being preached by the temperance unions were not being heard by the general population.

The Great War directly and indirectly increased support for national prohibition. With Germany as an enemy, many of the German Lutherans who were supporting the Wets came under suspicion. With the Wets' input either ignored or openly dismissed, the Drys' influence reached its apex.

The presidential campaign of 1916 saw both Democratic incumbent Woodrow Wilson and Republican candidate Charles Evans Hughes trying to avoid the prohibition issue. The Democratic and Republican platforms contained no position statement on the subject. Both parties had Wet and Dry factions within, and no one wanted to risk alienating any part of their base.

When election day came, the Drys trounced the Wets. As the 65th United States Congress met at the beginning of the session in March of 1917, the Drys controlled the congress by over a two-to-one advantage.

It was the Anti-Saloon League's Wayne Wheeler who conceived and drafted the prohibition bill. Wheeler, the attorney and general counsel for the Anti-Saloon League and its de facto leader, wielded considerable political power. Andrew Volstead, chairman of the House Judiciary Committee, served as the legislation's sponsor and facilitator and oversaw its passage through Congress.

On August 1, 1917, the United States Senate adopted a resolution for submitting a prohibition amendment to the Constitution. On December 17, the House of Representatives, by a vote of 242 to 128, adopted a resolution for an amendment to the Constitution prohibiting liquor traffic. Congress sent the amendment to the states for ratification, where it needed three-fourths approval. The amendment stipulated a time limit of seven years for the states to pass this amendment. Within thirteen months a sufficient number of states had said yes to secure ratification of the amendment that would prohibit the manufacture, sale, and transportation of alcoholic liquors.

Multiple breweries and distilleries throughout America immediately shut down. In Kentucky alone, thirty-three bourbon distilleries shut their doors, never to reopen. The story was the same in western Pennsylvania, where many of the producers of rye whiskeys closed down.

Some companies tried to survive outside the United States. Waterfill and Frazier, of Tyrone, Kentucky, moved to Mexico in order to make a go of it. Schenley brands diversifed, and reestablished their headquarters in Canada, with the hopes of coming back to the States if Prohibition were ever to be repealed.

Meanwhile, black marketers took over the whiskey business. Some folks tried their hand at making their own spirits, which they sold to others as "moonshine," "white lightning," or "white dog." While some called this bathtub gin, if they used a grain as their base, and allowed it to distill to less than 70 percent alcohol by volume, the spirit would have technically been a whiskey.

The moonshiners of the American South had a resource that the Irish and Scottish smugglers of the eighteenth century did not: the automobile. The lucrative trade of illicit whiskey provided them the resources to purchase the cars they needed to deliver their drink to their customers. The rebellious nature of the citizens of Appalachia, so present in the late 1700s, resurfaced, and a culture of illicit whiskey making and whiskey running became prevalent, lasting several years longer than Prohibition itself.

The moonshine runners started buying bigger and better cars, designed for speed and often modified to outrun the revenuers looking to shut down the production and smuggling of the whiskey. It became a point of pride to have the car that delivered the most alcohol, or clocked in at the fastest speed. Soon some of the runners began holding races to see who had the fastest car. These contests evolved into present-day stock car racing and the NASCAR circuit.

Much like home-brewed whiskeys of the past, many homemade whiskeys were of dubious quality, oftentimes produced with an eye for the quick buck. If one wanted quality in one's illicit whiskey, one had to buy from places that had no fear of American revenue agents. Places such as Canada and Scotland.

Due to the loophole introduced in the various laws on the books in Canada, distillers could sell to anyone who was exporting the product. The Canadian whiskey distilleries who were in close proximity to the American border soon found themselves playing host to an influx of tourists and businessmen of various classes and questionable backgrounds. In the first full year of prohibition, 900,000 cases of Canadian spirits were "exported" to the United States.

The smuggling trade was heaviest across Lakes Ontario and Erie in the early days of Prohibition. Hiram Walker, being directly across the river from Detroit, and Gooderham & Worts, located directly on the shore of Lake Ontario, were both particularly well situated to take advantage of this influx of dubious trade. Thousands of gallons of whiskey left these distilleries and ended up in the United States. Many customs officials on both sides of the border turned a blind eye after a decent bribe.

For a "businessman" to purchase Canadian whiskey, all that was needed was a BN-13 customs form stating intent to export the liquor purchased at the distillery, and the country to which it was being exported. If these two items were filled in, the distillery would load you up, regardless of the validity of the claims. At Hiram Walker, there's a tale about a smuggler who showed up in a rowboat, a document in his hand that said he was on his way to Jamaica. By law, Hiram Walker could not deny him his alcohol. The method of transportation was the small rowboat, and since the Detroit River eventually drains out into the Atlantic Ocean, which provides access to Jamaica, this met all of the requirements that the Canadian government needed to allow export.

Hearing about the large amounts of money smugglers were making, elements of organized crime soon became ensconced in the bootlegging business. Turf wars developed over locations that had easy access to Canada, or even over who had "rights" to specific distilleries.

Al Capone, based out of Chicago, seized upon this opportunity to make his name in organized crime, and established his fortune in bootlegging. He forged a business alliance with Sam and Harry Bronfman, who were manufacturing liquor in Saskatchewan after Prohibition had ended there in 1924. Reports of Capone making deals at Hiram Walker, Gooderham & Worts, and Seagrams have become part of the lore of each company.

Adding to America's smuggling problems was the fact that by the time of Prohibition in the United States, Canada was figuring out that its version wasn't working out. People claimed that it violated British traditions of personal liberty. Others stated that the referendum went against standard Canadian protocol of adding laws. Quebec rejected prohibition in 1919 and became popular with scores of tourists from the United States. People flocked to "historic old Quebec" and the provincial government reaped huge profits from the sale of alcohol.

In 1920, British Columbia voted "wet." Manitoba voted into place a system of government sale and control in 1923. Ditto for Alberta and Saskatchewan in 1924, and Newfoundland in 1925. Ontario and New Brunswick followed suit in 1927, as did Nova Scotia in 1930. As the various provinces added alcohol back to their bars, taverns, and store shelves, Americans close to the Canadian border soon found reasons to visit the Great White North.

In western Canada, liquor, mostly grain whiskey, was smuggled from several locations in the prairie provinces of Alberta and Saskatchewan. People in British Columbia got into smuggling liquor via shipping containers and cargo vessels into the states of Washington, Oregon, and California. Vancouver became the gateway for Canadian whiskey into the western states of America. Ships would leave Vancouver, travel south, and unload their cargo onto smaller American-owned crafts while still in international waters.

As the Prohibition era progressed, customs officials from both America and Canada became more diligent in their duties, and began to shut down the border smuggling. But the smugglers simply changed their tactics. The Canadian distillers exported their products legally to the French islands of St. Pierre and Miquelon, located off southern Newfoundland. There they could sell their products to French middlemen, and left the business of getting the product to the American market to the smugglers and bootleggers. With documentation in hand stating that they were off to such destinations as Cuba, the Bahamas, or Belize, the smugglers would instead head out to sea, where, just like the smugglers from British Columbia, once in international waters, they would unload the liquor into smaller, faster boats. These smaller boats would then deliver their wares, usually in the dead of night, to a variety of points on the Eastern seaboard between Boston and Atlantic City, New Jersey.

Canada was not the only country to take advantage of Prohibition in America. The Scottish saw a large increase in blended whiskey sales, particularly in their exports to North America. Though initially Prohibition resulted in a massive decline in Scotch whiskey sales, once the Scottish distillers saw how the Canadians were making money, they soon joined the gray market to fill America's demand.

Other distilleries made money selling whiskey legally into the United States market as medicine. Several bourbons and Scotch whiskeys were sold by pharmacies in America, chief among them Laphroaig, so heavily peated that regulators in America couldn't imagine anyone drinking it of his own free will.

There were many areas of the United States in which the Volstead Act was enforced with popular support. In the rural South and West, community standards and culture ensured that Prohibition was effective, and this has continued even up to the present day. However, these successes contrasted starkly against the failure of prohibition in other parts of the country. In big cities the law was flagrantly, and sometimes violently, defied. In smaller, blue-collar towns, the law was simply ignored.

In 1928, President Herbert Hoover made a campaign pledge to appoint a commission to investigate the effectiveness of Prohibition if he were reelected. When he won, he followed up on his pledge. In 1931, the commission summarized its findings, stating, "There have been more sustained pressures to enforce this law than on the whole has been true of any other federal statute, although this pressure in the last four or five years has met with increasing resistance as the sentiment against prohibition has developed." Without the support of the people, they continued, enforcement of Prohibition was near impossible. Yet the commission concluded that it did not support the repeal of the Eighteenth Amendment.

It took the election of Franklin Roosevelt to push the issue into Congress. On December 6, 1932, Senator John Blaine of Wisconsin submitted a resolution to Congress proposing the submission to the states of the Twenty-first Amendment, which would annul the Eighteenth. Two months later, on February 21, 1933, the following was sent to the state governors:

> **Section 1.** The eighteenth article of amendment to the Constitution of the United States is hereby repealed.
>
> **Section 2.** The transportation or importation into any State, Territory, or possession of the United States for delivery or use there in of intoxicating liquors, in violation of the laws thereof, is hereby prohibited.
>
> **Section 3.** This article shall be inoperative unless it shall have been ratified as an amendment to the Constitution by conventions in the several States, as provided in the Constitu-

tion, within seven years from the date of the submission hereof to the States by the Congress.

Less than a year after the Twenty-first Amendment was submitted for ratification, the necessary thirty-sixth state ratified the amendment at 5:32 p.m. on December 5, 1933. At 7:00 p.m., President Roosevelt signed the proclamation ending Prohibition.

7

Obsession Awakening

After all of the journeys we had taken thus far, and after all of the eras of whiskey covered, Krysta and I were finally ready to get acquainted with bourbon. Or reacquainted, in my case, for it was Jim Beam white label that I had intimate knowledge of as I pretended to be interested in college and my oh-ever-so-useful communications media degree. There were many nights during my tenure at Indiana University of Pennsylvania where I was more interested in how I was going to be able to make it to the bar for happy hour for one-dollar whiskey sours flavored heavily by Clermont, Kentucky's most popular beverage, than I was in writing my term paper regarding the importance of Marshall McLuhan. Sorry, Mr. McLuhan, but Mr. Beam provides a more compelling, if less mature, argument for a misspent young adulthood.

There's a perception about bourbon, which the liquor industry is far too eager to encourage, that the heritage of the Kentucky spirit marks it as the American whiskey, as pure as baseball, state fairs, and capitalism. The truth is that while bourbon has been made in one form or another in northern Kentucky since the late 1700s, the dominance of bourbon in the American whiskey market didn't really begin until after Prohibition and World War II.

This is why I waited so long until suggesting we head to the Bluegrass State. It didn't seem appropriate to visit until I had covered the reasons and areas that had allowed bourbon to become America's whiskey in the latter half of the twentieth century.

But the question that was most difficult to answer was this: Which bourbon distillery to visit first?

Jim Beam seemed the obvious choice, as it's the most popular, and they market the fact their brand has seen seven generations of the Beam family work at the company. But the Jim Beam brand, as we know it today, didn't start until 1934, after Prohibition.

That left Buffalo Trace. Their distillery and bottling plant can be traced back as far as 1865 (further, if we are to believe the lore told on the distillery tour), and the company was able to remain open during Prohibition as a bottler of medicinal whiskey. No other bourbon company today has as much evidence to support its claims to have been operating between 1920 and 1932.

Krysta and I arrived in Leestown, just outside Frankfort, Kentucky, at ten o'clock in the morning. What met us was unexpected— a scene of unmistakable industry. The Buffalo Trace Distillery was the first industrial-scale whiskey company that actually looked and promoted itself like an industry. The site boasted seventy-odd buildings, each with distinctive architecture, yet mismatched against the others, as each was built in a different time frame. Unlike the distilleries of Ireland and Scotland, these places were made neither with an aesthetic in mind nor with a nod toward pleasing any consumer who happened to walk onto the campus. This was a place where people made things, not where tourists came in to be coddled.

At least that's what I thought until we walked into the visitors' center.

"How y'all doin'?"

"We're doing great!" said an upbeat Krysta. "We'd like two for the tour." She plopped down the requisite money.

The tour at the Trace was . . . okay. It was good. But perhaps now that we were closing in on a dozen distilleries visited, new information was unlikely to be forthcoming. They showed a video that explained the process of distillation and (more importantly) killed ten minutes. We were shown the historical pictures of the company, which only muddled the ownership picture of Buffalo Trace. If my powers of observation and listening serve me, Buffalo Trace started out as Blanton's, then moved on to O.F.C., Old Taylor, George T. Stagg, Schenley (who were looking for a place to move from the Pittsburgh area), George Dickel, Ancient Age, and Leestown Distillers, until finally they were purchased by the Sazerac Company, which still owns them today. This company had changed hands more often than a bootleg copy of a Pearl Jam live performance.

It wasn't until we hit the barrel house that the tour deviated from the standard script followed by most. Sure, they highlighted the old barrels that were being stored. But they also were showing barrels that were filled with types of whiskey that Krysta and I had yet to come across in our journeys.

"You will see, on this row of barrels here, where Buffalo Trace is attempting to find new tastes and flavors of whiskey to sell to the public," said our matronly tour guide, who had led us around on this bright, shining morning. There, in barrels, was a bourbon made with corn and rice.

I nudged Krysta and mouthed, "Riced bourbon?!?"

"I know!" she mouthed back, her eyes as wide as my own.

Next to it was a whiskey that started off as a bourbon until it had been put in a sherry cask to finish, a practice common in Scotland, but less so in America. Next to that was a whiskey that was being finished in a cabernet cask. I stood there, awestruck by both the rarity of the whiskey in front of us as well as the temerity of Buffalo Trace to show whiskeys that might never see the marketplace.

I still am unsure what happened to me on that chilly yet sunny morning in Kentucky. But somewhere in the back of my head a switch clicked on that said: "I must have a bottle of one of these!"

It had to happen eventually, I suppose. There was going to be a point where I succumbed to the desire of "having to have," that driving force that makes a person cave into the dreaded "impulse buying." When it comes to the whiskey world, this typically means getting your hands on a bottle of something rare or new, no matter what the cost. There's not many things I know in this world. I know I have to pay taxes, I know I'll die at some point. And at that point at Buffalo Trace, I knew that I was going to leave Frankfort with a bottle of one of these whiskeys.

We walked into the bottling room, and all I could think of was this whiskey. The tour guide showed us how they check for impurities in their whiskey, and my mind was lost to the taste of whiskey finished in a cabernet cask. As Krysta took photos of the visitors' center, my mind raced ahead to the upcoming whiskey tasting, hoping that they would offer us a sip of this drink.

As we walked into the tasting room, I noted that no test product was available. They offered us a shot of Buffalo Trace, which I accepted gladly, as well as some vodka and other liquors sold by the Sazerac company. But no test products were to be found.

I examined my options. Perhaps we had to ask to purchase the whiskey. This was okay by me.

After the tour was completed and we had thanked the tour guide, I tracked down Meredith Moody, the marketing services director for Buffalo Trace.

"So, uh . . . it was a very nice tour," I said to her as she asked me about my book project. "Say . . . uh . . . do you happen to have any of those finished whiskeys for sale? Perhaps some on site for a tasting?"

I felt as subtle as a lounge lizard. She looked at me sadly, perhaps with even a little pathos.

"No. Unfortunately we have sent them all out into the marketplace," she replied.

She must have noticed my disappointment, for she quickly added: "However, there are some being sold nearby. There's a place called Capital Cellars, about a mile down the . . ."

"How do I get there?" I asked, interrupting her. She smiled and gave me detailed directions.

Ten minutes later, Krysta and I walked into Capital Cellers and scoped out the joint. A bottle of the cabernet whiskey was nowhere to be seen. I looked at the woman behind the wine tasting bar.

"Do you carry bottles of the wine-finished Buffalo Trace?" I asked hopefully. The petite woman smiled and said, "Of course!" and pulled down two bottles off the bar behind her. She started to pour a glass.

"No. No. Do you have bottles for sale?" I asked.

She looked at me glumly. "No. We've already presold all of our allotments." Crestfallen, I looked at the glasses in front of me. It was either this or nothing at all, as we had to leave for Tennessee in less than thirty minutes. "We'll have the drinks," I told her.

"This is Kate," Krysta said to the petite woman. "She's writing a book on whiskey." Once again, she played the "We're doing research" card. The woman behind the counter returned the introduction with a smile. "Hi, I'm Rachael," she said.

We began to talk about whiskey. We talked of the places we had been, and Rachael talked of her time working for . . . Buffalo Trace. The world once again showed how small it actually was. She poured us a glass of 6-year and 8-year cabernet franc whiskey.

A group of three middle-aged women overheard us talk about the book. The one closest to me turned and asked, "You're writing about bourbon?"

"Well, whiskey in general," I responded.

She laughed. "There are two things that a woman from Kentucky knows. The first is horses. The second, how to drink bourbon." All three of the women turned to us and we began a friendly conversation about drinking.

Soon Krysta and I were the center of the universe of Capital Cellars, exchanging bon mots and drinks with the group of women. I offered the women the opportunity to taste the cabernet-finished drink and we all commented upon what we liked about it and what we didn't.

As I was taking my third sip from the glass of six-year-old, Rachael came up to me and said, "You're not going to believe this. I just got an e-mail from one of the people who had reserved a bottle of this whiskey. He canceled his preorder, as he was able to pick it up from somewhere else."

I slammed my credit card down on the bar.

Rachael smiled. "I take it you want it?"

Buffalo Trace Whiskey Finished in a Cabernet Cask, 6-Year-Old (Available as a Special Order Only)
Buffalo Trace offers these special releases to only a handful of folks, so they are a rarity in the marketplace. I've always been a sucker for novelty.

Nose: The aroma leaves no doubt that this whiskey had seen a wine cask. A deep red grape aroma is matched with a nice floral bouquet.

Taste: Starts like a cola with orange bitters becoming prevalent soon afterward. The taste of the cask (both cabernet and oak) peeks its head through every now and then.

Finish: Long and with the taste of dark honey.

Character: This whiskey is like the friend of yours in college who liked to buy her clothing from thrift shops, and listened to New Order and The Replacements. Always seemed a fair bit different from everyone else. Very book smart, but had trouble communicating with those whose tastes were more mainstream.

I nodded like a child who had been asked if she wanted a cookie.

As we left, I turned to Krysta. "Do we have perfect timing or what?" This good karma from sharing the drink must have paid off. I was now a proud owner of a rare, fifty-dollar bottle of whiskey. I beamed for the rest of the day. The only question surrounding my purchase was that I did not know if I was going to drink it or save it.

Bourbon is the only American whiskey that found itself in an advantageous position after Prohibition had ended. Thirteen years was a long time for people to recall the history of a product that had all but disappeared, at least officially, from the public's consciousness. So once people had forgotten about the history of whiskey distilleries not located in Kentucky, bourbon marketers were quick to point out that their whiskey had been around since the start of the country, completely glossing over or even downright ignoring the evidence that there were whiskeys out there prior to Prohibition that not only were as popular as bourbon but in some cases even more so.

Many people believe that bourbon is the be-all and end-all of American whiskey history. Marketers, seeking to take advantage of this belief, have created ad campaigns and whiskey brands that cement these claims, ending in an almost infinite loop of marketers inventing history, the public believing it, and then marketers making more claims based on the history previously created.

This has left us Americans with a whiskey past that is more legend than fact. There are beliefs surrounding bourbon that need a quick dispelling. For example:

Bourbon is a blend of whiskey made of a mash of greater than 50 percent corn that has been aged in a newly charred barrel: It is now, thanks in large part to a law implemented in the late 1940s, but prior to Prohibition, there was no explicit requirement calling for the use of either corn whiskey or new barrels. The United States Pharmacopoeia had a regulation during Prohibition that stipulated that whiskey to be used for medicinal purposes had to be matured for four years, but that's as close as anyone got to legally defining an aging requirement. It was mostly tradition that dictated the bourbon recipe, and tradition often is altered on an individual basis to fit specific needs and resources. Many bourbons of the 1800s could not be labeled as such today.

Bourbon was invented by the Reverend Elijah Craig: The truth is that many farms in Kentucky were distilling in the late 1700s, and they all were using the grains on hand. Corn happened to be more plentiful and, thus, cheaper. Every farm in Kentucky during this period could and should lay claim to bourbon's history.

Bourbon is named after Bourbon County in Kentucky: Actually, as we have seen, it was likely named after the port where it hit the ships that were going downriver.

In other words, bourbon was just like any other American whiskey of the time. There were good ones and bad ones. It was likely that some bourbon was sold close to its departure from the still and never saw a day in a barrel. Others were put in barrels and shipped down the Ohio and Mississippi Rivers.

What really defined bourbon, as we know today, was how the Kentucky distillers responded after Prohibition. When many larger distilleries from other parts of the country had found homes and profits in other countries, this left a bit of a corporate vacuum in the American whiskey industry. It was the perfect environment for smaller distilleries to reestablish themselves.

The next morning we found ourselves in Bardstown, Kentucky, at the Bourbon Heritage Center, which sounds as if it is Kentucky's equivalent to the Scotch Whisky Heritage Centre that we had visited while in Edinburgh. In truth, it's more of an extension of the Heaven Hill brands of whiskey and liquor that they are responsible for.

Bardstown is a small town about forty miles south of Louisville. It proudly proclaims itself the bourbon capital of the world, when, in fact, the only bourbon distilled in Bardstown is by Barton Brands, which produces brands that don't really roll off the tongue of the general public, unless you happen to be a fan of such Kentucky bourbons as Barclay and Ten High. Jim Beam, the world's most popular bourbon, is distilled fifteen miles away, and in fact Heaven Hill *doesn't* distill in Bardstown, preferring to do so in Louisville, and then ship to Bardstown for bottling.

But as Bardstown is sorta-kinda centralized for all of the northern Kentucky distilleries, has a rich history of distilling, and has the small-town feel that the liquor wishes to be associated with, several Kentucky bourbon distilleries have adopted it as their own.

Heaven Hill itself became a bourbon distiller in 1934, after Prohibition. Today it's the world's second largest holding of aging Kentucky bourbon, and is the largest bourbon producer that is independently run and owned by the Shapira family, which has operated it since they opened their doors. They are also, they say proudly, the largest producer of bourbon distilled by someone named 'Beam,' as Jim Beam is represented by Fred Noe, and Parker Beam is the master distiller at Heaven Hill.

All of this we found out while walking around the Bourbon Heritage Center, waiting for Lynne Grant and Larry Kass to give us a brief tour of the place.

The tour had to be brief, as the distillery was forty miles away in the thriving metropolis that is Louisville. So we sat and went over the history of Heaven Hill with Larry, walked over to one of the many barrel houses they have on location, and then did a tasting led by Lynne.

Both Krysta and I were taken aback by Lynne's Scottish accent.

"You're not from around here, are you?" I asked.

Lynne laughed. "No. Heaven Hill hired me away from Glenturret."

"Home of The Famous Grouse?" asked Krysta.

She nodded.

"Wait a minute, wait a minute. You're responsible for the 'The Famous Grouse Experience'?" I asked. In my mind, I replayed the horror that was the interactive dancing with the anthropomorphic game bird.

"Yes, yes!" she responded. "That was me."

I looked at her, unable to determine whether I should hate her or not. As she was the one who was going to lead us in the tasting, I decided to silently forgive her.

She led us to the tasting room that was in the center of the gift shop. A circular room shaped to give the impression of the inside of a barrel, it was a warm, inviting place. Of course this could have been my own bias, based on the anticipation of the bourbon we were about to consume. The bar was also circular and able to accommodate two dozen people comfortably, giving the room a slight impression of the war room from *Dr. Strangelove*.

We sat at the bar, where we drank selected bourbons: Old Fitzgerald, Evan Williams Single Barrel Vintage, and Elijah Craig 18-year-old Single Barrel. Heaven Hill has no shortage of bourbons to sell to the general consumer. If you see Cabin Still, J. W. Dant, Echo Spring, Mattingly & Moore, J. T. S. Brown, T. W. Samuels, Kentucky Deluxe, or Kentucky Supreme, all of them come from Heaven Hill.

Out of all of the bourbons we tasted, there was one that made me very, very happy: Parker Beam's Heritage Collection. It's bottled at cask strength, which means that it's typically sold at a higher alcohol content than your average bourbon. Cask strength whiskey is essentially a whiskey that has not had water added to it after aging. As a whiskey ages and gets ready to be bottled, water is sometimes added in order to get the whiskey down to the magical 80 proof line. Cask strength whiskeys work under the assumption that added water detracts from the overall flavor, and that leaving the whiskey "as is" before it enters the bottle doesn't adulterate the flavor.

This has become what's known in the marketing biz as a "thing"—something that allows the company to up-sell the whiskey and mark up its price by a few dollars to get even more profit from the customer.

The problem lies in the fact that, depending upon a consumer's taste buds, alcohol is an anesthetic. As we have seen, if one were to have a drink and a sniff of a whiskey with too high of a proof, the taste buds and nasal receptors would become numb. And when these become numb, tasting—true tasting—becomes nigh impossible. The only way to prevent this from happening is to add water to the whiskey, and bring it down to a point where the alcohol doesn't numb the senses.

However, there are a few knuckleheads out there who don't understand the above issue. When they hear that water has been added to a whiskey, they look at you as if you just spat on a holy book. To them, let me say this clearly: If you want to taste a cask strength whiskey, you almost always have to add water. In fact, in the course of our travels, we've talked and drunk with dozens of whiskey professionals, from master distillers to professional tasters to shop owners. Every single one added some water to his drink. Not one ever drank it straight. Of course, the amount of water differed, but water was always added.

So what is the big deal surrounding cask strength whiskeys? From my experience, once you deal with the excess alcohol properly, what is there is a whiskey that is far more complex in flavor than what one typically finds on the bottom shelf of your liquor store. This is why I think that cask strength whiskeys deserve attention— not because they are a higher proof.

Parker's Heritage Collection Bourbon was the cask strength whiskey that caught my attention at Heaven Hill, and I had no problem in shelling out the $130 dollars for it after we had completed our tasting and said our good-byes to Larry and Lynne. As we taste tested it in the barrel room, this was the one that I was drawn to. I've found that some bourbons push their oaky flavors too far. Other distilleries strive to keep their spirits out of the barrels for an extended period of time due to this same fear. This bottle pushes that time limit as far as it can go, and the flavor never becomes excessively woody. It was one of the more complex bourbons I had come across in our journeys.

After we had parted ways with our hosts, we scoured the gift shop, where I quickly found the bottle encased in a leather bag. The bottle itself was autographed by Parker Beam. I took it up to the counter and paid for it in full.

As Krysta was looking at a shelf full of bourbon-flavored barbe-cue sauce, I showed the bottle to her. She nodded.

"You do know that you've spent close to two hundred dollars on two bottles of whiskey in the past two days."

I nodded back. Of course I knew. It was my debit card that had the skid marks upon it.

"Kate . . . ," Krysta paused, either out of concern or for effect. Either way, it caught my attention. "That's two hundred dollars . . . for two bottles."

Again, I nodded at her, this time more emphatically, as if that would convince her that I understood.

It was only then that it hit me. I had spent the equivalent of a modest stereo on liquor. My mind went quickly down a list of prod-ucts. With the money I spent, I could have bought seven compact disks, paid for thee months of cable television, or purchased a new computer monitor.

My eyes went glassy. I nearly dropped my bottle, which most as-suredly would have broken if not for the inlaid leather gift bag with extra padding that it came in. It was then that I realized what Krysta was trying to say. I had become Ms. Disposable Income, albeit on a smaller scale. Over the course of the past two days, I had desired two different bottles of whiskey, and had paid what some might con-sider to be an excessive amount of money for them.

I opened the leather inlaid bag, took out the bottle, and looked

Parker's Heritage Collection Cask Strength Bourbon

This is Heaven Hill's specialty small batch bourbon, sold without adding water in between the time it was removed from the barrel and bottled.

Nose: Hot and spicy, with a fair amount of oak present.

Taste: The oak is there, ever present, but it's not the dominant flavor. There's the sweetness of brown sugar, with raisin as well. There is also a bit of black tea in the flavor, supported with the tannins from the barrel.

Finish: Oak competing with a caramel/butterscotch sweetness for several minutes afterward.

Character: A heavyweight boxer who can show both agility and pure power. Can slug you as well as simply tire you out with continual jabs. Quite complex but also fun. This is the Muhammad Ali of whiskey.

at it. Was it worth it? Did I now understand what was going on in the head of the gentleman in Surrey?

As we drove back to our hotel by the Louisville Airport, I took stock of the situation. Yes, I had taken on some expense in the past two days. And perhaps, yes, two hundred dollars could be seen as an extravagance.

But I was doing research.

Somewhere in the back of my mind, a voice spoke up. "Using research is a cop-out. You're using it as rationalization for a purchase that you can't justify. You don't need two more bottles of whiskey when you already have thirty at home."

I silently told the voice to shut the hell up.

8

Small Batches and the Big Stage

The hotel still smelled of evil, but by our last day in Louisville, it was a manageable evil. At least the hotel staff recognized that the smell was apparent to all and tried to drown it in lemon-scented disinfectant.

Krysta and I packed the car, as we had one distillery to visit and then a three-hour drive to Nashville, where we were to stay before our subsequent trip to the whiskey areas of southeastern Tennessee.

It's a rough life, getting up at five a.m. in order to be in the car by seven, and then casually driving to breakfast before heading out to various whiskey distilleries. By now, Krysta and I were well versed in our routine—find an interesting eatery, discuss the itinerary, look over Krysta's tour book to see if there was anything interesting to do that was not whiskey-related, and then drive to our destination. Today our first destination was Woodford Reserve, a small batch bourbon distillery found in the rolling hills of Kentucky horse country, just outside of the city of Versailles.

"Ten to one it's pronounced 'ver-SAILS,'" I said to Krysta as we got closer to the distillery.

She nodded her disagreement. "No way. That's too back-country, even for Kentucky. Besides, they pronounce the 'Louis' in 'Louisville' the French way."

"Maybe. But my money is on them doing things their own way, not the way the French do them." I said. I had been around enough small American towns in my life to know their limitations in acknowledging namesakes properly.

"I think we should turn here," Krysta said. I was traveling down a back road looking for an unmarked road.

"Are you sure?" I said. We had forgone renting a GPS in the States, under the theory that we could find proper directions using both Google Maps and local map books. The benefit was that we would save about sixty dollars, and considering Molly's track record in Ireland, it made logistical sense as well.

Thirty minutes later, we found ourselves retracing our steps, trying to discern exactly where Google Maps had pointed us in the wrong direction. No matter which way we took, it seemed that we eventually ended up in downtown Versailles, which, while pretty, was notable mostly for the fact that Woodford Reserve was not located there.

If there's one trait that Krysta and I share, it's that we both need to be in control of our environments. Where we diverge is that Krysta likes to change hers through direct, precise, and near-constant alterations. I like a slower, more organic approach, affecting variables far earlier in the decision-making process, and then let things sort of "happen." This gives the impression that I have little input into what is going on, when, in fact, a fair amount of work went into getting things to happen exactly the way I wished them to. Krysta's approach allowed for quick improvisations when unaccounted-for variables appeared, such as closed roads due to construction, or finding new restaurants when initial choices were found to be closed. My approach set the long-term schedules, such as "We should be in Ireland on this date, and we should be in Kentucky on this one."

While these contrary approaches worked well for the most part of the trip, we did have to make a few accommodations. We found that it was better to let the person who rented the car drive it, rather than debate whose turn it was. We also allowed for the fact that the person who wasn't driving needed some responsibility, and thus she was in charge of navigation and music.

A failure in both of the maps had frayed both of our nerves. It was a variable that I had not accounted for, nor could Krysta's improvisational skills fix it.

"Okay, this is the third time that we've passed this intersection," I said, my frustration clearly beginning to show. Krysta stewed silently, letting me vocalize my displeasure, knowing that adding to it would only exacerbate the situation.

Not that it was horrible being lost in this area of the country. Horse farms dotted the landscape, with expensive barns and stables announcing to everyone that the people here had money to spare. What was missing from the horse farms was any sign of horses, to which Krysta mused that they were likely under strict regimens of diet and exercise, so it was unlikely that we would see any out in the fields unsupervised.

I did what I often do when things aren't going as planned. I let out an extended, passive-agressive sigh.

"We could ask someone how to get there," Krysta offered in a precise, well-controlled tone. It was in stark contrast to my own.

"No," I thought to myself. "I do not want to get other people involved." My rational mind kicked me in the back of my head. "You do not know where you are going," it told me. I decided to compromise. I stopped the car.

"Let me think about this for a second." I gathered my wits and regained a bit of composure. I took inventory of our surroundings.

"Okay, we know that the distillery is nearby. Where, exactly, we don't know," I said. Krysta agreed.

"The maps are worthless. They got us here, but that's where their value ended. So what do we know about Woodford Reserve?"

Krysta thought for a moment. "It's a distillery."

"Okay. So what do we know about distilleries?"

We both looked outside of the car for inspiration. Thoughts that were running in my head included a distillery's need for grain, a need for storage, a need for water . . .

"The creek!" Krysta yelled at the same time that I thought about it. Google had us cross a creek several miles back and turn right at an intersection after crossing it. What if it we had made a wrong turn. Was it as simple as that?

I put the car into gear. "Shall we follow the creek in the other direction?"

Krysta smiled at me by way of agreement. We got to the intersection where we had been told to turn right, and took the left turn instead. Several moments later, lo and behold, we found the entrance to the old Labrot & Graham Distillery, better known today as Woodford Reserve.

After I'd parked the car, three things became apparent. One, the stress of being lost went away immediately, as I find that the promise of bourbon does wonders to allay tension.

Two, the industrial environment so prevalent at places such as Buffalo Trace and Heaven Hill was nowhere to be seen. In its stead was a rolling estate, more akin to the pastoral distilleries of Scotland. The lawns were well manicured, the buildings well taken care of, and the visitors' center looked as if it could have been plucked from one of the several horse farms we passed when we were lost in Versailles.

Finally, the Woodford Reserve clientele seemed belong to a breed of people best described as country club folk. They were the types of people who would wear golf clothing without a hint of irony. They looked perfect. They had perfect teeth, perfect haircuts, and spoke with near-perfect diction, with only a trace of their southern drawl still perceptible.

Owned by Brown-Forman, Woodford Reserve provides an interesting contrast to another whiskey in Brown-Forman's stable, Jack Daniel's. Where Jack Daniel's can be considered an "everyman's" whiskey, Woodford Reserve seems to go out of its way to give the appearance of being "exclusive," in several senses of the word.

For starters, it is a small batch bourbon, so it's both higher-priced and harder to come by than the mass-produced bourbons of Jim Beam and Heaven Hill.

But Woodford Reserve is also the official bourbon of both the

Kentucky Derby and the Breeders' Cup, sponsoring both of these premier horse racing events. Considering both Jim Beam and Jack Daniel's sponsor NASCAR racing teams, it's easy to tell what type of person Woodford Reserve is being aimed at—upper- to upper-middle-class folks.

Judging from the pairs of well-pressed khaki slacks being worn by both the clientele and the distillery staff, I'd say their marketing was a success.

As we settled into the bus that was designed to drive us the five hundred yards between the visitors' center and the distillery, Krysta nudged me in the side.

"Does this place strike you as a bit . . . cultish?" she asked.

I shrugged. Sure, the clientele, us excluded, fit into a certain mold, but it was difficult for me to agree that Woodford Reserve did anything except try to make money on their bourbon, making them no different than the multitude of other distilleries out there. Their preference for WASPs was nothing more than a sales strategy, no different from Canadian Club selling their whiskey to blue-collar workers.

The tour guide was an affable older gentleman who looked like a cross between Dick Smothers and Gore Vidal. As we got out of the bus, he put on a small speaker into which a microphone was plugged, and he became his own portable PA system.

"I want to alert you that the first thing you'll notice as we take our tour is that no work is actually going on at the distillery today. Being a small batch bourbon distiller means that you're more often not working than you are. And today is one of those days when we're not."

He shuffled uncomfortably in his shoes, aware of how clumsy his turn of a phrase turned out to be. "Anyways, let's go into this door here, and remember to stay within the yellow lines."

As we started the tour, I thought for a bit about status and whiskey. Due to the many incarnations as well as the huge disparity in quality, whiskey lends itself to defining class and status quite easily. In this regard it has the same characteristics as wine, where one can be judged not just by the types of wine one drinks but also by the way one drinks it.

For whiskey, there are several distinct aspects to which a person can apply status. Price is the most obvious one, with people buying expensive whiskeys without having any knowledge of the quality or circumstances that make these bottles so expensive to begin with. People buy them because they can, and that ability gives them a leg up on a great majority of whiskey drinkers.

Knowledge is also a status setter, and often runs at odds with those who spend money on expensive bottles and drinks. As we have see, nothing exemplifies this better than talking with a whiskey expert about Johnnie Walker Blue. Typical bottles of the Blue Label can run as high as two hundred dollars, and a glass of the stuff can be had at high-end restaurants for one hundred dollars (if not more). In my opinion, it is the quintessential status whiskey. Many people who have only a passing interest in whiskey are aware of Johnnie Walker Blue and how much money the bottle costs.

But if you talk to someone who knows whiskey, the Blue Label will rarely be discussed. It's not that it's a bad whiskey, there are just other, more interesting whiskeys out there to get excited about.

This isn't to say that the connoisseurs know what is going on either. As with every social group, there are still status distinctions, sometimes based on nothing more than one's preference for the amount of water to add to any drink. There are fans of Scotch whiskey who won't let a drop of bourbon pass their lips. Within that group, there are fans of single malts who believe nothing good can ever come from a blended whiskey. Within the single malt group, some fans of the Islays believe that Lowland single malts aren't worthy to be on the same shelf. All in all, it makes for interesting discussions when whiskey experts get together in person or on the Internet. It is no wonder that snobs exist. Taste is subjective, and the sheer variety of whiskeys available allow for multiple interpretations of what makes a great whiskey and what does not.

I felt a familiar elbow nudge me in the side. "Kate!" Krysta hissed. I shook myself out of my train of thought. The tour guide was looking at me expectantly, having opened a path from me to the mash tun. I guessed at what he was asking and walked toward him and looked at the bubbling brew. I took in the aroma held within and smiled.

"Can I stick my finger in?" I asked.

"Oh, yes, yes," the tour guide responded. I poked the mash with my finger and pulled it out, giving my finger a small taste.

"It tastes like weak beer, doesn't it?" asked the guide, as he looked toward the other tourists. I nodded in agreement, not wanting to disrupt his tour. We continued on.

The distillery was beautiful, both from a historical point of view and aesthetically. It was at this location, back when the distillery was run by Oscar Pepper in the 1830s, that Dr. James Crow came up with the "sour mash" process. And it was this process of adding a part of the old mash to the new that many people regard as the moment that bourbon was created, distinguishing itself from other American whiskeys of the time.

As we walked along, the tour guide pointed out the copper pot stills, a rarity among American whiskeys, which tend to use the more efficient patent stills. I stood in awe of the stills, having not seen the likes of these types since Scotland. My respect for their bourbon leapt up by several steps.

The rest of the tour went by quickly. We saw the area where they filled the barrels, then walked over to the storage house, where they kept the casks, and met yet another cat who lurked in a distillery.

Krysta decided to walk back to the visitors' center, giving her the opportunity to take some pictures. I had no shame and entered the bus. As the the rest of the tour group and I went back up the hill, I couldn't shake the idea of how Scottish the Woodford Reserve Distillery felt, regardless of how much they talked up their ties to bourbon, horse racing, or the state of Kentucky. Here was a small brand whiskey, whose sales were so modest that they did not need to operate their stills on a regular basis, and which sat in a remote part of the backwoods. The distillery lacked the industrial feel that had been so pervasive at Buffalo Trace the day before.

I turned in my ticket at the tasting bar for my glass of their bourbon. As I sipped my whiskey, I thought that maybe I was a little tough on the marketing aspects of the spirit. Yes, they did promote themselves as a little exclusive. But in considering both their location and the quality of their bourbon, I thought maybe, just maybe, they had earned the right to be a little snooty. They were different from the Jim Beams of the world, so why not highlight that difference?

"Damn this is good," Krysta said as she placed her glass on the table, her camera hung off her shoulder. I nodded, acknowledging her return.

"Do you feel out of place here?" I asked her.

She looked at me with the look that said that my neuroses were kicking in.

"No, no. That's not what I meant. Take a look at the clientele here," I said.

She glanced around the tasting room, where people were standing on the wood flooring, and looking at the various exhibitions explaining the distillery process.

"What is the one thing they all have in common?" I said, prompting her to remember her earlier comment about the place having a cultish feel.

She shrugged, giving me a confused look. "What? They all like bourbon?"

Woodford Reserve Bourbon
A small batch bourbon from the producers of Jack Daniel's.
Nose: Smells of honey mixed with Werther's Original toffee candy.
Taste: Lightly spiced at first before a nuttiness appears, quickly followed by a light chai.
Finish: Long and yet subtle. Honey, spices, and then the oak.
Character: Woodford is all about finesse and precision, the lightness belying the complexity beneath. This whiskey is akin to a portrait by Al Hirschfeld.

I opened my mouth, looking to press the issue. I quickly shut it, realizing that Krysta's current perception was really the only thing that mattered.

The end of Prohibition did not end the difficulties surrounding the international whiskey industries. The economic depression of the era made it difficult for American distillers to restart their production. With the aging of whiskeys now a required production technique, many companies had to find other streams of income while their product sat in storage, taxed all the while. Imports from Canada and Scotland had no such concerns, as they had never ceased production while America sat dry.

By the time the Americans' product was finally mature enough to hit the market, production had to be stalled due to the sacrifices needed in order to feed a country and provide products for the armed services during wartime.

That's not to say that starting a new whiskey-making company was impossible during the time between 1933 and 1938. In 1933, the old operators of the Clear Spring Distillery in Bardstown looked upon the business venture that had kept them afloat during the lean years of Prohibition. The Sunbeam Quarries company had kept the Clear Spring folks comfortable during those years, but mining rock wasn't where their heart was. They wanted to get back into distilling.

The quarry owners were none other than Jim Beam and his, son T. Jeremiah.

They may have wanted to start up a new distillery, but they did have a bit of a problem. They had no money to start a new venture. So they turned to five Chicago businessmen to invest in their idea. The businessmen were to own the company outright, and the Beams were to run it. On August 14, 1934, the James B. Beam Distilling Company was incorporated.

It was also in the 1930s that whiskey started gaining in popularity in parts of the world other than those influenced by the Scottish and Irish.

Japan had known of whiskey for a few generations, likely when they started trading with the West during the mid 1800s. By 1910, the Japanese were producing "Yoshu"—essentially foreign liquors. Whiskey would have undoubtedly been part of that production.

But it wasn't until Masataka Taketsuru headed to Scotland in 1919 to learn the secrets of whiskey making that Japan got serious about the hows and whats of making scotch-style single malt whiskeys. With help from Shinjiro Torii, they started the modern-day whiskey industry of Japan when they introduced Suntory Shiro-fuda, Japan's first genuine whiskey, in 1929.

By the late 1930s, the imperial armies and navies of Japan were drinking the spirit to such a degree that, when many of the Japanese companies were being asked to make sacrifices during the time of their country's conquests, the Yoichi Distillery was designated a naval installation, and thus was free from sharing the burden of wartime sacrifice. It's likely that the distillery helped in making armaments, but it's also known that they still produced whiskey for the officers of the navy who had sought to protect them.

World War II influenced the whiskey industry in several ways, even when production became limited. This would include exposing many a young man to new and foreign lands. For the U.S. armed forces stationed in Great Britain, this meant exposure to Scotch whiskey. Carrying with them the zeal and appetite so common to young servicemen, they developed a taste for the liquor that they would carry back home.

Conversely, the British armed forces found that Scotch whiskey was the one treat they could count on, regardless of where they were in the world. They exported the virtue of their drink to remote parts of the world. As travel times shrunk, new international consumers of the drink could demand Scotch whiskey and be served by import and export laws that saw the restocking of bars and liquor stores on a regular basis.

After World War II, sales for all liquor increased, and the American market opened to new customers flush with cash from the post-war economic boom. Thirty-eight bourbon distilleries reopened and another fifteen opened for first time.

But it was a different world than that of the bourbon distilleries of the pre-Prohibition era. Whiskeys were competing not in regional but national markets, and sometimes international markets. Jim Beam Brands worked to ensure that the servicemen stationed in postwar Europe and later Korea and Vietnam would have access to whiskey from America. They made sure that their brand was sold wherever possible. Local shopkeepers close to the American bases, keen to make some money off American GIs, also sought out Jim Beam. Between 1952 and 1953, sales in Jim Beam rose thirty percent.

Canadian Club and Seagram's also saw increases in sales in the United States in areas of the country where rye whiskeys once ruled supreme.

But it was the Scotch whiskeys that saw the most significant increase in sales. With the demand of Scotch whiskey from countries that used to be British colonies, the Scotch whiskey industry had an export market already in place.

The more successful companies began buying out their competitors in whiskey and spirits. Some were bought out in the name of diversification, as when Heaven Hill purchased smaller regional whiskeys such as Old Fitzgerald, or Seagram's bought Gordon's Gin. Others were bought out to remove competition from the playing field. In 1987, Jim Beam Brands controversially purchased National Distillers, owners of Old Crow, which happened to be Jim Beam's closest competitor and, until 1970, the world's most popular bourbon. Jim Beam closed their old competitor's distillery so as to make Old Crow at their own place, and then were rumored to have altered the recipe in order to make it less appealing than their own brand.

Smaller independent distilleries, seeing other companies being bought out, looked for ways to distinguish themselves and their brands. Glenfiddich, noting that mostly blends were being sold in the United States and other areas of the world, took a risk and started exporting single malts, and helped foster the age of the international whiskey connoisseur.

Single malt whiskey is a whiskey from one single distillery, made from malted grain, and not blended with whiskey from any other distiller. It was a practice that had never ended in Scotland, even as blended whiskeys had come to dominate the marketplace. For many people outside Scotland, it was a forgotten practice. Once it was rediscovered, whiskey fans found products with deep, complex flavors that differed from year to year. This was far different from the lighter and more predictable flavors offered by the blended brands. The idea of single malts took off worldwide, and they now account for somewhere between 7 and 15 percent of all Scotch whiskey sales.

People sought out the different flavors from different distilleries, and many places in Scotland began to establish reputations for consistently producing interesting flavors. Scotch clubs, where people would get together and share their discoveries, soon became established, and word of mouth helped promote the lesser-known independent brands that were ignored by mainstream wholesalers.

Meanwhile, the era of bourbon had truly begun. By the late forties, the government clarified what defined bourbon—that it must be made in the United States, made of a grain mixture that is at least 51 percent corn, must be distilled to no more than 160 (U.S.) proof, must be 100 percent natural, and must be aged in new, American, charred oak barrels. The last bit was added after influence from Congressional Representatives A. S. J. Carnahan, a Democrat from Missouri, and Cleveland M. Bailey, a Democrat from West Virginia, both of whom represented states with timber companies and cooperage mills.

Bourbon's success after prohibition was completed in 1964, a mere thirty years after Prohibition's repeal, when Congress declared that it was "America's Native Spirit." The influence of rye whiskey was completely forgotten, ignored, or mistakenly thought of as Canadian.

Only one type of whiskey did not initially share in this increased popularity. But even Irish whiskey would get a new life.

At the beginning of the 1960s, the amount of Irish whiskey exported to other countries was statistically insignificant. The remaining distilleries left in Ireland looked to change that. In 1966, John Jameson & Son, Cork Distilleries, and John Power & Son merged to become the United Distillers of Ireland, and then changed their names to Irish Distillers Limited.

They modernized their production techniques, centralized their distilling and bottling at the newly opened Midleton Distillery, and started selling almost nothing but blended whiskeys. Their popularity rose.

Soon larger whiskey companies came looking to buy out the IDL. To prevent a massive buyout, IDL leveraged a deal that would give Seagram's 15 percent ownership; IDL would get Bushmills, which Seagram's owned. Seagram's used its weight to reintroduce Irish whiskey to the rest of the world. By 1988, their influence was still no match for the Scotch whiskey industry, but there was enough potential that Pernod Ricard purchased IDL in a hotly contested sale against Cantrell & Cochrane (which was owned jointly by Allied-Lyons and Guinness). The result? A great majority of Irish whiskey was now owned by the French.

That was until 1987, when the Irish government put up for sale an old Power Methylated Spirits plant located in County Louth, a few miles south of the Northern Ireland border. The government-owned plant found itself producing alcohol for the likes of Smirnoff Vodka, and wished to remove state involvement from such activities. They put the plant up for sale for a mere £106,000. John Teeling purchased it and started Cooley Distillery, creating the first independent Irish distillery in over one hundred years.

But the late twentieth century belonged to the multinational spirit corporations. Companies such as Seagram's, Pernod Ricard, and Fortune Brands ruled the industry. Companies such as Hiram Walker provide a great example of the unsteadiness of the managment of the brands. As of 2008, Hiram Walker was owned by Fortune Brands, owners of the Jim Beam bourbon brand. They were sold to Fortune Brands by Pernod Ricard, who had picked up the distillery when they bought out Allied Domecq. Allied Domecq came into being in 1994 when Allied-Lyons partnered with Pedro Domecq, the leading spirits marketer in Spain and Mexico. Allied-Lyons purchased Hiram Walker in full in 1988. Hiram Walker, as a side note, had purchased Gooderham & Worts in 1927.

Corporations were picking up brands like kids purchasing trading cards. Pernod Ricard owns brands of Scotch whiskey (Aberlour,

The Glenlivet, Chivas, Glendronach, Ballantine's, to name but a few), Irish whiskey (Jameson's, Power's, Midleton), bourbon (Wild Turkey) and Canadian (Walker's Special, Wiser's). Diageo, formed in 1997 when Guinness merged with Grand Metropolitan, has a similar portfolio. In 2000, when Vivendi (previously known as Seagram's) auctioned off Seagram's drink business, their operation consisted of around 250 drinks brands and brand extensions—whiskeys, gins, vodkas, and a variety of other alcoholic and nonalcoholic beverages.

Of the money being made, it is Scotch whiskey that has become king. According to the *Financial Times*, whiskey accounts for thirteen percent of Scottish exports, excluding oil and gas, and services 200 export markets. It makes up about a quarter of the UK's annual food and drink exports. More than 40,000 Scottish jobs depend on whiskey production, including cereal suppliers, bottling, labeling and packaging companies, and transport suppliers. Their success can be attributed too a variety of factors, including the quality of the product, the class status associated with aged single malts, even the climate of Scotland. But in my opinion, the primary reason for their success is self-inflicted setbacks in both Ireland and America. Had the Irish distillers embraced blending, or had America never gone into Prohibition, the whiskey world would be vastly different.

The Scotch Whisky Association knows this and has sought to protect itself, bringing lawsuits and filing complaints with legal authorities worldwide. In Canada, the association objected to a trademark application filed by Glenora distillery for Glen Breton Single Malt, stating that the use of the common Gaelic word "Glen" confused retailers and wholesalers into thinking that the Canadian single malt was Scotch whiskey. In 2008, the Canadian High Court agreed and refused the trademark application. In India, the SWA protested the use of the name Red Scot as a brand, for the same reasons, and an Indian court ruled that Indian whiskey manufacturers cannot use the words "Scot" or "Scotch" to describe their products, in compliance with World Trade Organization rules.

But for all of their status, and all of their legal wrangles, even the Scotch Whisky Association will admit that the world's top-selling whiskey does not come from either the islands or from Speyside. Nor is it a single malt or blended Scotch whiskey. They are likely loath to admit that the top-selling whiskey in the world is sold in a square bottle, has a black label, and comes from the rolling hills of Eastern Tennessee.

9

Way Down South

Out of all of the distilleries we had planned on visiting, the one that gave me the most apprehension was that of Jack Daniel's. There were two basic reasons for this. The first was knowing how vested the company was in their public persona. The whiskey is made in the small town of Lynchburg, Tennessee, and everything about the whiskey is painted with the stereotypes associated with the region. While most of the whiskey world markets themselves as a drink of the elite, of the cultured, Jack Daniel's markets themselves as the drink of the rebel, the hell-raiser, and the rural lower middle class.

The dilemma I was having was knowing that Jack Daniel's is owned by Brown-Forman, a company that also sold Stellar Gin, Finlandia Vodka, and Korbel Champagne. My concern was that the cynic within me was half under the belief that the marketing strategy of a "down-home, whiskey by the common man" theme so frequently associated with Jack Daniel's was simply a thin veneer, a marketing strategy that had been expertly crafted and implemented, allowing the brand to bring in a net income of a little over one hundred and twenty million dollars a year.

The second fear? If this wasn't a cynical marketing plan, then I was just about to walk into a whiskey company that has a reputation equivalent to that of fried baloney sandwiches and monster trucks. This would be a far cry from the Highlands of Scotland.

Krysta and I drove in from Nashville on a very wet morning, neither one of us knowing what to expect. All I had was an appointment time, a lunch date, and a name—Roger Brashears.

"Is he the master distiller?" Krysta asked me on the way into town.

"Nope."

"The owner?"

I shrugged. "I don't think so. I think he's in public relations."

Mr. Brashears, as it turned out, was indeed in public relations, but was unlike any PR person I had dealt with before. We entered his office, a paper-infested tribute to the history of Jack Daniel's, as he and his assistant were finishing their morning discussion about e-mail.

"I don't know why no one wants to read memos any more. That's what I'm used to," said a stout man with silver hair. An older gentleman, with a distinct southeastern Tennessee drawl, he carried a look in his eye that showed a level of mischief and respect. "This was supposed to lead to a paperless office, wasn't it? And yet what do most people do when they get an e-mail? They print it out." He chuckled at his own observation.

"We have this discussion every morning," his assistant said to us apologetically.

Turning to us, he said, "So you are the two young women I'm supposed to be talking to today?" Krysta and I both nodded.

"Oh, good. You both are far more attractive than most of the people I have to talk to." He laughed. "I much prefer to look at good lookin' women. They can get me into trouble, though. I was getting an annual physical, and the doctor told me that my heart rate was too high. I said that was his fault for having such a pretty nurse take my pulse."

He pointed us to two seats in front of his quite cluttered desk, and proceeded to reminisce. He spoke of the people he worked with and people he worked for. He told us a bit about the history of the company. "Jack Daniel's wasn't all that big, even through the fifties. In 1954, we were only producing about fifty thousand cases of whiskey a year."

"And how many do you produce today?" I asked.

"Well, we're expecting to hit ten million cases in 2009," he said.

"That's a lot of whiskey you're moving. How many people work here?" I asked.

"About half of them," said Roger. He smiled at his own joke.

"What happened between then and now?" Krysta asked.

"That'd be Brown-Forman." He pointed at some black-and-white photographs on the wall. "This is Mr. Smith, the smartest man I ever knew, who worked for Brown-Forman. I know he was the smartest man I ever knew," he added with a wink, "because he was the man who hired the man who hired me."

He moved his finger to point at a different picture. "The man he hired who hired me was Mr. Hancock, who happened to know a few things about marketing and selling. It was through these two men that Jack Daniel's became so popular."

The next hour was a collection of reminiscences of the history and legends of Jack Daniel's, as well as stories relating to how much he liked beautiful women. Mr. Brashears was a perfect example of how minor lasciviousness can be seen as a positive character trait.

"Now it's said that ol' Jack died when he came into work early one day, and couldn't get his safe open. He kicked it out of frustration, broke his toe, and that led to an infection that eventually led to his death. Of course he was sitting on his own supply of 'medicine', so he wasn't in too much pain. But it also goes to show that no good comes from coming into work early." Again he chuckled at his well-rehearsed line.

"This company couldn't exist with Lem Motlow," he said, pointing to yet another picture on the wall. "When Jack died, he passed the distillery onto Lem, who was Jack's nephew."

"Did you know Jack was buried here in town?" he added, changing topics in midthought. "He was buried down there in the city cemetery. Two chairs were put next to his tombstone so that all the women he flirted with could come to his grave and have a place to sit as they cried over his death."

He brought our attention back to Lem's picture. "Anyway, Lem made sure that the distillery made it through Prohibition and World War II. He made sure that the distillery would reopen, and when it did, he upped and died, leaving the distillery to his sons."

"Here's a picture of Lem's sons," he said, pointing at to a picture on the far wall. He paused for a moment, clearly in a reflective mood. He then looked at his watch and jumped. He said with a start, "Ladies, we're going to have to get you on your tour if we're going to have lunch together. After you're done, we're going to have lunch at Miss Mary's Boarding House. Best food in Lynchburg. I'll promise you that."

Roger drove us back to the visitor center, where we rushed in and were able to make the tour that was just starting.

We were greeted by a man in bib overalls. "Ah, good. I was told you two were coming." He sat us in a room with thirty other people, the largest group we had ever been on a tour with. We settled into the benches and looked toward the wall with the movie screen.

I leaned over to whisper to Krysta. "Really? Bib overalls? Why don't they let them walk around barefoot as well?"

Krysta gave me a look as if to say "Hush!" as the guide brought the lights down to show the standard corporate video. The screen flashed images of people hard at work, people smiling and waving at the camera, and then the recently retired master distiller of Jack Daniel's looking off into the distance while standing next to his pickup. The narrator voiced words such as "Quality" and "Family" and other nouns that evoked images of a down-home good time, and a company-wide passion to be the best.

The video display was nothing more than evidence of the fine line between company pride and propaganda. But it was no worse than any other videos we had seen. I flashed back to the videos of Jameson and the Scotch Whisky Heritage Centre. I said a small thanks to the heavens that the Jack Daniel's video wasn't as hokey as those two.

———

We were herded outside into a downpour of rain, and we were rushed from one distillery location to another.

The first stop of the tour offered something not seen on others: their charcoal filtering process, also known as the Lincoln County Process. They showed how they make their charcoal (essentially setting a lot of sugar maple timber on fire, putting it out at the right time, and collecting the remaining charcoal chips), and then the filtering process itself, in which the whiskey is filtered through a column of the aforementioned charcoal chips before going into the casks for aging.

Even in a downpour, the Jack Daniel Distillery is beautiful. The strong industrial buildings that were developed with slight aesthetic influences from both Victorian England and the rural South circa 1900 provide a stark contrast with the deep lush green of the hills of southeastern Tennessee. Walking from building to building with the rest of the tour group communicated two different messages.

One—image is just as important as the product. Time and time again, reference to Jack Daniel himself and the era in which he ran his distillery was made.

Two—they've made an exorbitant amount of money selling their whiskey. For all of their talk about Jack Daniel and the influence he had on the company, their growth occurred after the Eisenhower administration, and most of the buildings on site are less than fifty years old.

It was an odd juxtaposition, these two messages. But clearly both were being heard loud and clear by the fans of the whiskey. Tour buses shoved their way into the parking lot, tours running every fifteen minutes, and each tour was at or near capacity. The visitors' center was busier than many museums I have been to in my life, let alone other distilleries.

I took a quick sampling of our tour group. There was an older gentleman and his wife. Two folks from Japan, one from Canada, two from France. There were the two sorority sisters who had come over from the University of Tennessee. While Jack Daniel's may have a specific market they're aiming their advertising at, they are hitting more than the blue-collar worker from the rural South.

The tour hit all of the major stops of a distillery tour, with the mash tun and their stills, each on a larger industrial scale than Krysta and I were used to. By the end we were taken to the smallest of over fifty barrel houses they had on site. Each barrel is no longer painted or scored with the company name and date placed on its lid, as is the tradition in so many of the distilleries the world over. Instead, a little UPC code to be read by a computer scanner is now stapled to each barrel. Heritage may be important, but sometimes the future has to win out in the name of efficiency.

We met Roger outside the visitors' center. He was to escort us to lunch in Lynchburg. The rain was really pouring down at this point.

"Would you like to see downtown?" Roger asked us, after we shoehorned our way into the cab of his white pickup truck.

We both nodded.

He drove us past a few storefronts advertising either ice cream or pizza. We neared a red brick building with a white tower. This was clearly the town hall.

"Did you enjoy it? You didn't blink, did you?" Roger laughed as we turned off the side street to Miss Mary Bobo's Boarding House, where we were to have our lunch.

We sat down with a group of about a dozen other people, the majority of them strangers to one another, and we were served our lunch "boardinghouse" style. A dish was placed in front of each person. You passed off to the right when you had had as much as you wanted. We filled up with Tennessee ham, freshly made biscuits, green beans, and fried okra. All the while Roger provided entertainment to the tourists, regaling them with stories of Jack Daniel's past, and how he met his wife, and how his wife's cooking could never measure up to the meal in front of us.

And to drink? Iced tea or lemonade. Jack Daniel's was not on the menu, as Lynchburg is still famously dry. We did eat candied apples laced with Jack Daniel's , and that would be as close as we were to tasting the whiskey all day.

"Roger? I was wondering if we could impose on you one more time?" Krysta had pulled Roger aside after the meal, as everyone was putting on their jackets and getting ready to leave.

Jack Daniel's
The world's most popular whiskey. What more can be said?
Nose: Oaky with a bit of almond, like a peach pit.
Taste: Caramel/toffee flavors intermix with licorice and the oaks, all supported by the grains. Can be a bit rough if one is used to smoother whiskeys.
Finish: Long, without being overly so. There's a fair amount of toffee here, with the spiciness of the rye showing up as well.
Character: Jack Daniel's is lacking in pretense of any sort. Much like hard rock, it's appreciated by fans on an almost unimaginably large scale, yet it's appreciated by only a handful of critics due to Jack's rough approach to their medium.

"Sure! Sure!"

"Could you drive us to the cemetery so we can get a picture of Jack's tombstone? The one with the chairs next to it?"

"I'd love to," he said with the air of a southern gentleman.

We piled into his truck and drove four blocks from the restaurant. There was the cemetery, and there in the middle was Jack Daniel's tombstone, with two chairs beside it for the ladies to sit in as they mourned his death.

Roger drove us back to our car in the visitors' lot. As we said our thanks, he looked at us with a bit of seriousness.

"I want to thank y'all for comin' by. I do enjoy it when the ladies stop by for a visit. The last time I took two women in my truck, people started askin' me 'how my date wuz'," he said, embellishing the southern drawl.

"That's okay, Mr. Brashears. If anyone asks, we'll tell them what really happened," I said.

"Now why would I want you to do that?" he asked with an evil grin. "I want them to think I still have the way with the ladies."

10

Reflections

We had taken our seat in a high-end Chinese restaurant in Toronto. The waitress came over and asked us for our cocktail orders. It was our last night on the whiskey tour, and I was a little unsettled. I felt a little guilty for ending our tour on such a non-whiskey note, but it was clear that both Krysta and I had a lot to digest. Hopefully a moment away from the spirit, where I didn't have to feel as if I had to taste the drink, let alone judge it, would give me just enough space to collect my thoughts.

We had spent the day back in Canada, specifically in Ontario, visiting Kittling Ridge Winery, home of Forty Creek Whisky. More importantly, it was the home of John Hall, the man behind the whiskey. His approach to creating and distilling had led to his being named Pioneer of the Year in 2006 by *Malt Advocate*, a quarterly magazine aimed at whiskey aficionados.

John Hall, to me, represents the future of whiskey. While the major corporations buy up labels and brands, a new breed of distiller is coming along, looking to create something new and different.

These risk-taking distillers are a recent phenomenon here on the left side of the Atlantic. As Prohibition-era laws are updated to better reflect the state of alcohol production and consumption, new distillers are arriving on the scene, either offering unique takes on whiskey or revisiting the way things used to be done before the politicians and corporations took over. These are the kinds of people who are doing to the whiskey industry what microbreweries were doing to the beer world not two decades ago.

The Forty Creek Distillery is unlike any of the other places we had visited. For one, instead of being located in a scenic location, à la Glen-fiddich, Jack Daniel, or, heck, even Canadian Club, Forty Creek Distillery is found off a service road accessible from the Queen Elizabeth Highway, a multilane highway that connects Niagara with Toronto. When the view from the distillery makes you long for the picturesque backdrop of downtown Detroit, you know that impressing visitors with the grandeur of whiskey making is not on the top of their priority list. The building that houses the distillery itself could easily be mistaken for the multitude of tractor dealerships that pepper this region of Ontario.

We parked the car, which we had left unnamed, and headed into the shop.

"Oh, you were the one we had scheduled to meet with John yesterday!" said a helpful woman in the gift shop after I had introduced myself. "He had to reschedule his interview with Jim Murray, because we never heard back from you."

Wait, what?

I swallowed hard. Hearing that I had inconvenienced Jim Murray, the reigning king of whiskey writing, was akin to hearing that I had made life difficult for Prince Charles; or, more frightening, Martha Stewart.

I had recently had a series of e-mails gone missing from my mail server, both those sent to me and those I had sent to others. It was embarrassing to tell them that my mail server had gone down, as it sounded as authentic as such statements as "The check's in the mail" and "No really, the bridesmaids' dresses look beautiful!" My face must have looked panicked, as she worked to reassure me.

"No, it's no big deal, really. He has about an hour to spend with you today. We can sneak you in." We were herded into a conference room and were soon introduced to a soft-spoken man with blond hair. He gave the impression of being more like a toymaker than a whiskey distiller, an image that lasted just until we got him speaking about the whiskey business. As we listed the places we had been, he focused on Canadian Club.

"So you went to Hiram Walker?"

"We did."

"I bet you didn't know that I am from Windsor, and had wanted to work there after high school," he said with a smile. He opened the door and proceeded to play Willy Wonka to our Violet Beauregarde and Veruca Salt.

The contrast between the Forty Creek Distillery and the recent large-scale distillers such as Jack Daniel and Canadian Club could not have been more noticeable.

As we walked, he explained his distillery processes to us. "For Forty Creek whiskeys, each single grain whiskey is aged in its own special barrel. We then use a different type of oak barrel for each of the grain whiskeys. Lightly toasted oak barrels are used to enhance the fruitiness and spiciness of the rye whiskey. Medium toasted barrels are used to enhance the nuttiness of the barley, and heavy charred barrels enhance the smoothness and body of the maize."

"It doesn't sound like the processes we've heard about at other distilleries," said Krysta. This was true. None of the several places we had visited where they used several different types of grain in their spirits had aged each grain whiskey separately.

John paused before responding. "I respect the traditions surrounding whiskey," he finally said. "But coming from a winemakers' background, I am not tied to them."

As we passed his stills, the same point came across when he explained that he used a German still. Up until now, we had only seen either Scottish-made swan neck stills or the massive column stills that made Aeneas Coffey a legend in the whiskey world. Instead of the beautiful copper stills that one typically associates with whiskey distillers, in front of us sat something akin to a washing machine from a steampunk novel.

"Does using this still provide a different taste to your whiskey?"
I asked.

John smiled. "I'd like to think so. Let's go find out," he said as he
led out us out of the production area and back to the conference room.

There we sat down in front of four different glasses of whiskey, a
setup we had seen several times before at our other tastings. Or so I
thought. Typically when at a tasting, the company either offers tastes
of several different house brands or pairs their whiskey with several
competitors. As I looked at the setting in front of me, I saw that this
was neither. Instead I saw a glass labeled "corn whiskey," one labeled "barley," and still another labeled "rye." These were the indi-
vidually aged whiskeys now sitting in front of me.

"What I do," said John, noticing my examination, "is take a bit
of the corn . . . for the sweetness." He picked up the corn whiskey,
swirled and nosed it, and then took a sip.

"The barley provides a bit of nuttiness." He repeated the ritual,
this time for the barley whiskey.

". . . and finally, the rye provides a bit of spice and fruitiness."
He drank from the rye, and a small smile crossed his lips. It was
clear that he had done this demonstration many times.

"I then blend the three whiskeys here to get . . . ," he looked
down at the fourth glass. ". . . Forty Creek."

I've seen several people do the work of the salesman when they
do tastings, and John was no different. But beneath the subdued
P. T. Barnum sell was a strong sense of pride.

"How much time does the whiskey take up of your day compared to your winemaking?" I asked.

"Almost all of it."

I got the sense he wouldn't have it any other way.

I thought about John Hall as Krysta and I sat in the Chinese
restaurant, waiting for our drinks, reliving the places we had been,
determining which place we enjoyed the most, and which whiskey
we liked the most. Throughout the entirety of the trip, the one constant theme had been that of heritage, of being true to one's past.
Whether it was Jameson telling us how Ireland changed when John
Jameson moved to Dublin, Dennis Malcolm telling us stories of the

Forty Creek Three Grain

If you want to imagine what whiskey could taste like from a winemaker's perspective, this is a great place to start. John Hall is one of the handful of folks who have the potential to bring Canadian whiskey back to the age of innovation.

Nose: The grains mixed with a bit of dates and raisins gave me a granola cereal type of image.

Taste: Sweet fruit, almost peachlike, mixed with spiciness from the rye.

Finish: The grains appear again on the finish, which evaporates quickly into a fennel/oak taste in the back of the mouth.

Character: Sweet and very approachable, this whiskey is the aunt who came from humble beginnings and ended up as the next big thing when she got to the city. She prospered where her most ardent supporters never suspected her small-town roots. Think Audrey Hepburn as Holly Golightly in *Breakfast at Tiffany's*.

major at Glen Grant, or Dan Tullio talking about Al Capone and Prohibition, each place went to great lengths to tell us how long they'd been around and, by extension, how good their whiskey must be because of their ability to stay in the market.

And here was John Hall, essentially saying that anyone with passion could make a decent whiskey. In fact, more and more people are rediscovering that making good whiskey is not a difficult process. Heritage, to him, was a liability.

People with similar passions are creating new and unique types of whiskey. Companies such as Highwood Distillers out of Calgary, Clear Creek out of Portland, Oregon, and Stranahan's out of Denver, Colorado, have all provided new takes on the old farm product. Thanks to San Francisco's Anchor Distillery, even pure rye whiskey is being made again, through the use of nineteenth-century processes once thought lost to Prohibition.

Do the bigger distilleries and well-established producers feel threatened by the newcomers to the scene? If the Scotch Whisky Association's recent lawsuit against Glenora Distillery of Nova

Scotia is any indication, they are at least keeping a wary eye on them.

Are these new whiskeys superior? This depends on one's taste. But they do shine a light on the rickety presumption that only big, well-established distilleries can make good (if not great) whiskey.

Americans' perception of whiskey has changed over the past generation. Thanks in large part to the reintroduction of single malts from Scotland in the late 1960s and early 1970s, and then the introduction of small batch bourbons from the folks at Jim Beam in the 1980s, the American whiskey consumer is realizing that whiskey can have a vast spectrum of flavors. Much like the microbrewery revolution, the addition of new whiskeys has increased the options available, and has, in turn, made whiskey a spirit with nuance and character. People are no longer exclusively looking to Scotland for the best whiskey, and countries such as New Zealand, India, and Japan are all challenging the perceptions of what whiskey is. And Irish whiskey, long thought dead or dying, is now seeing its popularity rise.

I thought back to Mr. Disposable Income, and the £35,000 he spent on his night out. Did he get his money's worth? Was it a memorable experience for him, one that would last a lifetime? I thought back to the whiskeys I had partaken of over the course of the past few weeks. Which ones would come to my mind several years from now?

Drinking my age at Glenfarclas was pretty cool, and having Dennis Malcolm shamelessly flirt with Krysta and me was certainly high on the list. Brian Quinn offering us a drink of the 63-year-old whiskey came to mind, as did the coincidences that occurred during the search for Buffalo Trace's special release. There were the tastings at Jameson and Bushmills, Heaven Hill and Canadian Club, each teaching me something new and each allowing me to meet some wonderful people. Which one of these could possibly be said to be the best? They were all memorable and each had value to me.

I thought back again to Mr. Disposable Income, whose splurging on a bottle of expensive whiskey brought me on this journey. It was then that a thought crossed my mind.

It's rare that an epiphany occurs in such clarity. But I had one while waiting for my cocktail. Mr. Disposable Income was not merely buying a whiskey. He was buying a memory; the whiskey was simply the means

Whiskey with a friend
Yes, it's a tad sappy, but none of the whiskeys I tasted over the course of our journeys would have been as memorable if I did not have Krysta there to share the experience.
Nose: Sometimes it's best to simply ignore the aroma, and instead listen and laugh with those with you.
Taste: Any way you like it.
Finish: The finish lasts forever.
Character: It's the trip of a lifetime. Easily taken for granted until it isn't there. Best served with laughter and camaraderie. Highly recommended.

in which that memory was allowed to occur. In all likelihood, it was celebrating something, likely to do with money, perhaps gaining a windfall through some means. The whiskey was the way he had treated himself.

And in some ways, we had done the same thing. But instead of celebrating a windfall, Krysta and I celebrated whiskey itself, going from its start in Ireland to this little distillery off the shores of Lake Ontario. We had chronicled, not just the distilleries, but how history had shaped the way that allowed places such as Forty Creek to be created today. Mr. Disposable Income may have had his windfall and celebration, but we had traveled to many of the places that had influenced Mr. DI's purchase.

And I was reminded of a note I received from Shannon Briggs, self-proclaimed Scotch chick, and one of the contributors to the Web site Scotch Chicks. "Life is too short to drink bad whiskey. Do some research or have a really good mentor helping you pick your first single malts, and then savor the experience."

Krysta and I had done exactly this, in ways that many people never have done. I wondered if Mr. DI could make the same claim.

I chuckled to myself as the waitress arrived with our drinks.

"What?" asked Krysta, picking up her glass.

"I think we just kicked Mr. Disposable Income's ass, without even knowing it."

Krysta laughed as we toasted our experience.

Glossary of Whiskey Terms

Aqua Vitae   Latin for "water of life," it was the name given to many distilled spirits during the Middle Ages, including grain whiskey.

Blending   A whiskey that is the end result of mixing several different distillations. Unaged grain whiskey is a large part of the mixture, along with several aged single malts.

Bourbon   It used to mean whiskey that came from the docks of Bourbon, Kentucky. Now it means any American whiskey made from a mash containing at least 51 percent corn, distilled to 80 percent alcohol by volume, and then aged in a newly charred oak barrel starting at a strength of no more than 62.5 percent alcohol by volume.

Column Still   The continuous still first made popular by Aeneas Coffey. Allows for cheaper and quicker whiskey production.

Dram   A small volume of liquid, typically whiskey. Larger than a shot, less than a glass. Often served in a short, stout, fluted glass.

Gauger   An exciseman whose job was to collect taxes from whiskey producers.

Grain Whiskey   All whiskey is made from grain, so the term now mostly refers to unaged whiskey that usually has a higher percentage of alcohol. Often used in blends.

Grist   Grounded grains used for the mashes.

Malt   A grain that has been soaked in water in order to promote germination. Barleys are the most common, but rye and and wheat can also be malted. Corn is never malted, as there are already enough sugars within it to foster fermentation.

Mash   The liquid one gets when the grist is mixed with hot water, and then allowed to cool before being sent to the fermenter.

Maturation   The aging of whiskey in a cask.

Moonshine   Grain whiskey made without oversight from a government. Illegal whiskey.

Peat   Solid compressed vegetable matter that appears dark brown. Used as a fuel source. Provides a very distinct aroma, especially when used to dry malted grains.

Poteen   Irish moonshine with the added distinction that some of it may have been aged.

Pot Still   Copper pots used for the process of distilling. Can be of many sizes, from that of a gallon to one that is twenty feet tall.

Rye Whiskey   Typically, it's a whiskey that has rye as the primary grain used (at least 51 percent). A rye whiskey can be a single malt, but usually they are made more in line with bourbon techniques, with rye replacing corn as the primary grain.

Single Malt   Malt whiskey made from a single distiller and unmixed with grain or pot still whiskey.

Usquebaugh   Gaelic for "water of life." It was the term for whiskey in the sixteenth and seventeenth centuries. In fact, the word "whiskey" comes from this term.

Vatting   Mixing of malt whiskey from a single distillery or multiple distilleries.

Wash   The beer that is needed in order to distill the whiskey. Technically, it is "the wash" as soon as the yeast is added for fermentation. However, it is generally regarded as wort after fermented.

Wort The liquid from the mash tun. It is the liquid that is in the fermenter but has yet to be fully fermented. Wort is the liquid that gets the yeast added for fermentation. Wash is the result when the yeast has fully converted the sugars of the wort into alcohol.

Visiting the Distilleries

Over the course of writing this book, I ended up at almost two dozen different distilleries, both large and small, some not mentioned herein. Below is a list of contact information.

CANADA
Canadian Club
Canadian Club Brand Heritage Centre
2072 Riverside Drive East
Walkerville, Ontario, Canada
N8Y 4S5

Telephone: 519-973-9503
http://www.canadianclubwhiskey.com/

May–December
Wednesday–Saturday, 12:00 p.m.–6:00 p.m.
Sunday, 12:00 p.m.–4:00 p.m.

Forty Creek
Kittling Ridge Distillery
297 South Service Road
Grimsby, Ontario, Canada
L3M 1Y6

Telephone: 905-945-9225
http://www.fortycreekwhiskey.com/splash/

Visitor tours are offered at no charge from June to September.
Tuesday–Saturday, 2:00 p.m.
Sundays & holidays, 11:00 a.m.

Gooderham & Worts:
The Distillery Historic District
55 Mill Street, Building #58, Suite 200
Toronto, Ontario, Canada
M5A 3C4

Telephone: 1-866-405-8687
http://www.thedistillerydistrict.com/

NORTHERN IRELAND
Bushmills
Antrim, County Antrim, Ireland
BT57 8XH

Telephone: 44-28-2073-3272
http://www.bushmills.com

March–October
Monday–Saturday, 9:15 a.m.–5:00 p.m.
Sunday: March–June & October, 12:00 p.m.–5:00 p.m.;
July, August, & September, 11:30 a.m.–5:00 p.m.

REPUBLIC OF IRELAND
Jameson's (The Old Jameson Distillery)
Bow Street Distillery
Smithfield, Dublin

Telephone: 353-1-8072355
http://www.jamesonwhiskey.com/
Open 7 days, 9:00 a.m.–6:30 p.m., including bank holidays (last
tour at 5:30 p.m.)
Closed Good Friday & Christmas holidays

Jameson's (The Midleton Distillery):
The Jameson Experience
The Old Distillery, Midleton
County Cork

Telephone 353-21-4613594
http://www.jamesonwhiskey.com/
November–March, 1:30 pa.m.–5:00 p.m.; April–October, 10:00–
4:00 p.m., Including bank holidays
Closed Good Friday & Christmas holidays

Locke's Distillery Museum
Kilbeggan
County Westmeath

Telephone: 353-579-33-2134
http://www.lockesdistillerymuseum.ie/

April–October, 9:00 a.m.–6:00 p.m.;
November–March, 10:00 p.m.–4:00 p.m.
Groups please book in advance.

Tullamore Dew Heritage Centre
Bury Quay
Tullamore
County Offaly

Telephone: 00-353-506-25015
http://www.tullamore-dew.org/default_flash.asp
Monday–Saturday, 9:00 a.m.–6:00 p.m.; Sunday, midday–5:00 p.m.

SCOTLAND
Auchentoshan
Dalmuir
Clydebank
G81 4SJ

Telephone: 044-01389-878-561
http://www.auchentoshan.co.uk/

Monday–Saturday, 10:00 a.m.–5:00 p.m.;
Sunday, 12:30 p.m.–5:00 p.m.

Glen Grant Distillery
Elgin Road
Rothes
Moray
AB38 7BN

Telephone: 044-01542-783-303
http://www.glengrant.com/

March–October
Monday–Saturday, 10:00 a.m.–4:00 p.m.;
Sunday, 12:30 p.m.–4:00 p.m.

Glenfarclas
Marypark
Ballindalloch
Banffshire
AB37 9BD

Telephone: 044-01807-500-245
http://www.glenfarclas.co.uk/

April–June
Monday–Friday, 10:00 a.m.–5:00 p.m.
July to September
Monday–Friday, 10:00 a.m.–5:00 p.m.; Saturday, 10:00 a.m.–4:00 p.m.
October–March
Monday–Friday, 10:00 a.m.–4:00 p.m.
For Christmas and New Year holiday opening hours, please call.

Glenfiddich
Dufftown
Banffshire
AB55 4DH

Telephone: 044-01340-820-000
http://www.glenfiddich.com/

Monday–Saturday, 9:30 a.m.–4:30 p.m.; Sunday, 12:00 p.m.–4:30 p.m.

Glenturret
The Hosh
Crieff
Perthshire & Kinross
PH7 4HA

Telephone: 044-01764-656-565
http://www.thefamousgrouse.com

January and February
10:00 a.m.–4:30 p.m.

March–December
9:00 a.m.–6:00 p.m.

Open seven days a week, all year, except Christmas, Boxing Day, and New Year's Day.

Oban

Stafford Street
Oban
Argyll & Bute
PA34 5NH

Telephone: 044-01631-572-004
http://www.malts.com/en-us/Malts/summary/Oban.htm

January–February
Monday–Friday, 12:30 p.m.–4:00 p.m.

March
Monday–Friday, 10:00 a.m.–5:00 p.m.

Easter to June
Monday–Saturday, 9:30 a.m.–5:00 p.m.

July–September
Monday–Friday, 9:30 a.m.–7:30 p.m.; Saturday, 9:30 a.m.–5:00 p.m.; Sunday, 12:00 p.m.–5:00 p.m.

October
Monday–Saturday, 9:30 a.m.–5:00 p.m.

November
Monday–Friday, 10:00 a.m.–5:00 p.m.

December
Monday–Friday, 12:30 p.m.–4:00 p.m.
Closed between Christmas and New Year

The Scotch Whisky Heritage Center
354 Castlehill
Royal Mile
Edinburgh
EH1 2NE

Telephone: 0131-220-0441
http://www.whiskey-heritage.co.uk
September–May
10:00 a.m.–6:00 p.m.

June, July, August
9:30 a.m.–6:30 p.m.

UNITED STATES
Buffalo Trace
1001 Wilkinson Boulevard
Frankfort, KY 40602

Telephone: 502-223-7641
http://www.buffalotrace.com/

Monday–Friday, 9:00 a.m.–3:00 p.m.; Saturday, 10:00 a.m.–
    2:00 p.m.
Closed Thanksgiving Day, Christmas Day and New Year's
    Day

George Dickel
1950 Cascade Hollow Rd.
Normandy, TN 37360

Telephone: 931-857-3124
http://www.dickel.com

Tuesday–Saturday, 9:00 a.m.–4:00 p.m., except major holidays

Heaven Hill
1064 Loretto Road
Bardstown, KY 40004

Telephone: 502-348-3921
http://www.bourbonheritagecenter.com/

Tuesday–Saturday, 10:00 a.m.–5:00 p.m.; Sunday, 12:00 p.m.–
4:00 p.m. (March–December only)

Jack Daniel's
182 Lynchburg Highway
Lynchburg, TN 37352

Telephone: 931-759-4221
http://www.jackdaniels.com/

9:00 a.m.–4:30 p.m.
Open every day except Thanksgiving, Christmas Eve, Christmas,
New Year's Eve, and New Year's Day

Jim Beam
149 Happy Hollow Road
Clermont, KY 40110

Telephone: 502-543-9877
http://www.jimbeam.com

Monday–Saturday, 9:00 a.m.–4:30 p.m.; Sunday, 1–4 ET
Closed New Year's Day, Easter, Thanksgiving Day, Christmas Eve,
and Christmas Day; closed Sundays in January and February

Maker's Mark

3350 Burks Spring Road
Loretto, KY 40037

Telephone: 270-865-2881
http://www.makersmark.com

Monday–Saturday, 10:00 a.m.–4:30 p.m.; Sunday, 1:00 p.m.–4:30 p.m.
Closed New Year's Day, Easter, Thanksgiving Day, Christmas Eve,
  and Christmas

Woodford Reserve

Labrot & Graham Distillery
7855 McCraken Place
Versailles, KY 40383

Telephone: 859-879-1938
http://www.woodfordreserve.com

Tuesday–Saturday, 9:00 a.m.–5:00 p.m.; April–October only Sunday,
  12:30 p.m.–4:30 p.m.
Closed major holidays

West Overton Distilling Co.

West Overton Museum
1000 Overholt Drive
Scottdale, PA 15683

Telephone: 724-887-7910
http://www.westovertonvillage.org/

Tuesday–Saturday, 9:00 a.m.–4:00 p.m.; Sunday 1:00 p.m.–
  5:00 p.m.

References

Blue, Anthony Dias. *The Complete Book of Spirits: A Guide to Their History, Production, and Enjoyment.* New York: Harper Collins, 2004.

Brown, Lorraine. *The Story of Canadian Whiskey: 200 Years of Tradition.* Markham, Ontario: Fitzhenry & Whiteside, 1994.

Burns, Eric. *The Spirits of America: A Social History of Alcohol.* Philadelphia: Temple University Press, 2004.

"Calgary & Southern Alberta." *University of Calgary.* The Applied History Research Group. http://www.ucalgary.ca/applied_history/tutor/calgary/Ft1875.html#ft1875.

Cecil, Sam K. *The Evolution of the Bourbon Whiskey Industry in Kentucky.* Paducah, KY: Turner Company, 1999.

Cowdery, Charles. "Articles About American Whiskey." http://home.netcom.com/~cowdery/bour4.html.

Cowdery, Charles K. *Bourbon, Straight: The Uncut and Unfiltered Story of American Whiskey.* Chicago: Made and Bottled in Kentucky, 2004.

Daiches, David. *Scotch Whisky: Its Past and Present.* Glasgow: Fontana/Collins, 1969.

Delves, Stuart. *Great Brand Stories—Scotch Whisky: Creative Fire—The Story of Scotland's Greatest Export.* London: Cyan Books, 2007.

Dillon, Patrick. *Gin: The Much-Lamented Death of Madam Geneva.* Boston: Justin, Charles & Co, 2002.

Gabányi, Stefan. *Whisk(E)y.* New York: Abbeville Press, 1997.

Getz, Oscar. *Whiskey: An American Pictorial History.* New York: David McKay Company, Inc., 1978.

Gibson, Sally. "Evolution of the Distillery District Site 1830s to 1890s." http://www.distilleryheritage.com/.

Gray, James H. *Booze.* Toronto: Macmillan, 1972.

Heron, Craig. *Booze: A Distilled History.* Toronto: Between the Lines, 2003.

Hume, John R., and Michael S. Moss. *The Making of Scotch Whisky.* Edinburgh: Canongate Books Ltd., 1981.

Krass, Peter. *Blood and Whiskey: The Life and Times of Jack Daniels.* Hoboken, NJ: Wiley, 2004.

Lamond, John. *The Whiskey Connoisseur's Companion: Facts, Fables and Folklore from the World of Whiskey.* Leith: The Edinburgh Company Ltd., 1993.

Lender, Mark E., and James K. Martin. *Drinking in America: A History.* New York: Free Press, 1982.

Lipman, John, and Linda Lipman. "American Whiskey: John and Linda Lipman's Adventures in Bourbon Country." http://www.ellenjaye.com/.

MacKinnon, Tanya. "The History of the Molson's Distillery: A Foundation for the Brewing Empire." *Bacon,* Spring 2008. http://www.frymybacon.com/articles/articles.php?articleID=216.

MacLean, Charles. *Scotch Whisky: A Liquid History.* London: Cassell Illustrated, 2005.

———. *Whiskey Tales.* London: Little Books Ltd, 2006.

Magee, Malachy. *Irish Whiskey: A 1000 Year Tradition.* Dublin: The O'Brien Press, 1980.

Malcolm, Elizabeth *Ireland Sober, Ireland Free: Drink and Temper-*

ance in Nineteenth-Century Ireland, Dublin: Gill and Macmillan, 1986.

Maurer, David W. *Kentucky Moonshine.* Lexington, KY: University Press of Kentucky, 1973.

McBain, C S. *Glen Grant: A Distillation of 150 Years.* Aberdeen: Aberdeen University Press, 1989.

McGrew, Jane L. "History of Alcohol Prohibition, 1913–1933: National Prohibition—Prologue and Finish." *Schaffer Library of Drug Policy*, April 2008. http://www.druglibrary.org/schaffer/Library/studies/nc/nc2a_5.htm.

McGuffin, John. *In Praise of Poteen.* Belfast: Appletree Press, 1978.

McGuire, E. B. *Irish Whiskey: A History of Distilling, the Spirit Trade, and Excise Controls in Ireland.* Dublin: Gill and Macmillan, 1973.

Mulryan, Peter. *The Whiskeys of Ireland.* Dublin: O'Brien Press, 2002.

Murray, Jim. *A Taste of Irish Whiskey.* London: Prion Books, 1997.

Pacult, F. P. *American Still Life: The Jim Beam Story and the Making of the World's #1 Bourbon.* Hoboken, NJ: Wiley, 2003.

Quinn, John F. *Father Mathew's Crusade: Temperance in Nineteenth-Century Ireland and Irish America*, Amherst: University of Massachusetts Press, 2002.

Rorabaugh, W. J. *The Alcoholic Republic: An American Tradition.* New York: Oxford University Press, 1979.

Rothbaum, Noah. *The Business of Spirits: How Savvy Marketers, Innovative Distillers, and Entrepreneurs Changed How We Drink.* New York: Kaplan, 2007.

Slinn, Iain. *Whiskey Miscellany.* Inverness: Hospitality Scotland Ltd, 2004.

Standage, Tom. *A History of the World in 6 Glasses.* New York: Walker & Company, 2005.

The Glenlivet. http://www.theglenlivet.com/theglenlivet.php.

Townsend, Brian. *The Lost Distilleries of Ireland.* Glasgow: Neil Wilson, 1997.

"Welcome to the Distillery District." http://www.thedistillerydistrict.com/frameset.html.

Weir, Ronald. *The History of the Distillers Company, 1877–1939: Diversification and Growth in Whisky and Chemicals.* Oxford: Clarendon Press, 1995.

Wishart, David. *Whiskey Classified: Choosing Single Malts by Flavor.* London: Pavilion Books, 2002.

Acknowledgments

While writing a book may seem like a solitary pursuit, the truth is that it would be quite impossible for one to be written and published without the help of many talented and giving individuals sparing their time and resources. This book would not exist without those contributions.

My gratitude goes out to David Hynes and John Teeling of Cooley, who went out of their way to show me what Irish whiskey means to them. David Williamson of the Scotch Whisky Association also proved to be an invaluable resource, and it was him and his information that led me to talk to the many people I came across while in Scotland. Also in Scotland, I have to thank Dennis Malcolm (Glen Grant), George Grant (Glenfarclas), and Brian Robinson (Glenfiddich), who helped me understand their passion for both whiskey and the distilleries where they work.

Back in North America, I'd be remiss if I didn't give thanks to Nicole Chardavoyne, who helped arrange the Hiram Walker visit, and Rob Hoskins, who helped with the one with Jack Daniel's. Each of these locations helped shine a light on aspects of our whiskey heritage that I had difficulty getting a handle on.

From the publishing point of view, I have to thank both my agent, Jon Malysiak, and the folks at St. Martin's Press, for taking a chance on what I wanted to do. I am especially grateful to Daniela Rapp of St. Martin's, who had the unenviable task of breaking me of my bad writing habits. Additionally, I want to thank the folks in the food and spirits blog community. It is their sites that challenge and inspire me on a daily basis.

Finally, I have two personal acknowledgments. Thanks go out to my partner, Tara, who has put up with the various tidbits of trivia about whiskey that I foisted on her over the course of the development of this book. No one should be subjected to this sort of behavior on a daily basis, and she has responded with love and understanding.

But my greatest thanks go to my friend Krysta Scharlach, who gladly accepted my invitation to join me on these journeys. She kept me focused and open to moments of last-second improvisation, and filled the long car drives with talks about literature, rock 'n' roll, and the Internet. I am thrilled to have shared an experience of a lifetime with her.

Index